GIVE AND TAKE

Also by Reynold Levy:

NEARING THE CROSSROADS
Contending Approaches to
American Foreign Policy

GIVE AND TAKE

A Candid Account
of Corporate Philanthropy

REYNOLD LEVY

HARVARD BUSINESS SCHOOL PRESS

Boston, Massachusetts

Printed in the United States of America

03 02 01 00 99   5 4 3 2 1

Library of Congress Cataloging-in-Publication Data

Levy, Reynold.
    Give and take : a candid account of corporate philanthropy /
  Reynold Levy.
        p.   cm.
    Includes bibliographical references.
    ISBN 0-87584-893-1 (alk. paper)
    1. Corporations--Charitable contributions--United States.
  I. Title.
  HG4028.C6L48   1999
  658.15'3--dc21   98-52016
                                                            CIP

The paper used in this publication meets the requirements of the
American National Standard for Permanence of Paper for Printed
Library Materials Z39.49-1984

For my wife Elizabeth and our
children, Justin and Emily

Your support made this book possible.

Shall we devote the few precious days of our existence only to buying and selling, only to comparing sales with the sales of the same day the year before, only to shuffling our feet in the dance, only to matching little picture cards so as to group together three jacks or aces or kings, only to seek pleasures and fight taxes, and when the end comes to leave as little taxable an estate as possible as the final triumph and achievement of our lives? Surely there is something finer and better in life, something that dignifies it and stamps it with at least some little touch of the divine.

My friends, it is unselfish effort, helpfulness to others that enobles life, not because of what it does for others but more what it does for ourselves. In this spirit we should give not grudgingly, not niggardly, but gladly, generously, eagerly, lovingly, joyfully, indeed with the supremest pleasure that life can furnish.

— JULIUS ROSENWALD, 1923

January 1, 1984, will stand in the annals of American corporate history as the first day in the life of the new AT&T, created by the breakup of the Bell System. At about the same time, a less heralded but notable event took place: The AT&T Foundation was born.

America is unique in its dependence upon voluntary organizations for the delivery of human services, for the generation of knowledge, for the preservation of our heritage and for the protection of our highest ideals. Thus, AT&T believes it important to support private institutions of higher learning, social welfare and the arts and culture. When they flourish, our employees, our customers and our shareowners—indeed society as a whole—benefit.

It was no accident that AT&T, even in the midst of a massive corporate reorganization, paid attention to its broad responsibilities to the community. Such commitment is rooted in our heritage and values. The AT&T Foundation is one measure of that commitment, and we take pride in it.

— CHARLES L. BROWN, Chairman, AT&T, 1985

Contents

Preface

SIGMUND FREUD CALLED BIOLOGY DESTINY. In philanthropy, biography is destiny. Behind every donor is a personal story of accomplishment and caring, of personal interest and community need, of advancing a favorite cause and "giving something back" to society. Philanthropic acts engage us. They reflect who we are and what we are about.

Each year, almost two thirds of all adult Americans donate their time and treasure to charities. Millions serve on the boards of directors of nonprofit institutions. Tens of millions are served by them—the church and the synagogue's congregants, the community center's members, the university's students, the hospital's patients, the day care center's infants and the advocacy group's aggrieved. Those American clients and consumers are also the employees of commercial firms. They are customers, suppliers, partners, and regulators. They are us.

When Americans leave their homes in the morning destined for the workplace, they may lock their valuables behind. But they take their values with them to the office. One of these values is helping those who need it most. Another is improving the quality of life in the communities in which they live and work.

The corporation can advance just such ends in fascinating, inventive, and powerful ways. It can do so without damaging the profit-making mission of the firm. Indeed, staying in close touch with customers and with key societal trends that influence the course of business is critical to corporate success. Meaningful interaction with America's Third Sector is indispensable to aligning a company's strategy to its fast-changing environment.

Consisting entirely of the nation's nonprofit organizations, America's Third Sector is estimated to employ about 14 million people, or one out of every seven white-collar workers. Its assets include more than 10 percent of the value of the nation's real property and hundreds of billions of dollars of endowment and capital plant resources. Nonprofit institutions spend more than $600 billion annually. In 1996 they raised more than $150 billion in charitable contributions, the balance of their budgetary needs being satisfied by earned income and by government grants and purchase of service contracts. Their collective output amounts to 6 percent of the nation's Gross Domestic Product.[1] In most cities, nonprofit hospitals, universities, and cultural institutions are among the top twenty employers. In all places, they are objects of civic pride. More often than not, the budgets of nonprofits and their employment numbers exceed the size of the municipal budget and the public payroll in the nation's cities and suburbs.[2]

Neither the Fortune 500 chief financial officer nor the small business owner can afford to ignore such numbers. Nonprofits represent markets and distribution channels that no self-respecting vice president for sales would gainsay. They incubate ideas and social action movements that no strategic planner or marketing specialist can neglect with impunity. They nurture talent that corporate human resource professionals and recruiters relish. And they provide services that enrich our communities and our personal lives.

It is no surprise, therefore, that as the size and impact of the Third Sector grew in America, so too did corporate contributions to its constituent organizations and causes. What are the key whys and wherefores of corporate philanthropy? What does it accomplish in realizing social objectives and satisfying business needs? How broad a concept of business social responsibility is likely to emerge at the dawning of a new century? These are the leading questions this book endeavors to address.

Give and Take is the product of my personal experience. The views presented here were formed during my tenure as president of the AT&T Foundation and as a senior officer of the company. The AT&T I joined in 1984 enjoyed an extraordinary legacy of directing private resources to

public service. In 1983, before AT&T divested itself of the Bell Companies, the firm employed more than a million people and became the first
company in the world to earn a billion dollars of profit in a single quarter
of business. It was also the world's most generous corporate philanthropist, giving away $73 million in cash alone for calendar year 1983. Con-
verting that corporate philanthropy from an obligatory function of a
government-blessed monopoly to a discipline whose mission was to identify the most significant intersections of business interest and societal
need fell to me.

Could the broad exercise of corporate social responsibility offer the
firm a sustainable competitive advantage as well as serve the public good?
The challenge and privilege distilled in that question was my preoccupation. More than any others, five colleagues enabled me to contribute to
writing a new chapter in AT&T's history of contributions to society.
Charles L. Brown, James Olson, and Robert E. Allen, the chairmen of
AT&T during my tenure, offered all those associated with the AT&T
Foundation the opportunity to direct the company's cash contributions
without interference or second guessing.

We enjoyed their confidence and worked hard to merit their trust.
They provided unfailing support.

Ed Block and Marilyn Laurie were two of my bosses at AT&T. Ed
took a chance and hired me. He usually didn't engage in such rash acts.
Ed believes that corporations can become dangerously insular places.
Exposure to the nation's vibrant Third Sector would help to keep the new
AT&T abreast of important social change. Ed also set an example of
bold, inspired assistance to nonprofits. It was he who suggested to Charlie
Brown that AT&T might make it possible for two respected journalists to
lead in the creation of the nation's most intelligent, informative, and civil
television news program. For fourteen consecutive years and at a total
cost of more than $90 million, AT&T underwrote public television's
MacNeil-Lehrer News Hour. It was a gifted and consequential act of
generosity.

Marilyn Laurie left an indelible mark by provoking those associated
with the AT&T Foundation to think long and hard about how philanthropy could help position a newly competitive firm to sell its products
and services. How could philanthropy add luster to AT&T's new brand?
Anonymous giving may have been exalted by the philosopher and phy-
sician Maimonides as the highest form of an individual's generosity, but

corporations and their needs were unknown to him. Laurie gently reminded us that it would be well for AT&T to be visibly and tastefully associated with its corporate contributions.

Two sets of colleagues are too numerous to mention individually. But they gave me the courage of my convictions about how a corporation could contribute to addressing the social challenges in its midst. By virtue of the efforts of the staff and trustees of the AT&T Foundation, the exercise of corporate social responsibility won an honored place in the new firm that emerged after the 1984 divestiture of the Bell Companies. Challenged competitively on every front for the first time in its hundred-plus-year history, AT&T since 1984 has experienced wave after wave of restructuring, reorganizing, merging, and downsizing. Consequently, the company has had to set aside reserves for facility closures, inventory liquidations, and the like. Under such circumstances, had philanthropy and civic commitment gone largely neglected, it would have been difficult to render too harsh a judgment.

About one hundred men and women worked especially hard to prevent that outcome—AT&T Foundation staff and trustees. They were indispensable to ensuring that their company lived up to its philanthropic heritage. They made all the difference.

This candid account of corporate philanthropy is a tribute to their leadership.

Give and Take owes its existence also to the generosity of model donors. AT&T, IBM, Levi-Strauss Corporation, the Horace W. Goldsmith Foundation, the Mimi and Peter Haas Fund, the Blanchette-Hooker Rockefeller Fund, the Rockefeller Brothers Fund, and a source that prefers to remain anonymous provided grant assistance. Their collective judgment that the growing role of corporations in American philanthropy is a tale worth telling in book-length form offered much encouragement. Their no-strings-attached support is a writer's wish fulfilled.

Two universities provided me with invaluable material and psychological support. Indiana University's Center on Philanthropy has emerged in the past decade as an indispensable source of teaching and scholarship on America's Third Sector. My appointment as Distinguished Professor of Philanthropic Studies facilitated access to an impressive faculty, student body, and library. In Bob Payton, the center's founder and guiding spirit, and Warren Ilchman, its first executive director, one could hardly find more nurturing and resourceful colleagues.

The New School for Social Research was my intellectual refuge in New York City. As a Presidential Fellow, I enjoyed contact with a welcoming faculty and an additional reason to meet with Jonathan Fanton, the New School's accomplished CEO and a wise counselor.

Special thanks are also reserved for the good friends and colleagues who read all or parts of the manuscript. Their comments and reactions improved the work, sparing the reader everything from inaccuracy to infelicity and saving the writer from error and oversight. I enumerate these volunteers alphabetically with a deep bow of warm appreciation and respect: Ed Bligh, Ed Block, Jonathan Fanton, Warren Ilchman, Sarah Jepson, Milton Little, Tim McClimon, Elizabeth McCormack, Fred Tipson, and Burt Wolder.

Nessa Rapoport is an author's muse. Present at the inception of the idea for *Give and Take,* Nessa knew just whom to coax, prod, persuade, and offer a dollop of praise. Her careful reading of the manuscript and well-placed criticism frequently sent me back to my desk, eager to clarify my thinking or illuminate a point of view. This book is much the better for Nessa's benevolent guidance.

The energy and skill of the people at Harvard Business School Press helped to improve the book as it assumed final shape. I'm particularly grateful to Nikki Sabin. Her enthusiasm for *Give and Take* was abundant. Her suggestions for improvements in the text were exacting and welcome.

I am among the many grateful clients of James Levine. He is an able agent and a resourceful collaborator.

This book was written in an old-fashioned way—at home, in long hand, with blue pen, on long thin-lined white pads. Alan Freed typed these virtually indecipherable jottings with speed, a keen eye for errors of omission and commission, and good humor.

For the full length of my service at AT&T, Margie Borrero served as my secretary. It was she who decoded my scrawl, guided this newcomer through the intricacies of a dauntingly complicated company, and assisted thousands of solicitors of funds. She also flawlessly saw to it that I arrived at the right place, on time, literally all over the world. *Muchas gracias, mi amiga. ¡Vaya con Dios!*

My wife, Elizabeth Cooke, has been a stalwart supporter. As a former president of the Bronx Museum of the Arts and current executive director of the Parks Council, two important nonprofit organizations in New York City, she understands how critical corporate philanthropy can be to assisting needy causes and advancing the public interest. She warmly encouraged the idea of revealing what goes on behind the closed doors of firms for the benefit of both philanthropists and grant seekers. Her experience and commentary are woven throughout *Give and Take*.

Our kids, Justin and Emily, cheered me on at every turn. No author could wish for a more supportive family.

Introduction

Of late, leaders of the nonprofit sector have become concerned that support flowing from corporate America has reached a plateau and will decline or, at best, level off. It is feared that corporate chief executives today are motivated solely by bottom-line concerns; that mergers and acquisitions are thinning the ranks of major corporate givers; and even that some companies are viewing many nonprofit organizations as marketplace competitors.

I sincerely hope that we are not witnessing a lessening in the commitment of business to support the nonprofit sector. By any precept and example, AT&T will do what it can to counter any such trend. . . . The men and women who guide AT&T firmly believe that our business has the responsibility to contribute to the long-term well-being of the society of which it is a part.

—ROBERT E. ALLEN, Chairman, AT&T, 1987

THIS BOOK IS THE PRODUCT OF A JOURNEY that has taken me from a seven-year tenure as the executive director of a major nonprofit institution in Manhattan to more than a decade as a senior executive at one of the world's largest companies. That excursion, from the 92nd Street Y, a cultural, educational, recreational, and community center of some repute, to AT&T, a multinational telecommunications firm, has been exhilarating. It has taught me much about the dynamics of both America's free enterprise system and its Third Sector.

The Third Sector is the name often given to the more than 600,000 tax-exempt nonprofit institutions in America that are eligible to receive tax-deductible gifts. They are the fastest-growing part of the nation's economy, employing one out of every seven of the nation's white collar workers and spending about $600 billion annually. In 1996, they received about $150 billion of charitable contributions, 90 percent of which came from the volitional acts of close to two thirds of Americans. They also benefited from the voluntary service of tens of millions of people.[1] If donations of money and time are to Third Sector organizations what voting is to democracy, it is worth observing that more than twice as many Americans participate in nonprofit life as cast a ballot in the 1996 presidential elections.

These impressive numbers reflect the indispensable work of organizations performing such vital societal roles as service provider, problem identifier, advocate of causes, guardian of values, and source of social capital.[2] They offer a dazzling variety of choice in education, health, social services, and the arts. They embrace social action movements, think tanks, self-help groups, gardening clubs, and veterans' organizations. They are as familiar as the American Association of Retired Persons, the Parent-Teacher Association, the Boy Scouts, the Sierra Club, the nearby private college and the local community center, and as specialized as the Philatelist Association of America and the Sherlock Holmes Society. It is a very rare and deprived American who can go for very long without becoming a customer of or a contributor to a nonprofit organization or cause.

The label "Third" is intended to distinguish nonprofits from the realm of government, on the one hand, and the for-profit activity of businesses, on the other. As a practical matter, these spheres of life often blend. My career is an illustration of that reality. I began a twelve-year stint at a Fortune 10 company serving as the architect and first CEO of its nonprofit foundation. I concluded by serving as a senior executive performing purely business functions.

The AT&T Foundation was created in 1984 as the principal vehicle for postdivestiture philanthropy when AT&T separated from the regional telephone companies, dubbed the Baby Bells, under court order. The local telephone companies, also known as the Regional Bell Operating

Companies or RBOCs, acting as monopolies, were assigned responsibility for providing customers with local calls. AT&T, by contrast, was to compete for domestic and international long-distance customers and for the manufacture and sale of telephone equipment for large telephone companies, businesses of all sizes, and individual users.

By the time I left the company, in 1996, I had been the managing director of AT&T's government relations outside the United States. In that same year, the U.S. Congress passed the Telecommunications Reform Act, sanctioning a virtual free-for-all among corporations seeking to enter new markets. Subject to meeting certain conditions, AT&T is free to offer local calling capability to all American businesses and consumers; local companies are free to offer intrastate, interstate, and international long distance. When the act is implemented fully, all telecommunication firms will be free to provide cable television services. Current cable providers may enter any and all parts of the voice and data communications market.

As managing director, it was my responsibility to help AT&T win permission to engage in business outside the United States. Doing so requires affirmative government consent everywhere in the world. Moreover, because most telephone companies abroad are owned by the public, government is not only the regulator but also the dominant potential customer. As a result, I was viewed as both a public affairs operative and an extension of AT&T's sales teams around the world. I carry in my wallet an airline frequent flyer card signifying my having traveled well over 1 million miles as part of the privilege of playing that dual role.

Between directing the myriad activities of the AT&T Foundation and the international government responsibility, I performed other business functions in advertising, sales and marketing communications, media relations, employee information, community relations, speechwriting, and brand management.

These business experiences enriched immeasurably the quality and the credibility of corporate philanthropy. After all, the purpose of business is to make money, not give it away. To the extent that staff associated with corporate philanthropy could also be seen as tangibly adding value to the firm, by demonstrating how charitable activities also served business objectives or by virtue of discharging other job responsibilities, so much the better for the impression left by foundation-like activity. The best way to keep philanthropy vibrant, well regarded, and well funded in a corporation is to demonstrate its regular contributions to business success. That means good corporate philanthropy incorporates both business interest and societal need. To find those areas of confluence requires knowing a company's businesses, as well as its customers, competitors, markets, and driving forces. And one must understand the charitable institutions and causes seeking a share of corporate wherewithal.

At first blush, becoming part of AT&T's business seemed to run the risk of my losing sympathy with the needs of the nonprofit sector and those it serves. Having been hired on the strength of my track record as chief executive, trustee, teacher, consultant, author, and public speaker in various nonprofit venues, would I now, at the age of thirty-eight, become a cog in the profit-generating wheel of a $75 billion corporate behemoth? Was promoting AT&T's business fundamentally incompatible with a philanthropist's calling—advancing the commonweal?

What I soon discovered was that the special value of corporate philanthropy resides in the business perspectives and the array of resources it brings to addressing societal needs. To understand the points of view of business and to garner those resources required me to be in *and* of the company. Nothing less could win the respect and confidence of colleagues. After all, this was no plain-vanilla philanthropy I had been chosen to lead. Although any corporate foundation is chartered by law to help achieve public purposes, AT&T's philanthropists could only do so by being true to the company's distinguished history, its values, and its compellingly new business interests.

While on this corporate journey, I was acutely aware of the absence of a decent guidebook. There are no Fodors or Birnbaums—let alone Michelin Guides—to corporate philanthropy. Why there is such a vacuum of helpful literature is puzzling. On a cash basis in 1996, America's companies gave away only 28 percent less in contributions than did all of its private foundations—$8.5 billion compared to $11.83 billion.[3] And if one adds up the dollar value of many other additional sources of corporate support to nonprofits—from advertising and marketing assistance to equipment donations; from gifts of products and services to participation in benefits, galas, sports fundraisers, and the like; from the use of facilities to pro bono executive volunteer time—for-profit firms may well contribute more to the Third Sector than any other single source, save the time and treasure of individual Americans. What has been written about private foundations can fill a small library. In contrast, filling a single shelf with first-rate books on the corporation and philanthropy is impossible. Until quite recently, no book-length treatment of the subject has ever been written by anyone who practiced the craft. Aware of that deficiency, I left AT&T in part to write candidly about the contemporary corporation and the Third Sector from the perspective of someone who has been an appreciative inhabitant of both worlds. This book redeems that pledge.

The goal of *Give and Take* is to reveal the underlying dynamics of philanthropy and the sources of its appeal in the context of modern business realities. It also aims to help practitioners and volunteers to solicit funds effectively and corporate benefactors to give wisely and well. That the corporation can help bridge the gap between critical social needs and the resources available to satisfy them is widely understood. Less well accepted is the view that philanthropy can contribute meaningfully to business success. I am a strong proponent of both contentions.

Philanthropy can help minimize potential damage to a firm's performance and to its reputation. Philanthropy can please customers, strengthen brand recognition, bolster morale, express the values of a business, and provide employees with leadership development opportunities. Philanthropy can also enhance the quality of life in communities where employees live and work and encourage key executive relationships with opinion leaders, customers, and government officials. Not least, philanthropy can help expose leading executives to new ideas, important social movements, and points of view they might not otherwise encounter.

In short, corporate philanthropy can help win friends and influence people. When executed well, the process and outcome of contributing to nonprofit institutions strengthen the donor as much, if not more, than the donee. Philanthropy can be no less than a source of sustainable competitive advantage difficult to attain by other means. It can energize, enrich, and sustain nonprofit causes in ways simply unavailable to private foundations and individuals.

Such claims are not intuitively obvious to the business executive who believes that the shortest distance between two points is the bottom line. "Giving money away" to nonprofits is still viewed by many inside companies as at best an innocuous—although some would charitably concede a virtuous—distraction from the central mission of a business: increasing the value of the shareholders' investment.

Nor is the proposition that business interests ought to be advanced by philanthropy greeted with open arms by all supplicants or scholars.

Many read into any corporate advantage from philanthropy a taint that devalues the gift, as if it were the fruit of a poisonous tree.

The first part of this book is devoted to the fundamentals of corporate philanthropy—its norms, roles, players, and craft. In the opening chapter on the dynamics of corporate philanthropy, my aim is to demonstrate that neither skepticism nor cynicism is warranted. In its many guises and manifestations, corporate philanthropy can add value to the firm *and* advance the commonweal. Indeed, only by doing both can it prosper. How that can happen, and the ways in which corporate philanthropy resembles and differs from individual and private foundation giving, are discussed. The array of resources available to corporations and the multiple stakeholders to which they are accountable help to explain their distinctive discharge of social responsibility.

Chapter 1 notes how these large realms of American life—the Third Sector and for-profit companies—relate to one another. Moving from the Y to a huge corporation is a voyage—from gemeinschaft to gesellschaft, from supplicant to benefactor, from psychic rewards to nonqualified stock options. Appreciating the continuities is as important as respecting the differences. To preside over a corporate foundation is to attempt to maintain a nonprofit entity in a for-profit firm. Whether this nonprofit tissue grafted to a commercial body is rejected or welcomed by its host depends on how well the properties of both are understood and their needs accommodated.

Chapter 2 turns to the art and craft of corporate philanthropy. What constitutes the world-class practice of philanthropy? What are the most common sins of omission and commission to be avoided and the most admired virtues to be embraced? How should a corporate philanthropist's performance be judged? Does the quality process and methodology have much to say about how to practice philanthropy professionally? These questions preoccupy reflective practitioners, I have found. My responses will, I hope, withstand scrutiny and be helpful to those whose unusual livelihood is centered on giving money away.

In Chapter 3 general principles and precepts of corporate philanthropy are illustrated by AT&T's own processes and practices. Oliver Wendell Holmes once observed that "in the life of the law, an ounce of experience is worth a pound of logic." In this space are offered a few of the lessons of my experience as both grantee and grantor. In the first role, acting as employee or trustee fundraiser, I've raised tens of millions of dollars for nonprofits. In the second capacity, acting as corporate donor, it was my privilege to be involved in the giving of almost $1 billion of cash and in-kind assistance to nonprofit institutions and causes.

If business philanthropy can be found where a firm's interest and societal need intersect most significantly, what precisely are those interests? How are they identified, and in what ways are they served by charitable contributions? Besides opportunity-based motivations, there are equally important obligation-based factors driving a firm's philanthropy. Three distinctive dimensions of corporate philanthropy are examined: how it is governed, how it engages employees, and how it can galvanize many other company resources.

The second part of the book analyzes in detail some of the workings of corporate philanthropy—its conduct, politics, and general condition.

In Chapter 4 the special manner in which corporations can relate to nonprofits for mutual benefit is examined from the perspective of the arts. How can giving to this cause be justified in view of the many compelling and competing demands on firms for a share of their charitable giving? The attraction of the company to the arts and of the arts to commercial support is grounded in sound experience and argument. Unfashionable though it may be to advance the case for the arts anew, firms would be mistaken to dismiss its persuasive claims on a share of their philanthropic support.

Chapter 5 considers the politics of philanthropy. From the ideological right come frontal challenges to the allegedly liberal bias of corporate giving programs. It is claimed that corporations, whether advertently or unknowingly, allow themselves to provide grant assistance to the very organizations that support excessive taxation, regulation, and litigation, thus clogging the arteries of annual earnings. It is asserted that companies, whether willfully or in fits of absentmindedness, philanthropically support nonprofits that propagate values detrimental to the free enterprise system. How, then, does such conduct serve the interests of the shareowners, implore the outraged?

AT&T is among those organizations consistently ranked by some partisans as leading allies of the left wing. Nor has the company escaped being accused of having become the pawn of right-wing, religious zealots. In 1991, AT&T found itself under attack by Planned Parenthood for having discontinued grant support after a quarter century of supplying consistent aid. Full-page advertisements in the nation's leading newspapers, annual-meeting proxy proposals, and telephone and letter-writing campaigns were among the tactics deployed in an unsuccessful attempt to compel AT&T to reverse course and resume philanthropic assistance.

Refuting the accusations of extremists on the right and rebutting the contentions of true believers on the left helped shed light on their some-times irresponsible tactics. My attempt to steer a course between the Scylla of charges of failing to understand corporate self-interest and the Charybdis of being perceived as the captive of a reckless, feckless right wing did not go without criticism. I take the occasion to separate the digestible wheat from the rhetorical chaff and mark the ground on which reasonable men and women can differ.

Chapter 6 assesses the current condition of corporate philanthropy. Will it continue to grow in real terms in the face of relentless short-term earnings pressure? How is it combating the continued principled opposi-tion of some to its raison d'être and the indifference of others to its daily operations? If corporate philanthropy is to bridge the gap between its potential and its performance, what obstacles need to be overcome?

The third part of the book turns the table. Corporate philanthropy is viewed entirely from the perspective of its beneficiaries and aspirants.

Sound corporate philanthropy sustains an open dialogue between donor and donee. At a minimum, both are parties to a mutually benefi-cial transaction. At the optimum, both are enriched by a continuing rela-tionship. Central to healthy exchanges of view and of value is empathy—the capacity to identify and help satisfy the needs of the other. Therefore, indispensable to an appreciation of corporate donor objectives, motiva-tions, and procedures is viewing them from the perspective of applicants.

In Chapter 7 I divulge "insider trade secrets" by providing pro bono advice to those seeking corporate philanthropic support. The secrets and rewards of asking well are fully disclosed. How do you capture the atten-tion of the right people in a firm? What is the best way to formulate and then communicate proposals? How do you know how much to request? How should you measure success (or the lack of it) in corporate fundrais-ing? Do you ask enough or only the minimum from an ample number of well-researched targets of opportunity? What is the role of the nonprofit board in soliciting corporate funds? Do these processes of asking differ from those for raising funds from individuals and private foundations? If so, how?

Seen from the vantage point of potential nonprofit beneficiaries, how corporations direct their largesse remains something of a puzzle.

Chapter 8 reconstructs some of the most frequently asked and incisive questions put to me by AT&T Foundation grantees and solicitors. These earnest and disarmingly straightforward queries deserve responses in kind. The resulting dialogue is intended to offer useful guidance to grantors as well as to would-be grantees.

The fourth part of the book offers a glimpse at the future of corporate philanthropy. Chapter 9 identifies some of the leading trends that are likely to shape the course of giving and asking in the decades ahead. Among them are the democratization of the workplace; the continued globalization of the economy; more frequent competition and collaboration among the commercial, charitable, and public sectors; the rising importance of small business and privately held companies as philanthropic players; and the primacy of the individual donor. These driving forces will help determine the magnitude, direction, and impact of overall philanthropy and of the corporation, its latest protagonist.

IN ITS SPIRIT RATHER THAN IN ITS PARTICULARS, corporate philanthropy advances a claim to being at the heart and soul of the firm.

At the heart of a firm in that giving away money well is impossible without being in close touch with a company's operating objectives, key executives, and vital interests. Philanthropy should connect to the very core of the corporation's preoccupations. Charitable matters should flow through the auricles and ventricles of a firm. If instead they are being processed at its extremities, that is a sign of philanthropic downgrading or performance failure.

At the soul of a firm in that philanthropy at its best is a noble expression of the values of a company and its people. How a company discharges its social responsibilities is an important manifestation of what it stands for. Another measure is whether employees, retirees, and shareowners can proudly tell their friends and colleagues about its good works. When a company aligns itself with the aspirations and beliefs of its employees, powerful sources of energy are unlocked, deeply felt identity with something larger than self emerges, and common bonds are discovered. In such a process, America, its companies, and all those with a stake in their welfare are very well served.

The nation flourishes when problem-solving energies and initiatives are nurtured. A healthy Third Sector protects the freedoms and promotes the interests of citizens by standing between them and a sometimes neglectful, even oppressive, state. A healthy Third Sector offers people choices for satisfying educational, recreational, cultural, health, or social needs by remedying market failures or excesses.

In essence, pluralism is indispensable to how America conducts its affairs, even its philanthropy. *Give and Take* demonstrates that corporations have earned their position at the center of the nation's philanthropic enterprise. Relatively new as benefactors, they have become a force to be reckoned with, important players in and of themselves but also worthy partners and willing collaborators. No discussion of how America copes with its leading challenges can any longer be complete without reference to its corporations and their exercise of social responsibility. At the table of philanthropy, corporations merit an honored place.

PART ONE

The Fundamentals of Corporate Philanthropy

I

The Dynamics of Corporate Philanthropy

> For what a business needs the most for its decisions—especially its strategic ones—are data about what goes on outside of it. It is only outside the business where there are results, opportunities, and threats.
>
> —PETER F. DRUCKER, 1982

Corporate Philanthropy: Its Powerful Potential

A COMPANY, LIKE A NATION OR AN INDIVIDUAL, is driven by its interests. These interests, in turn, are determined by the content of its business, the nature and number of its customers and competitors, the degree to which its operations are regulated or monitored by government, and the expressed needs of employees at its principal physical locations.

The raison d'être of companies is to earn a profit, continually increasing the value of the shareowner's stake in them. Theoretically, all of a for-profit's activities should contribute to this end, directly or indirectly, in the short run or over the long term. Although a company's philanthropy occasionally marks the difference between a customer gained or lost, such occurrences are rare. More often, philanthropy enhances a firm's capabilities.

For example, employee pride in the values of the company relates powerfully to whether and how those values are expressed in philanthropic acts. Such pride also instills loyalty to the firm.

Contributions activity is frequently regarded as an investment in a firm's brand identity—the degree to which it evokes such attributes as trust, caring, reliability, and fairness among customers.

3

The reputation of the corporation as a good citizen of the cities, states, and nations in which it operates is in part a function of its philanthropic performance. The body politic gives fuller rein to businesses that demonstrate commitment not just to profit but to employees, customers, and community. Corporate giving is one form of discharging a broader social responsibility.

Cultivating important relationships in the Third Sector can help advance such ends as favorably influencing government officials, recruiting outstanding students and mid-career personnel, and tapping the thinking of the best and brightest talent in the nation's think tanks and universities. All of these and many other connections are facilitated by walking through the doors philanthropists can open.

Exposure to the ideas that percolate in the nation's social action movements—consumer, environmental, civil rights, feminist, labor, free trade—can provide clues about market opportunities worth seizing and hazards to avoid. And the chance for corporate managers to assume important civic roles as nonprofit board members and volunteers and to grapple with nonprofit leadership challenges can be invaluable to the education of future senior executives.

From the plethora of companies exploiting philanthropy's powerful potential, I have selected four examples to illustrate how contributions-like activity can be put to imaginative use.

Dayton-Hudson Corporation is well known for its record of consistently generous charitable contributions. It regularly donates 5 percent of its pre-tax net income to charity—almost four times the percentage of the average company that contributes cash to nonprofits. It is also highly regarded for the extensive involvement of its retail department store managers in determining which community-based organizations receive charitable contributions of funds and employee volunteer time. Such widespread participation of key employees adds value to philanthropy. Employee morale rises. Sales and marketing objectives are advanced. Dayton-Hudson's good works become more widely known because its employees are proud believers.

The skillful use of corporate charitable connections by Levi-Strauss Company to cushion the blow of extensive factory closings and employees layoffs is worth noting. By providing negotiated access to nonprofit sources of job placement, social service counseling, and child care, Levi-Strauss helps its employees through a rough transition in practical and meaningful ways. Facility consolidations and personnel cutbacks that elsewhere are the subject of intense criticism become objects of praise. Levi-Strauss executives merge philanthropy and community relations with a high level of civic consciousness from which employees and towns across the nation and around the world manifestly benefit.

The formation of key relationships with government and private sector officials is critical to the advancement of American business, particularly abroad. Few companies have been as energetic and adept at cultivating those relationships with the aid of Third Sector institutions than the American International Group (AIG). AIG's chairman, Maurice "Hank" Greenberg, is legendary for the size of his Rolodex, the range of his associations, and the ubiquity of his presence in nonprofit venues. While hardly confined to think tanks and country-specific or region-specific organizations, Greenberg and his key lieutenants understand that the meeting rooms of the Council on Foreign Relations, the Asia Society, and the Institute for International Economics, among others, are filled with diplomats, politicians, ministry officials, and corporate leaders without whose cooperation AIG's marketing and sales objectives cannot be fully achieved. The extraordinary civic energy of AIG's executives is put to work as well in strengthening the governance, operating budgets, and balance sheets of these and other nonprofit associations.

IBM Corporation is strongly identified with philanthropic efforts to advance public school reform and the use of technology as a learning tool. Both undertakings cannot help but improve IBM's brand recognition and create a receptive environment for the sale of its products and services. Elementary and secondary schools across the nation and the children who attend them are both the beneficiaries of IBM largesse and an important customer base that merits the company's attention.

Mutual Benefits Beyond Philanthropy

Through a wide variety of means, commercial firms relate to nonprofit institutions to significant mutual advantage. The benefits that flow from a corporate-nonprofit relationship can be highly complex and multifaceted. To characterize them as if they transpired exclusively between a donor and a donee is to miss the point. Calling a company a "grantor" trivializes not only its relationship to nonprofits, but also to society more generally.

Calling a nonprofit a "grantee" reduces its identity to fundraiser and diminishes its status to that of perennial supplicant. Doing so confuses the tail with the dog.

Consider the many connections between the corporation and the university. A company like AT&T looks to universities as a primary source of knowledge that can nurture its own research and development capabilities. It views universities as a critical source of employees, several thousand of whom are recruited from college campuses each year. It depends on universities for their important contribution to the quality of life in communities where employees, retirees, and shareowners live and work. It recognizes that its employees are graduates who often display a fierce loyalty to their alma maters. And what is more important, it knows that universities—including administration, faculty, students, and alumni—house vital customers of high technology products and services. In all these manifestations of corporate-university interaction and mutual regard, AT&T is hardly alone.

To be sure, the university is a special kind of customer. One of its distinctive qualities is its eligibility to receive tax-deductible gifts. Companies are very aware of that attribute, which universities remind them of on numerous occasions.

In 1996, America's corporations contributed $2.7 billion in cash to higher education. That figure is nearly 31 percent of the total cash donations of for-profits to charity ($8.5 billion) and approximately 21 percent of the $14.25 billion raised by colleges and universities in that year.[1] Such gifts are important to the schools that receive them. But they co-exist with and are in no small measure the byproducts of many other interactions between the university and the company.

Each year, universities enjoy the attendance of tens of thousands of students whose tuition and fees are partly to fully subsidized by companies. Universities facilitate the placement of students in part-time and full-time jobs of commercial firms, and faculty members benefit from summer internships in and sabbatical leaves at the nation's businesses. In turn, companies buy services from the university, including research and development and commissioned studies of all kinds. Companies serve the university and its constituencies as customers supplying goods and services, often at discounted rates. And the university is an outlet for the civic energy of company executives who serve it in a myriad of leadership roles, from company volunteer to curriculum development adviser and from member of a distinguished visiting committee to trustee.

The philanthropic relationship between the corporation and the university is animated by all these transactions. It does not stand independent of them. Indeed, the nature and magnitude of corporate grant-making to the university cannot be understood apart from these other mutual benefits and interactions. Philanthropy is the consequence of such positive exchanges between the corporation and the university even more than their cause.

Neither private foundations nor individual benefactors engage in nearly so many exchanges of value between themselves and the nonprofits they support. Therein lies a critical difference between what it's like to practice philanthropy from inside a company and to perform the same function elsewhere. There are many others.

The Singularity of Corporate Philanthropy

Beyond the multitude of its interactions with nonprofits and the plenitude of the resources it can bestow on worthy causes, corporations bring to their philanthropy a distinct perspective. Companies certainly do exhibit diverse philanthropic agendas and ambitions. But they are virtually united in affirming that although nonprofits are clearly distinguishable from profitmaking firms, there is no reason why they cannot conduct their affairs in businesslike fashion. Careful attention to the efficiency and effectiveness of nonprofits are characteristic of corporate giving.

Corporate executives expect clarity about the mission, objectives, strategies, tactics, and anticipated outcomes of nonprofit work, whether the request is for general institutional assistance or for project support. Businesspeople expect grantees to be accountable for achieving promised results. They expect goals to be expressed in measurable terms, milestones to their realization identified, and timetables explicitly noted.

Many corporate managers much admire the nobility of purpose that animates the activity of many nonprofits. But managers must also place emphasis on the sharp execution of sound operational plans. Lofty goals must be closely aligned with practical ways and means to realize them. It's acceptable for nonprofit leaders to have their heads in the clouds as long as their feet are planted firmly on the ground. For grand dreams to be ful-filled, mundane deadlines must be met.

Businesspeople believe that they bring to their engagement with nonprofits a set of disciplines and methodologies that allow idealism and pragmatism to serve one another. A vision will remain just that unless it is bound to the real-world challenge of reaching a desired destination.

An episode from my experience illustrates the point. In warning me about the risks of leaving the CEO post at the 92nd Street Y, a well-known and well-regarded nonprofit, some friends wondered aloud whether I'd survive the border crossing to AT&T. The Y is a charitable institution, they reasoned. It must therefore be mission-driven, process-ridden, and averse to measurement. Presumably, authority must be unclear. The line between the policy-making prerogatives of the board of directors and the operational discretion of the professional staff surely is blurred. The Y enjoyed neither a bottom line nor a ballot box to periodi-cally assess its progress. How, then, could I adjust to a starkly different environment—one characterized, these friends assumed, by straightfor-ward profit objectives, clear patterns of authority, and an intolerance for cumbersome decision making?

The concerns of my well-motivated friends were largely misplaced, I soon found, and based on invalid presumptions and assumptions. These emerged full blown from a view of the Third Sector and of for-profits that was more akin to caricature than portraiture. As it happened, the powers that be at the Y judged the organization to be reasonably well managed. Figures on endowment size, cash reserves, earned and contributed income, per-unit costs, and subsidy per user were frequently employed as analytical tools to judge organizational performance. As guides to action, such tools are every bit as exacting and useful in their milieu as are earn-ings per share, gross margins, revenue generated per employee, and accu-mulated debt on the balance sheet in a corporate environment.

If the Y's trustees occasionally erred by involving themselves exces-sively in operational matters, corporate governance is often criticized for being too relaxed and too detached. Not infrequently lacking in company boardrooms is a tough-minded review of business performance. Directors of profit-making firms are often accused of yielding too much unfettered discretion to senior management.[2]

So at odds with reality is the excessively sharp contrast usually drawn between nonprofits and for-profits that I arrived at AT&T some-what startled by what I found. The company's state of affairs included an abundance of group process and more than a little ambiguity on the subject of who is responsible for what. There was also a surprising lack of clarity on the part of many employees about what they were expected to do to help achieve business objectives.

I was also pleasingly taken aback to discover that the first profitmaking firm in the world ever to earn a billion dollars in a single quarter was driven by more than financial goals. AT&T had formulated a mission as important, as well articulated, and as moving as any I'd encountered among organizations in the Third Sector:

> We are dedicated to being the world's best at bringing people together—giving them easy access to each other and to the information and services they want and need—anytime, anywhere.3

AT&T, it turned out, possessed not only business interests but also business values. By living them, shareowners, customers, and employees would be rewarded amply. Those values remain "Respect for individuals; dedication to helping customers; the highest standards of integrity; innovation and teamwork."4

Just as nonprofits have widely recognized the need to adapt sound business principles and practices, corporations recognize that employees are motivated by values as well as interests and by a mission that speaks to more than profitability. To be sure, differences between for-profit businesses and nonprofit institutions—cultural, legal, managerial, behavioral—abound. But there are important and growing areas of convergence. Indeed, much learning now occurs across these once more distant and more distinct realms of American life.

For example, that roughly three quarters of the 92nd Street Y's revenue was earned income—from tuition, fees for service, and ticket purchases—meant that the place simply had to be market-oriented and customer-driven. Key staff looked to profit-making firms for guidance on product and service attributes, pricing, and promotion.

For example, that AT&T had been a government-blessed, private monopoly for more than a century meant that its employees considered themselves not just businesspeople but also public servants. AT&T people understand that in a democratic society, corporations operate ultimately by citizen consent. Business firms are creatures of law, not products of nature.

Under such circumstances, the assignment I'd accepted of building a nonprofit charitable foundation in a for-profit firm was not greeted with the howls of derision nor the scowls of disrespect that more than a few of my friends had predicted. Still, giving away cash and in-kind gifts is hardly regarded as conventional business activity. Who could blame the average AT&T employee for viewing philanthropy with a mixture of healthy curiosity and heavy skepticism?

The Setting for Corporate Philanthropy

The assessment of a corporation's record of social responsibility varies with the eye of the observer. Surveys of consumers, businesses, reporters, and public officials reveal a fairly broad consensus, however, about what constitutes responsible behavior by a for-profit enterprise.

Companies are expected to make money. In emphasizing the centrality of profit in the mission of any free enterprise firm, Peter Drucker put it well:

> Economic performance is the *first* responsibility of a business. A business that does not show a profit at least equal to its cost of capital is socially irresponsible. It wastes society's resources. Economic performance is the basis; without it, a business cannot discharge any other responsibilities, cannot be a good employer, a good citizen, a good neighbor.[5]

Profitable companies are expected to be law-abiding. They are expected to tell the truth about operational and financial performance and about their products and services. They are expected to pay their bills and their taxes.

A corporation is also expected to treat its employees fairly. Employers should pay a fair wage and fringe benefits, maintain good working conditions, including a safe workplace, and provide opportunities for training and promotion to worthy employees. Survey respondents report that they often take their cues about a company's social responsibility from the expressed views of insiders. If a company's own workers hold it in high regard and tout its accomplishments, that's a solid sign of good corporate conduct.[6]

Responsible companies are expected to focus on their customers. It is anticipated that they will provide safe products and services, delivering what they promise at fair prices. It is also presumed that companies will disclose key information about items for sale. Their employees or agents are obligated to stand behind claims about product or service performance should something go awry.

Only after these minimum conditions are satisfied do most Americans take into account other manifestations of good corporate citizenship. Does a firm participate actively in the civic life of the communities in which its employees live and work and its principal customers reside? Does it incubate a charitable contributions program that supports critical nonprofit organizations and causes? Do its hiring, purchasing, and supplier management procedures provide opportunities for women and minorities to compete for treasured jobs and contracts?

The answers to such questions surely influence the perception of a firm's citizenship. But if it is thought to violate or skirt the law, if there is evidence that it sells an unsafe product, misleads its customers or investors, or treats its employees unfairly, then the most generous philanthropic programs, the most spirited community-involvement projects, and the most praiseworthy diversity efforts will be for naught.

Ralph Nader's well-documented allegations in the 1960s that American-made automobiles were "unsafe at any speed" damaged severely the reputation of car companies.[7] The organized resistance of General Motors, Ford, Chrysler, and American Motors to such safety measures as seat belts and air bags challenged claims of social responsibility by these car manufacturers for several decades.

The many sins of commission and omission leading up to and following the massive oil spill in Alaska from the *Exxon Valdez* tarnish to this day that oil company's desire to be regarded as a solid citizen.

When Prudential's senior management stands justly accused of having tolerated sustained misrepresentations to customers by its sales force, the good deeds of its foundation pale in comparison.

As seven chief executive officers of America's tobacco companies— Philip Morris, Liggett Group, RJR Nabisco, Brown and Williamson among them—testify under oath that to the best of their knowledge and belief smoking is not addictive, the socially responsible activities of their firms are badly damaged by the derision that greets such a bald public misrepresentation.

And when AT&T announced an intention to reduce its workforce in 1996 and 1997 by forty-thousand employees in the wake of reporting record earnings for 1995 and in the same period when its CEO was scheduled to receive record-setting compensation, an exemplary history of corporate social responsibility was blemished in the minds of many.

The content of this book is corporate philanthropy. Its context finds corporate philanthropy housed in an enterprise with many other capacities to advance or retard the common good. A firm can contribute handsomely to nonprofits that train women and minorities for employment but hire few for its own workforce. A company can take philanthropic leadership in supporting initiatives to improve primary and secondary education while lobbying the state capital in its headquarters location for tax cuts that inevitably result in reduced resources allocated to assist public education. An industrial enterprise can support environmental nonprofits in exemplary fashion but fail to offer its employees such alternatives to driving to work as busing, car pooling, mass-transit vouchers, and telecommuting options; or to provide a serious recycling program for solid wastes; or to reduce the level of pollutants emanating from its own manufacturing processes.

Conversely, companies can perform ably in a given field internally and virtually ignore societal needs in the same areas of endeavor. Some are known to provide state-of-the-art educational training programs for their employees while offering little philanthropic support even to those colleges and universities from which many of their own workers have graduated and others will be recruited. Some firms own fine art collections and pay lavish attention to the design and packaging of their products but virtually ignore the needs of artists and the many community institutions that nurture the visual and performing arts.

Corporate philanthropy is one major component of a firm's relationship to society at large. In a very well run outfit, much of the work of contributions should be aligned with a firm's operations and with the positions it advances before governmental bodies. Indeed, at their best, philanthropic staff and trustees should be able to influence company policies and practices in overlapping and adjacent fields of endeavor. Axiomatically, the converse is also true. Key company executives should be positioned and invited to help set philanthropic objectives and to participate in formulating charitable contributions policy.

Suffice it to state that such careful, deliberate orchestration of a company's complex processes and personalities is not routine. Harmony, though highly desirable, should not be assumed. To assess thoroughly a for-profit enterprise's track record of social responsibility requires examining all the critical dimensions of its conduct.

2

The Art and Craft of Philanthropy:
A Practitioner's Credo

Every individual endeavors to employ his capital so that its produce may be of greatest value. . . . He intends only his own security, only his own gain. . . . By pursuing his own interest he frequently promotes that of society more effectively than when he really intends to promote it.

—ADAM SMITH
The Wealth of Nations, 1776

It is certainly not a good citizen who does not wish to promote, by every means in his power, the welfare of the whole society of his fellow citizens.

—ADAM SMITH
The Theory of Moral Sentiments, 1790

The Purists, the Utilitarians, the Pragmatists

THE RELATIONSHIP OF COMPANY PHILANTHROPY to the pursuit of business interest is a subject at once fascinating and controversial.

On the one side, there are the purists, who contend that the favorable tax status accorded charitable gifts, if nothing else, must impel businesses to use contribution funds in the public interest. This school of thought holds that corporate philanthropists must judge applicants at arm's length and on their merits. They are obliged to resist pressures from customers, colleagues, and senior management to use charitable funds to advance short-term business interests. A sharp distinction is to be drawn between the use of eleemosynary resources and corporate expense budgets. Philanthropic funds are intended first and foremost to benefit society; any business advantage accruing from such expenditures should be incidental. General corporate funds are spent in the interests of shareowners. Any public interests served at the same time are utterly coincidental.

Philanthropists, who are among those charged with embodying the corporate commitment to society writ large, are therefore expected to be *in, but not of,* the business.

On the other side, there are the utilitarians, who regard contributions as a necessary evil, devoid of redeeming business value except insofar as philanthropy is but another means to achieve short-term business objectives. Contributions are considered tolerable if they advance business self-interest in a manner indistinguishable from, say, buying research or consulting services, or print ads, or public affairs influence. In this conception, those who direct philanthropic activity are not unlike their advertising, marketing, and lobbying colleagues.[1]

Neither line of argument holds theoretical appeal. Neither commends itself to the practical mind. Neither should constitute the aspiration of effective corporate philanthropists, whose calling lies on that continuum between the poles of idealism and the undiluted pursuit of institutional self-interest.

Much More Than Cash

Corporate philanthropy is distinct from private foundation and individual giving. Corporations employ millions of people. A company's charitable dollars can therefore reinforce or stimulate voluntary activity of all kinds—from service on nonprofit boards to matching employee gifts; from provision of pro bono financial, legal, advertising, public relations, and management assistance to leading fundraising campaigns and loaning executives to Third Sector organizations.

A company can authorize the use of facilities, donate surplus or state-of-the-art equipment, hire meaningful numbers of graduates of universities or research institutes, and stimulate continuous interaction between beneficiary and donor. Neither foundations nor individuals can so readily harness these powerful sources of assistance to nonprofits.

If these forms of help to nonprofits and the corporate perspective on society are important ingredients of the "value added" of business to philanthropy, then how is their utilization to be energized and directed? How can contributions staff engender in their colleagues an appreciation of the business *and* societal reasons to give of themselves and of the resources under their control to compelling Third Sector causes, projects, and institutions?

To start with, corporate philanthropists must understand their business and its people. To be in *and* of the company. Private foundations are in the business of charitable activity. Companies are in business to earn a profit for their shareowners. Those who forget or understate the importance of this distinction run the risk of losing support in their own bailiwick for the philanthropic enterprise.

Corporate contributions staff can ill afford to be isolated or divorced from the complex business that nurtures philanthropy. But even if they could be, they shouldn't. For the quintessential value of *corporate* philanthropy is its capacity to stimulate support to the Third Sector that neither individuals nor private foundations are as capable of generating. And the perspectives that inform such giving—the business perception of societal need and nonprofit worth—are part of that donor pluralism which is to be valued, not denied, ignored, or gainsaid.

Relating to the Third Sector

Corporate philanthropy is not "a thing apart." Rather, it is intimately related to a host of other interactions between corporations and the Third Sector. Flowing from an appreciation of that reality, strong professional relationships can develop within companies, and key employees can encounter nonprofit life for the first time or experience it differently. Enormous "value added" can accrue to donees.

A company's relationship to the Third Sector is only partly charitable in impulse. In varying measure, nonprofits represent markets, sources of employees, pools of research and expertise, and sources of community goodwill for companies.

To ignore the business interests served by interaction with the Third Sector is both flawed conceptually and fatal in practice. Acts of pure altruism are rare. Individual donors also seek to do good for institutions, causes, and people. But why do they?

Does the social status such acts confer, the business opportunities they create, the guilt they relieve, the impulse to immortality they satisfy, or the visibility with which they are associated often have something to do with donor motivation? Of course. And foundation executives and nonprofit board members, or at least those I've been privileged to know, are not themselves devoid of institutional, personal, and professional interests that they wish to advance. Only infrequently do such motivations diminish the value of the gift. In short, the complexity of motivations that give rise to charitable gifts is not confined to corporations. To assume otherwise and to pursue some archetype of "pure" philanthropy is to deny reality. Donors are not just idealists. They are pragmatists, too. Prototypically, philanthropy reflects both donor interest and grantee need. The philanthropist, whether individual or institutional, seeks to advance those interests and help satisfy those needs.

Dangers and Risks

But what of the dangers and risks of being so enveloped by company objectives and so entangled by collegial perceptions of company self-interest that the discipline of philanthropy is lost in the welter of contending forces pushing at and within for-profit firms?

To exert a measure of control over the real dangers and risks, contribution officers must not only know the business of which they are a part but also bring to it the conviction that corporations don't direct their largesse to mere charitable objects. By understanding fully the multifaceted contributions of the Third Sector to American life, philanthropic officers can demonstrate how corporations are enriched by that sector's vital presence.

The soundness of society and the comfort, health, and welfare of corporate employees are dependent on the viability of the sector. Were it crippled, our culture, our intellect, and our polity would be critically deprived.

Joining Company Forces

To succeed in profit-making firms, philanthropists must know their stuff. Of course, they need to be experts on the contributions nonprofit institutions offer to the welfare of society and to the companies that employ them. But required as well is an understanding of what their colleagues inside the business are endeavoring to accomplish. Without the cooperation and assistance of others inside the company, the only resource at the disposal of the philanthropist is the charitable contributions budget. Gaining access to other important assets that nonprofits relish requires teamwork.

Corporate philanthropists must be skilled advocates. They must cultivate their corporate gardens, not just by example but by precept. They should also encourage corporate colleagues and opinion leaders to become eyewitnesses to what philanthropy makes possible. When the support and understanding of senior company officers are secured, then the opportunity to integrate a corporate contributions program with other aspects of the business will naturally follow. It will then be possible to relate philanthropy on its own terms to such activities as marketing, advertising, community relations, and public affairs.

So diverse, wide-ranging, and porous is the Third Sector and so overlapping are the corporate functions relating to it that no one activity, in isolation, can be effective. Call the whole *external affairs, corporate social responsibility,* or just plain *good corporate citizenship,* and suddenly the tidy compartments by which complex institutions organize themselves fade in the face of their common interests and the abilities of those who manage them.

To be sure, life would be simpler if one could just parachute the pure or semi-pure altruists into a corporation to do their thing unencumbered, blithely ignorant of their environment, and, moreover, virtually unaccountable. But that's not possible or even desirable. Developing firm philanthropic roots in a company does not require diverting resources or distracting attention from critical business concerns. Rather, it demands addressing them even as social needs are served.

Striking the balance between idealism and self-interest is, I believe, the calling of those who hold the truly unusual vocation of giving away funds from organizations whose basic purpose is to earn them. That challenge demands skilled practitioners who stay the course. It is noble and ennobling work for people who are very privileged. With those privileges come profound responsibilities.

The Donor: Temperament Matters

Among those responsibilities is to recognize that funders are means to ends—servants, not masters of causes. Corporate donors hold funds in trust for service to their firm and to grantee beneficiaries. They do so by extending grants to people and organizations much closer operationally to concrete problems in a given field than are their corporate colleagues.

This basic view of a donor is laden with operational meaning. It calls for humility. It suggests that the most important single attribute of a corporate funder is the capacity to listen well to clients and applicants. It argues that although there is always room to invest in new organizations, no sound philanthropic strategy can safely ignore the potential for renewal and innovation in existing institutions.

Because corporate executives have access to resources that nonprofits cherish, people pay heed to what they say, often profess to agree and offer compliments, deserved and otherwise. Some donors are reputed to bask in the flattery, and from an aspiring grantee's perspective, some even fall into the trap of arrogance. Others are simply remote—difficult to reach by phone, unavailable for meetings. Too many funders act as if their role as grantmaker bestows on them the right not to listen but to lecture, not to question but to posture, not to assist but to demand. Properly conceived, however, philanthropy is not so much an act of one-way giving as it is an informed transaction between those in a position to investigate a problem, satisfy a need, or resolve an issue and those possessed of the resources to help finance such tasks.

Good fundraisers search for the common ground between societal need and business interest. So do good donors. But forcing it—asking a nonprofit to do something outside its mission—converts the grant into a club rather than a carrot and makes the corporate donor an intruder rather than a benefactor.

Most of the time, grants fill spaces in the life of a grantee. With perseverance, the spaces filled can grow and endure. But major changes rarely come swiftly. Grants that have lasting impact frequently require what the Japanese call "patient capital."

The quick fix and the fad are ephemeral. The philanthropic equivalent of the summer soldier and the sunshine patriot rarely accomplishes much. Good philanthropists are more like long-term investors and venture capitalists than speculators and gamblers. They take prudent and calculated risks. And they keep their grantee portfolio sufficiently diversified to balance various approaches to solving problems. In other words, they are realistic enough to recognize that not all grantees will succeed and results-oriented enough to establish appropriate measures for the return on their charitable investments.

Good philanthropists are eager to learn. They read widely and deeply. They enjoy meeting people inside and outside the firm. They are curious and alert to internal and external opportunities. They enjoy getting out of the office, site visiting, seeing the world as others do. In short, they possess the capacity to empathize—a rare gift, indeed.

Rarer still is knowing how to say no to those who seek financial support. Like one hand clapping, the sounds of the letter of inquiry unread or unacknowledged, the phone call unreturned, and the solicitor's question unaddressed are deafening in their silence. The art of saying no—considerately, helpfully, promptly—is much neglected.

Effective corporate philanthropists pay attention to much more than giving and getting. They carefully weigh the whys, wherefores, and hows of a request declined. They bring together corporate colleagues or nonprofit staff where collaboration is necessary to solve problems. They regard themselves as cheerleader and publicist of favored institutions and causes. They provide advice, counsel, and technical assistance where needed.

Modesty, curiosity, attentiveness, helpfulness, empathy—these are some of the leading personal characteristics of admired funders.

The Grantmaker's Challenge: Promising Philanthropic Techniques

The situation facing a corporate philanthropist is typically characterized by grand goals and limited means.

From a company's perspective, those goals might include strengthening the brand, broadening and deepening the customer base, facilitating the formation of relationships with key government and Third Sector leaders, helping to compete effectively for able employees and for entry into new markets, and strengthening its overall reputation. Those are no small aspirations for any firm's philanthropy to embrace.

From a philanthropic perspective, more often than not what's at stake is contending with a significant social problem or opportunity, one that is insufficiently recognized and inadequately addressed. Powerful forces support the status quo. They are tenacious and resourceful. To successfully overcome resistance to change is a battle against the odds.

Put simply, the classic challenge of the corporate philanthropist is to apply limited resources to move people and events in a new direction toward objectives that benefit both the firm and society.

One of the powerful tools of the philanthropic trade to help seize that challenge is a practice known as "conditioning the gift." The conditions come in many forms. All are insufficiently used by companies.

The Matching Condition. The company offers a challenge grant to a nonprofit institution. The gift is advanced only when an agreed-upon sum is raised from others toward the same purpose. To strengthen the grantee, sometimes the challenge is addressed not only to the aggregate amount others should contribute but also to the identity of those sources. For example, a given nonprofit might be challenged to find more supporters from alumni or parents or those who reside in a certain state or country. Or family foundations, small businesses, or large corporations might be the right targets for improving the nonprofit's fundraising performance.

The Evaluative Condition. A company provides a specified sum only when institutional or project effectiveness is satisfactorily demonstrated.

The Multi-Year Pledge. A company extends a grant in several installments subject to the nonprofit having reached clearly stated milestones.

The Operational or Governance Condition. The gift is given on the condition that the institution receiving it change in some way not necessarily related to the purpose of the grant.

Governance conditions are usually the most controversial. Many view them as intrusions on the prerogatives of independent nonprofit institutions. To condition a grant on behavior unrelated to its specific purpose is to risk accusations of overreaching on the part of the donor. Crudely applied, governance conditions often evoke a "how dare they?" reaction. Institutional resistance to broad attempts to impose from the outside changes in basic internal structure and process can be very strong.

For example, various levels of government and the Ford Foundation have for years importuned nonprofits to show evidence of ethnic and racial diversity on their staffs and boards of trustees. Though the intention may be admirable, the results of such efforts are unclear, largely undocumented, and certainly unaudited. They haven't been warmly received.

The successful application of any of these conditions is generally the outcome of a partnership between donor and donee. The power of the grantor is less to order than to induce, less to exhort than to explain, and less to control than to influence. The prudent exercise of that power demands a clarity of purpose. It also calls for mastery of the dynamics of activity in a given nonprofit field and in the benefactor firm.

A second underutilized tool of the corporate philanthropic trade is the cultivation of collaborators, both inside and outside the firm. Demonstrating the benefits of cooperation to sales, marketing, human resources, government relations, and line colleagues to advance a philanthropic project is often painstaking work. In any large institution, divisions and units tend to establish highly focused goals and to pursue them with their own resources. Jealous of prerogatives, protective of turf, and wary of offers of assistance, corporate executives have a will to autonomy that is very strong. But overcome it by mastering a colleague's needs, providing proof of the capability to help satisfy them, and cultivating trust through effective relationship building and—bingo!—all kinds of help will be on the way.

Inside the *same* firm, centripetal forces are by definition stronger than the centrifugal. It should therefore not come as a surprise that the obstacles to sustained cooperation *between* companies and *among* companies and private foundations is formidable. Philanthropic actors highly prize their autonomy. Institutional donors generally find it difficult to address major societal challenges collectively.

It is not difficult to encounter large private foundations whose officials believe that with their brainpower and other people's money, the right solutions are at hand. Funding sources eager to leverage the resources of others can always be found. And identifying corporations willing to collaborate as long as the program carries their brand name is not a tough assignment. The ability to cooperate on the takeoff of a project (not just its landing), a willingness to occasionally be leveraged by others, and a proclivity to follow as well as to lead are qualities not found in abundance in philanthropic circles. Break through the philanthropic parochialism and you'll likely find unusual sources of power to address large-scale social problems.

Another perspective on collaboration takes the view that institutions almost always house enlightened individuals identified with progressive change. Corporate philanthropists must find them not only within their own firms but within their nonprofit grantees. Locating those "children of light," shaping grants to support and highlight their work, and providing them with much-needed recognition can be an important philanthropic strategy.

The tendency of corporations and foundations to pursue courses of action independent of one another is generally no less true for nonprofits. To foster connections between similarly situated or challenged institutions is a role philanthropists can ably play. Unfortunately, the magnitude of so many social problems is such that disseminating information and promoting networking among the like-minded barely begins to establish the kind of sustained cooperation needed to fashion solutions. Philanthropists can use their grant funds to require project collaboration. They can request that applicants show evidence of such collaboration in their request for support. They can decide to fund only collaborative projects involving several organizations. They can insist that not only the CEOs but the board chairs also sign letters of intent, secure in the knowledge that partnerships rarely work without a high level commitment of both staff and board.

A third philanthropic driving force flows out of this notion of partnerships between donors and enlightened parties within nonprofits. It's necessary to acknowledge that after all the data on social causation have been compiled, after all the hypotheses have been tested, after all the eligibility and review criteria have been finely honed, grants are given to people. Gifted, driven, imaginative people, it is hoped. People possessed of passion, whose judgment and values merit trust. Finding such individuals, offering them encouragement, and connecting them to like-minded colleagues and sources of assistance is no small part of a corporate philanthropist's work.

For the attentive philanthropist, institutional transitions offer yet another critical opening for influence. There are defining moments in an institution's life when well-placed funds will make a special difference. For example, such an interval occurs when the CEO or board chair is scheduled to be replaced. Leadership change can be a wonderful period, ripe with the promise of reassessment and reappraisal. Positive change may be in the offing even when an organization experiences economic hardship, personality conflicts, or environmental pressures. In such cases, insiders are also suddenly open to ideas that will help them move to a new and better place. Crisis breeds opportunity.

Setting a Framework: Grant Guidelines

Every company needs to shape its philanthropic vision, mission, and values. Every corporate philanthropist needs to craft annual objectives that serve the firm and the public interest. Appropriate variations of these articulated needs find their way to grant guidelines.

Those guidelines are an important tool. They indicate to a carefully defined universe of nonprofits the purposes for which a company will entertain funding and the steps to take in inquiring further or applying for support. Every corporate grantmaker receives far many more applications than available funds can satisfy. If philanthropy is to generate good will, the tactful treatment of those who won't receive funding is essential.

Both needs are served by setting forth clearly guidelines on what is (and is not) eligible for funding. Aggressive fundraisers are like commuters by car in one of the nation's large cities; they find it very difficult to take no for an answer. To dispel any grounds for confusion about what is or is not acceptable, clarity helps. New York City, for example, has at least three kinds of no-parking signs. There's the sign that reads "no parking under certain circumstances." There's another that says "no parking at any time." And there's yet another that warns, "Don't even think about parking here." Grant guidelines are incomplete without very clear "no funding" signs.

When the corporate donor describes openly and fully the kind of applications to be entertained, the ingenuity and creativity of the responses from nonprofits are frequently impressive. But too often, the mail and the telephone message stack seem like an albatross round the necks of beleaguered donors who somehow never clear their desks. Instead such donors would do well to eagerly read that mail and return those calls. The correspondents and message leavers often have ideas that match in uncanny and unpredictable ways the very corporate and societal objectives a philanthropist wishes to pursue. And even if that doesn't come to pass, among those solicitors are real or potential customers, supporters, and allies. Treat them as courteously, thoughtfully and promptly as possible.

Stimulating Competition

Beyond the mailbox and the telephone, corporations should avail themselves of another technique—requesting competitive proposals from a "by-invitation-only" cluster of institutions. Describe a problem or a challenge, and prescribe a basic direction to help address it. Invite institutions to apply, making clear how many applicants have been solicited and how many grants will be awarded. Consider appointing a panel of peers in a given field to review and rank order the applications for your consideration.

Properly formulated, this kind of RFP (request for proposal) process can work extremely well. It discloses your philanthropic intentions to a far larger number of institutions than will actually receive grants. To the degree that even those you decline to assist take the preparation process seriously, there is a likelihood that applicants' energies have been engaged sufficiently to impel a search for other sources of funding and even to self-finance newly devised projects. The resulting multiplier effect is a significant philanthropic bonus. Assuming a sound and well-led review process, those who don't win rarely blame the grantor. And those who become beneficiaries are honored by having prevailed in an exacting, competitive process. Overall, such an approach leaves the company identified with an initiative likely to be remembered for the exercise of leadership.

But companies resist the RFP process. They are concerned that invitees who get turned down will be angry at having been put to work for naught. Moreover, justifying the ultimate list of winners and losers is always problematic. And setting in motion such invitation-only competition is time consuming, beginning with selecting which organizations you'll encourage to apply.

Still, those who have used the RFP find that its benefits far outweigh its costs and risks. If the company is an authority on the subject matter of the field, few nonprofits will question its grant choices. When the company isn't an expert, the selection of recognized outside authorities to help evaluate applicants is usually well received. Assuming that the area selected for attention is carefully chosen, applicants are probably active in it already or want to become so. When the process is handled sensitively, far from becoming upset at not receiving a grant, applicants are honored to have been invited into the small circle of competitors.

At AT&T, the RFP mechanism was utilized fairly extensively. One example—for AT&T's OnStage, a new play competition that has been in continuous existence since 1985—is reproduced in full in the appendix to this book. The proposal demonstrates the versatility, impact, and creative freedom achieved by this approach to soliciting applications.

Threshold Questions

Every foundation needs to grapple with some basic questions in giving away funds. Only some of the issues these questions raise are likely to be fully resolved in published guidelines, however. The following questions are essential to the execution of a sound philanthropic strategy.

- To what degree will our foundation be inner-directed and to what degree will it be responsive?

- In how many fields of endeavor will we attempt to make a serious difference?

- Do we favor a broad-based, (inter)national program, or will we focus on just a few regions of the world or of the United States?

- Should we provide fewer, larger grants to a relatively small number of recipients or a greater number of smaller awards to a wider circle of grantees?

- In our giving pattern, to what extent do we favor large institutions over small, the established instead of the aspiring, and renewal grants for existing donees over new funding relationships?

- What's our policy toward funding direct service rather than advocacy, policy studies or technical assistance? What's our position on providing operating as against project support? Under what circumstances, if any, will contributions to endowment be entertained?

- How much of company philanthropy will be directed to assist poor people and poor communities, society's most needy and disadvantaged?

Questions about philanthropic scope and scale, about the range and type of beneficiaries, and about the kind of grants to be awarded are basic to the funding process. There are rarely right or wrong answers. So much depends on the detailed circumstances and situational setting of each business as it weighs social need and entrepreneurial opportunity. Indeed, the answers are likely to change over time for any particular firm. And in any given period, solutions may well vary from program to program inside the same corporate foundation or contributions department.

Although the answers may differ from business to business, what all responsible funding sources must be certain of is that such questions are addressed squarely, thoroughly, and openly. The consequences and implications of choice are profound. Hence, their spirited exploration should not be neglected. Corporate senior officers and foundation trustees must pay ample attention to them, or they can stand justly accused of failing to discharge their responsibilities as stewards of a public trust.

These professional choices and techniques are all highly relevant to corporate philanthropists. To sense when and how to deploy them and to aid in the measurement of one's work, the philanthropist should give serious consideration to so-called quality management tools.

Quality Management and Philanthropy

Many business observers believe that the adoption of quality management practices is responsible for a significant improvement in the productivity of American companies. They credit quality processes with having contributed meaningfully to the increased competitiveness of the American economy in the last decade. Rivalry among companies for the much-coveted Malcolm Baldrige awards conferred annually by the U.S. Department of Commerce is but one indicator of the wide adoption of quality precepts.

Basic to the quality process is the insistence that every corporate employee identify the customer for each piece of work undertaken. Corporate philanthropy has a dual perspective: its customers are both the business units and leading departments of the firm and the nonprofits in the outside world. Whenever an internal or external customer cannot be identified for a piece of work—a report, an activity, a set of meetings or processes—then the work must be eliminated.

When the major customers for the work are named, it is necessary to determine their needs and requirements. These cannot be assumed; they must be documented by the simple act of asking. The specification of customer requirements will reveal gaps between what is now done and achieved and what is expected by the people who matter most—customers. The question that remains is how to measurably bridge the gap between customer expectation and supplier performance, year over year. The answer is formulated in the organization's plan of record.

Managing by quality precepts entails an unremitting focus on the customer. The unyielding commitment is to continuous improvement. The center of the process is a constant dialogue between customer and supplier. The discipline and the pleasure reside in testing oneself against targeted, measurable objectives. The bias is to informed, speedy and corrective action.

What can these basic quality precepts add to the philanthropic techniques we reviewed above?

By its insistence on customer focus, the quality process helps philanthropists to look inward to clients for direction and appraisal as much as outward to societal needs and the nonprofit institutions that can satisfy them.

By its concern for acquiring regular feedback and for measuring results, the quality process thrives on conditional gifts and multiyear pledges. Setting milestones for professional and philanthropic achievement and checking on progress at regular intervals are hallmarks of quality.

By its emphasis on the need for constant communication with customers and suppliers, the quality process immeasurably eases the formation of philanthropic partnerships, collaborations, and alliances inside and outside the company.

By its inclination to trial and error or, as quality practitioners might put it, by the propensity to "do, check, act, repeat," the quality process encourages the pre-testing of grant guidelines with focus groups of non-profits as well as with internal clients. Attention to guideline development is critical to the soundness and clarity of the ultimate work product. And no part of that process is more important than customer and client consultation.

Of course, not all world-class corporate philanthropists are familiar with, let alone consciously employ, quality methodologies. There were great engineers before the invention of the slide rule, after all. Memorable writers scrawled in long hand by candlelight without benefit of electricity, not to mention the word processor or computer keyboard. Outstanding mathematicians worked with the abacus, long before the advent of the supercomputer. Quality zealots notwithstanding, American industrial accomplishments during and after World War II dazzled the world without benefit of the teachings of Messrs. W. Edward Deming and Joseph M. Juran, two leaders of the quality movement. Besides, their ideas, it is often claimed, are far more valuable in manufacturing than in service firms and in line rather than staff jobs.

Nonetheless, in its fundamentals, quality methodology offers a congenial management system for corporate philanthropists. It provides a common vocabulary for communication with fellow workers, many of whom are quite familiar with quality language and routines. It both certifies and attests to client and customer satisfaction—the preconditions for ample funding of charitable contributions and for company-wide support of the philanthropic function. One could do a lot worse than to consider the many attributes of quality as a management system.

The CEO as Philanthropic Ally: Necessary, Not Sufficient

Conventional wisdom has it that philanthropy derives its authority from the chairman and CEO of a company. As the most powerful and often most visible corporate figure, it is to him or her that appeals for cash contributions, equipment donations, executive loans, and marketing, sales, and advertising support are often directed. These appeals arrive by post, e-mail, fax, telephone, and personal solicitation. They are mentioned during golf games and mealtime conversations, or at breaks between business meetings. They come from peers, suppliers, customers, friends, associates, school chums, retirees, hometown nonprofits, and shareowners. Responding with grace and intelligence and in accordance with a policy framework supported by the CEO has always been an indispensable part of a corporate philanthropist's job description.

The CEO of any firm should personify the company's values and embody its social responsibility. As such, CEO support remains a necessary condition for a professionally healthy philanthropic concern. In its absence, senior executives are tempted to treat philanthropy as a discretionary activity and philanthropic staff as their secretariat. Without CEO support, charitable budgets will wax and wane with swings in earnings and changes in senior management. Unless a company chairman is a true believer, a culture conducive to charitable giving will be very tough to sustain. Tolerance for risk-taking will be low, and funds for adequate staffing, travel time, and continuing professional education of contributions staff will be scarce.

A CEO's support should never be taken for granted. It is utterly necessary. But in and of itself, such support is no longer sufficient. Philanthropy is not exempt from the strong movement in corporate America to equip fully employees closest to the marketplace with all the resources they need to prevent customer defections, strengthen customer loyalties, and enlarge the customer base. The delegation of responsibility and the sharing of power throughout many firms has been extensive throughout the 1990s.

Hence, many CEOs look to their senior colleagues and to the soundness of the philanthropic process to validate the function and to ensure that its activities remain worthy of support. In turn, the confidence of businesspeople engaged in philanthropy is likely to be higher if they are meaningfully involved in the firm's processes, policies, and activities. The question is often asked whether philanthropy adds value to the firm and to society. For that reason, corporate philanthropists should know how decisions are reached, how business leaders are engaged, and how business needs are met through the medium of philanthropy.

Employee Engagement in Philanthropy

The standard operating procedures of the quality process, it has been suggested, can go a long way toward engendering needed internal consultation, collaboration, and involvement in philanthropy. Whether quality management is embraced or neglected, the methods of employee engagement at the philanthropist's disposal are exciting in their variety:

- Ensure that the contributions function is governed by a representative group of trustees or caretakers who enjoy the respect of their company colleagues and command access to resources that will advance the objectives of corporate philanthropy.

- Have key employees advise on grant guidelines and program priorities and serve on applicant review panels.

- Seek in-house counsel on grant applications requiring expert advice.

- Encourage high levels of participation in employee matching-gift programs.

- Challenge employees to match company grants with their own funds or fundraising.

- Decentralize a portion of grants activity so that community-based, field employees can complement and supplement gifts originating from headquarters.

- Offer opportunities to company officers and future leaders to provide pro bono advice, technical assistance, or board service to meritorious nonprofit institutions and causes.

- Provide incentives to employee giving and volunteering.

- Introduce key business leaders to nonprofit counterparts whose knowledge, experience, and track record of activity are relevant to their own professional or personal goals.

- Seek to align philanthropy with corporate policies affecting employees and retirees, and with corporate positions on public issues, wherever possible.

- Direct nonphilanthropic company resources to the benefit of society and the business.

- Communicate with employees, clearly and compellingly, early and often, on the what, when, why, where, and how of philanthropic programs.

The generous application of such tactics will cultivate understanding and support for philanthropy well beyond that of the CEO. Philanthropy that is widely shared, not closely held, will most likely enlist productive energy and resources. It will also be more likely to endure beyond the current generation of senior management.

The Protagonists of Corporate Philanthropy

For the philanthropic function inside a company to thrive and endure, much depends on the experience, entrepreneurial drive, business savvy, and qualities of mind of its practitioners. There cannot be extraordinary art and craft without gifted artists and craftspeople. Little is more important to building a reputation for excellent philanthropy than the selection of first-class professionals, those who combine a dedication to company and to society, who have wed knowledge of the business to an intimate awareness of nonprofit issues and challenges.

Successfully managing the demands of philanthropy's multiple stakeholders inside and outside the company is a complicated task. In contrast, private foundation officials and individual benefactors needn't concern themselves with customers, shareowners, and employees, to name only three constituencies unique to corporate philanthropy.

In corporate philanthropists, listening and communication skills are at a premium. A sense of humor and a tolerance for ambiguity rise to the level of job requirements. A zest for continuous learning is mandatory. Moreover, conflict-resolution skills are unlikely to suffer from lack of use.

Filling job vacancies with a judicious mix of business insiders predisposed to the Third Sector and nonprofit veterans attuned to the inner workings of corporations is a challenging hiring formula. Generally, companies offer candidates high expectations, heavy demands, long hours, and under the pressure of relentless cost cutting, diminished support. But they also hold out extraordinary opportunities for service. Resourceful recruiting of a combination of talents and experiences will enable the philanthropy of the host company to shine. Leading the way, often behind the scenes, is that unusual figure in business life—the professional corporate philanthropist. Everyone else is assigned the task of making money. Only contributions staff actually get paid to give it away.

Practical Guidance: Sins to Avoid, Questions to Ponder, Books to Read

Corporate philanthropy is a youngster compared to the experience with giving of private foundations and of individual Americans. Some date its legitimacy in modern form to a 1953 New Jersey Supreme Court case, *A. P. Smith Manufacturing Co.* v. *Barlow,* in which the court upheld the tax deductibility of a $1,000 charitable contribution to Princeton University, arguing that "the corporate power to make reasonable charitable contributions exists under modern conditions, even apart from express statutory provision."[2]

If this be a fair vintage date, we have less than fifty years of relevant history to consult in reflecting on the dynamics of modern corporate philanthropy. Indeed, corporate philanthropy is just beginning to evolve as an important force in business and nonprofit decision making. The application of business resources to public needs is a relatively new discipline. As a contribution to its coming of age in the form of philanthropy, I offer some sinners and some winners. More precisely, what follows are my candidates for the top ten sins to avoid and the winning questions to ask. The most valuable books to read are recommended in the bibliography to this book. All are intended to help elevate the art and craft of philanthropy.

The Corporate Donor's Sins: A Top Ten

1. *Failure to return phone calls* and acknowledge mail promptly and to reach and communicate grant decisions with all due deliberate speed.

2. *Failure to secure adequate financing* of the foundation's asset base and of cash for adequate, annual corporate contributions from the chief financial officer and chief executive officer, among other corporate authorities.

3. *Failure to listen attentively* to clients, colleagues, and grant seekers.

4. *Failure to get out of the office* and visit grantees where they live and work.

5. *Failure to involve employees* in philanthropic decisions and processes and to promote volunteering for nonprofit institutions and causes.

6. *Failure to balance continuity* with change in the content of philanthropic programs and in the identity of their beneficiaries.

7. *Failure to understand* the inner dynamics of the business and the fields chosen for philanthropic activity by reading broadly and consulting experts regularly.

8. *Failure to collaborate* with others in the firm or with "outsiders" having common interests—other corporations, foundations, individuals, or government officials.

9. *Failure to communicate* about philanthropy internally and externally and about how audiences can connect meaningfully to corporate charitable activity.

10. *Failure to exhibit respect* and consideration for the time and expertise of others and to demonstrate ample curiosity, energy, and empathy.

The Corporate Donor's Checklist: Questions Worth Pondering

1. Are you consciously trying to avoid committing any of the corporate donor's top ten sins?

2. Part of a corporation's distinctiveness in philanthropy is its ability to tap budgets beyond the charitable for the benefit of nonprofits (e.g., sales and marketing, customer entertainment, memberships, management, and general). Part of what sets a corporation apart is its capacity to donate equipment, products, and services; facility space; and the pro bono time of its people. Still another special feature of corporate philanthropy is the almost universal availability of a corporate matching gift program, whereby employee contributions to prescribed categories of nonprofit organizations are matched dollar for dollar or more by the firm. What role do you play in catalyzing and expanding the total resource output that the firm directs to the Third Sector?

3. To what extent would you call corporate philanthropy, as you practice it, a team sport? Are there hundreds of colleagues engaged in the process of grant decisions and in the corporate-inspired giving of money, time, and in-kind resources by dint of

your efforts? Is the corporate contributions function in your company widely shared or closely held?

4. Are you clear about the identity of the internal corporate customers for philanthropic work? Do you know enough about their requirements and whether you are satisfying them effectively and efficiently? Have you identified any shortfalls and developed a mutually acceptable plan to bridge the gap between client expectation and philanthropic performance?

5. What constitutes a solid year of achievement for you and your colleagues? How do you know if you are successful or if you fall shy of desired results? Can you name the three most important objectives you wish to accomplish this year and do so in measurable terms?

6. How important is philanthropy in your own corporation? Is its standing reflected adequately in the understanding of the chief executive and other high-ranking colleagues? Do they become involved in policy setting and performance monitoring? Are you doing everything possible to call to the attention of senior colleagues the opportunities and benefits of corporate philanthropy? Are grants budgets adequately funded and foundation assets satisfactorily maintained?

7. How many of the following publications about aspects of the Third Sector do you regularly read: *Chronicle of Philanthropy, Chronicle of Higher Education, Foundation News, Corporate Philanthropy Report, Harvard Business Review?* Do you actively participate in the deliberations and forums of organizations like the Contributions Council of the Conference Board, the Council on Foundations, the Independent Sector, Business for Social Responsibility, and the relevant Regional Associations of Grantmakers? Do you often enough engage in public speaking and writing about philanthropy inside and outside your company?

8. Are you actively engaged in efforts to inform employees, retirees, and the attentive public about your corporation's philanthropy? Do you measure the effectiveness of the foundation or corporate contributions annual report, grant guidelines, and other publications? How about its media relations and advertising programs?

Are the awareness and knowledge levels of your target audiences about philanthropy increasing adequately?

9. A person unknown to you, representing an organization you never heard of, sends an intelligent, unsolicited grant proposal containing an attractive idea that neatly fits your guidelines. Does such a newcomer possess a decent shot at overcoming the barriers to entry into that charmed circle of your grantees?

10. The lifelong friend of the socially active and aware spouse of the chairman of the board sends you a pedestrian request on behalf of a mediocre nonprofit organization. The chairman has encouraged this VIP to approach you. Really, does such a person have much of a chance of being denied funding?

3

The Distinctiveness of
Corporate Philanthropy

The life of money-making is one undertaken under compulsion, and wealth is evidently not the good we are seeking, for it is merely useful for the sake of something else.

—ARISTOTLE
Nicomachean Ethics, ca. 350 B.C.

It is nearly always easier to earn one million dollars honestly than to dispose of it wisely.

—JULIUS ROSENWALD, 1927

DURING THE DOZEN YEARS THAT I WAS PRIVILEGED to be involved in the conduct of AT&T's corporate philanthropy and associated activities, the company's donations amounted to roughly a billion dollars.

When most people think about charitable gifts, they have in mind cash. In grant dollars alone, AT&T regularly found itself ranked as one of the top five corporate donors for the period 1984–97. But unlike other philanthropic entities, companies can complement their cash giving with many other resources eagerly sought after by nonprofit organizations. At AT&T, used and state-of-the-art equipment, telecommunication services, advertising, cause-related marketing, promotional and sales gifts, loaned executives, real property, and use of facilities were all donated in various combinations.

This capacity to call on a very wide range of human and material resources to advance philanthropic ends is one of the features that distinguishes corporate from private foundation and individual donors.

What else differentiates corporate giving from any other kind? In what ways can a corporation's potential contribution to the society and to business success be fully exploited?

I have selected three of the key differentiating dimensions of corporate philanthropy for thorough exploration here. One is how philanthropy can best be governed in a large business. Another is how workers at all levels can be motivated to participate in Third Sector organizations and causes through the good offices of their employer. The third is how integrating a company's disparate resources helps achieve societal objectives and generate unparalleled charitable energy on a scale to which no other philanthropic actors can aspire.

In drawing directly on the lessons of experience, I employ frequent references to AT&T. It is, of course, quite possible to govern philanthropy and engage employees in a very different way from what has been the case at AT&T while justifiably claiming a mantle of excellence. Indeed, a philanthropist can, for example, entirely ignore the possibility of synergy in the application of a company's resources to a societal need and still do well for the firm and good for society. There are many roads to Rome.

Nonetheless, some of those roads are more enduring, safer, and more conducive to carrying the traffic of a company's attributes than are others. Consider the merits of one well-tested approach. Then borrow what makes sense. Discard what doesn't fit.

Governance: Philanthropy Widely Shared, Not Closely Held

Procedures embody principles. AT&T paid lots of attention to the process for devising and approving philanthropic policies and for implementing philanthropic decisions. The roles and responsibilities for AT&T's philanthropy flowed from both the company's mission statement and from one of its core values—teamwork. Here is what AT&T meant by teamwork:

> We encourage and reward both individual and team achievements. We freely join with colleagues across organizational boundaries to advance the interests of customers and shareowners. Our team spirit extends to being responsible *and* caring partners in the communities where we live and work.[1]

Figure 3-1 depicts the roles and responsibilities of all key players engaged in philanthropy at AT&T as it was organized at the end of 1996. The overall structure embraces the notion of corporate philanthropy as the process of identifying where business interests and social needs intersect.

The AT&T Foundation, governed by a diverse group of eighteen trustees, receives broad guidance from senior management and the company's board of directors. The foundation invites hundreds of subject-matter experts from throughout the company to participate in its activities. It also stimulates the volunteer activity of thousands more. Such consultation and participation help AT&T to define its business interests and to clarify the corporation's point of view.

The structure also permits the foundation sufficient independence for nonprofits' needs to be assessed by a professional staff free to establish grant guidelines and exercise judgment, within certain boundaries. Those guidelines, in turn, leave ample room for thematic grantmaking conducted at the foundation's initiative as well as for responding to the needs of nonprofits.

Addressing both business imperatives *and* nonprofit appeals is one important principle of operation. Another is balancing the company's responses to short-term, local needs with responses to institutions and causes of regional and national consequence. At AT&T, the foundation handled the latter. Executives responsible for corporate cash contributions throughout the business managed the former.

Both sources of funding foster employee involvement in philanthropic discussions and decision making. Both encourage employee volunteerism. Both place a high value on openness, accessibility, and equal opportunity.

A corporate foundation too insulated from business realities and perspectives is unlikely to garner the needed internal support and to generate optimal levels of cash and other-than-cash resources for nonprofits. Under such circumstances, it is also less likely that a foundation will receive the recognition and other public relations benefits that may accrue from exercising this form of corporate social responsibility.

A corporate foundation too enmeshed in day-to-day business developments runs the risk of losing its capacity to make effective philanthropic decisions. Judgments will tend to the short term and the idiosyncratic and will often depend too heavily on the pre-existing community relationships of company executives. The structure of roles and

FIGURE 3-1. AT&T's Philanthropy and Corporate Contributions Roles and Responsibilities

AT&T BOARD OF DIRECTORS

AT&T CHAIRMAN AND/OR VICE CHAIRMAN

- Reviews major foundation policies and priorities
- Decide on corporate contribution to foundation assets, if any, based on chief financial officer's advice and consent
- Approves annual corporate contributions and foundation budget
- Approves corporate contributions from $100,000 to $1,000,000, as needed

CORPORATE PUBLIC POLICY COMMITTEE

- Approves formation of AT&T Foundation
- Receives reports on AT&T Foundation, corporate contributions and other public service activity
- Sets guidelines for and receives reports on AT&T contributions to foundation assets
- Determines overall level of company philanthropy
- Approves annual corporate contributions budget
- Approves schedule of authorizations, including contributions
- Approves any corporate contribution in excess of $1,000,000
- Counsels senior management on prospective changes in program priorities and other matters of consequence

SENIOR VP, PUBLIC RELATIONS, AND CHAIRMAN, AT&T FOUNDATION

- Review major foundation policies and priorities
- Monitors efficiency and effectiveness of corporate contributions
- Recommends annual corporate contributions budget
- Recommends annual foundation budget
- Approves corporate contributions up to $100,000

AT&T FOUNDATION TRUSTEES

- Determines program priorities of foundation
- Determines grant policies
- Reviews all grants $25,000 or less
- Approves all grants in excess of $25,000
- Recommends annual grants budget
- Reviews foundation expenses

Committee on University Special Purpose Grants in Science
Committee on University Manufacturing Engineering Grants

FUNCTIONAL
COMMITTEES:

OTHER PROGRAM
COMMITTEES:

FUNCTIONAL COMMITTEES:	OTHER PROGRAM COMMITTEES:	
Executive	Arts	International
Budget	Environmental	Pre-College
Nominating	Health Care	Education

AT&T FOUNDATION STAFF

- Approve all grants up to $10,000
- Approve all grants between $10,000 and $25,000 with concurrence of foundation executive committee (five of eighteen trustees)
- Recommend annual grants budget and expenses
- Proposes program priorities and grant policies
- Held accountable for efficiency and effectiveness of corporate contribution activities
- Represent AT&T to nonprofit leadership
- Determine content of thematic grants programs and responds to unsolicited proposals

responsibilities depicted in Figure 3-1 highlights both dangers. It provides a set of protective checks and balances.

This overall method of philanthropic governance worked for AT&T. It erred on the side of inclusion, involving outside directors, very senior management, foundation trustees, company subject-matter experts, and employee volunteers. It assumed a broad view of what philanthropy might accomplish when linked with many other company resources and talents. It endeavored to ensure that the next generation of senior management was exposed to corporate philanthropy early on in their careers. It sought to satisfy business imperatives while addressing societal needs.

Other firms, of different missions, sizes, and views of corporate social responsibility, might well design different governance structures. Indeed, AT&T constantly altered many of its procedures and accountabilities to fit changing circumstances. Whatever a company's situational setting, I would urge adherence to these four basic precepts:

1. That philanthropy not be handled as a discretionary fund for the CEO and senior management to spend, treating philanthropic staff as a secretariat.

2. That a large zone for professionalism be protected, to allow societal need and business interest to find creative and measurable expression in philanthropy.

3. That attention be paid not simply to today's governance requirements but to a future beyond tomorrow. If philanthropy is an investment in the future and if its payoffs are long term, then it will function best when the processes that guide it are sound, enduring, and secure and when successors to senior management are exposed to the fundamentals of charitable contributions. Unless the next generation of business leaders appreciates the value of philanthropy, a company's charitable profile is likely to lower rapidly with the retirement of a few veteran loyalists.

4. That the willingness of employees and their families, retirees, customers, and shareowners to give and volunteer be acknowledged and reinforced.

No one governance system fits all. But any that are disrespectful of these four basic signposts will ill serve a company and its principal constituencies.

Engaging Employee Energy and Commitment

The notion of corporate philanthropy as both an expression of employee values and a means to engender employee participation in matters of concern to them, their customers, and their communities was central to AT&T's belief system. AT&T consistently encouraged employees to participate in the community organizations that mattered most to them and to the business.

Involvement began with AT&T's most senior management. If the Third Sector and its relationship to the health of society were to be taken seriously by employees, those highest ranked needed to do more than preach volunteerism—they needed to practice it. If engagement with nonprofits brought back to the company useful ideas, exposure to opinion leaders, good will, positive contributions to the AT&T image, and more seasoned, better informed managers, then its most senior executives should themselves find time for meaningful involvement.

In 1984, it should be recalled, AT&T was a completely new entity. It emerged from a Bell System in which local telephone companies had been assigned almost exclusive responsibility for community relations, media relations, advertising, philanthropy, and the like. In late 1983, only 7 percent of Americans associated AT&T with what it was to become a few months later—a competitive provider of long-distance services and a supplier of consumer and business telephone equipment. The strict division of labor that characterized the Bell System made the job of quickly forging a new corporate identity formidable. For example, AT&T had virtually no civic presence in cities around the country or in Washington, D.C. It needed to be created.

The conviction of foundation staff was that there was no better way to solidify the relationship with nonprofits than to enlist senior executives in joining boards of organizations compatible with their background and interests. Sometimes the fit between business executive and nonprofit was natural and easy. On other occasions, matchmaking required persuasion, encouragement, and lots of staff guidance. The results benefited the executives, the nonprofits whose boards they joined, AT&T, and especially the company's philanthropic enterprises. No slide presentation or document can convey the importance and the drama of nonprofit work nearly as well as observing it up close and having a measure of accountability for the outcome.

At first glance, the following nonprofit institutions seem to have little in common:

Columbia University

Duke University

George Washington University

Johns Hopkins University

Lincoln Center for the
Performing Arts

The American Enterprise
Institute

The Brookings Institution

The Council on
Foreign Relations

The Japan Society

The Massachusetts Institute of
Technology

The National Council for
the Achievement of
Minorities in Engineering

The New York City Ballet

The New York Philharmonic

The New York Public Library

The Trilateral Commission

The United Way of America

But they are among the Third Sector organizations that warmly welcomed AT&T's most senior executives to their boards in the years immediately following divestiture.[2] AT&T people contributed their time, talent, and funds. They also advocated for AT&T support of all kinds including, of course, philanthropic assistance. The company's trustees and volunteers gained at least as much as they gave, however. They networked with colleagues from all walks of life, learned about some of the leading issues of the day, and maintained close relations with many of the country's opinion leaders.

Similar associations with nonprofit boards were established among officer and upper-middle-management ranks throughout the company and around the country. In all, several hundred institutions benefited from AT&T employees serving on their boards of directors. Thousands more enlisted in other volunteer capacities. Participation was wide, reflecting the breadth of AT&T's employee and business interests. Participation was deep, reflecting AT&T's heritage and seriousness of purpose.

In the category of AT&T's historic charitable legacy, there was a valued trinity of groups to be supported. They boasted the broadest and deepest participation from AT&T during its monopoly years and their immediate aftermath.

The United Way. In the years immediately following divestiture, AT&T people collectively contributed, on average, as much as $35 million per year that was directed to more than 150 local chapters around the country. AT&T executives led dozens of annual campaigns. To these same United Way chapters the AT&T Foundation extended annual corporate grants of about $7 million.

The American Red Cross. In donations of money, time, and blood, AT&T and its people never failed to be ranked among the top ten institutional supporters of the Red Cross.

The Telephone Pioneers of America. The Pioneers is a nonprofit membership organization that undertakes projects like building parks, playgrounds, homes, and equipment for the physically handicapped and tutoring youngsters. It boasts chapters and clubs all across America. It claims a membership of 830,000, consisting of Bell system retirees, post-1984 AT&T and RBOC retirees, and current employees in the telecommunications industry. If the number of volunteer members of the Pioneers is impressive, so too is the financial support that emanates from the originating firms and from member dues. In 1995 both sources totaled $23 million, supporting what is estimated to have been no fewer than 29 million hours of voluntary service.

At AT&T, employee involvement was encouraged not just in outside organizations but also from inside the company. That internal activity was generated by the AT&T Foundation through other public service volunteer activity. The foundation's eighteen trustee slots were much sought after. The positions were held by senior officers, key figures in each of the company's business units and in such support divisions as law, public affairs, human resources, and public relations. In the recruiting of trustees, general attention was paid to high potential managers, up and comers from around the company. Specific attention was focused on gender, race, and ethnicity to ensure diversity of representation. Care was also taken to obtain a global perspective by including executives with responsibility for markets outside the United States.

Owing to changes in position, retirements, and the desire for some term limitation, almost one hundred executives served in a trustee capacity from 1984 to 1996. Meeting as a group for four hours once per quarter, they formulated policies, approved program priorities, set the total annual grants and administrative budget, and voted on all proposed assistance of more than $25,000. In addition, all trustees served on functional or program committees, along with subject-matter experts from throughout the firm, to conduct the work of the foundation.

Scientists from Bell Laboratories served on a committee that recommended grants to universities for research and teaching in various disciplines of active interest to the company. Engineers and factory heads drawn from around the company's lines of business made up the committee that recommended grants related to manufacturing engineering. Still other engineers, as well as lawyers and experts on occupational health and safety, advised on grants in industrial ecology and the environment. Executives posted overseas helped to shape an approach to philanthropy extending beyond America's borders. Grants for preventive healthcare, wellness programs at the workplace, and AIDS research were reviewed by a group of AT&T physicians and human resource experts. Separately established child and elder care funds for employees were managed by yet another group of company executives.

These pro bono employee assignments generated gratifying levels of commitment, passion, and energy. To be asked by the company to offer professional expertise for both AT&T's benefit and to advance the public good was regarded as a special privilege. With very rare exceptions, the request for participation was honored with enthusiasm. Pre-circulated reading materials were studied carefully. The quality of board and committee discussion was high. Trustees and volunteers contributed to the deliberations both their overall experience and the perspective of their business unit. They brought back to their unit an enhanced appreciation for the exercise of social responsibility and how the resources they controlled might supplement or complement the AT&T Foundation's philanthropic choices.

AT&T has several voluntary employee groups organized around racial, ethnic, and gender-based lines. There is a strong association of African-American employees (Alliance of Black Telecommunication Workers). There is also HISPA (Hispanic Association of AT&T Employees). There are the 4As (Asia-Pacific American Associates of AT&T). There is WAT (Women of AT&T), LEAGUE (Lesbian, Bi-Sexual and Gay United Employees of AT&T), ICAE (Inter-Tribal Council of AT&T Employees), and IDEAL (Individuals with Disabilities Enabling Advocacy Link).

All these organizations are devoted to the continuing education and professional advancement of their members. They provide opportunities for networking and for public service and, they nurture leadership dedicated to these ends. To their credit, these groups have avoided divisiveness and sectarianism. They have been energetic, constructive forces operating with the full support of senior management.

AT&T Foundation staff and trustees came to know each of these groups quite well as their leadership considered how best to connect with their distinctive constituencies and make a difference for the better. Their ideas and views were solicited eagerly. Direct participation was sought in foundation projects for which employee association volunteers proved invaluable.

All these kinds of employee engagement influenced the expenditure of AT&T Foundation grant funds. Managerial involvement was also triggered by devolving a part of the contributions function to regionally deployed executives in the United States and overseas. They were allocated a corporate contributions budget to expend in accordance with company priorities determined by locale. Literally hundreds of executives became engaged in this delegation of power. In addition to spreading ownership by geographic location, some business units and line managers set aside budget funds for philanthropy or its close cousins, the better to advance specific community relations, government relations, and human resources objectives.

The chairman of AT&T looked to the AT&T Foundation staff to ensure that all of these resources, from whatever source derived, were spent conscientiously and effectively. The staff was charged with counseling and monitoring the flow of funds to nonprofit organizations. This oversight function assumed many forms: advertising placement; new and used equipment give-aways; the use of facility space; loaned executives; discounted products and services; and, cause-related marketing. Within certain guidelines, managers were free to cultivate their own charitable gardens.

The employee involvement reviewed thus far involves voluntary efforts to intelligently spend company resources or to encourage pro bono support of nonprofits. Another method of engaging employees in philanthropy is to stimulate or reinforce their own charitable contributions of cash or common stock. Corporate matching gift programs were designed with this idea in mind. Almost universally among Fortune 1000 companies, employee gifts either to charitable organizations writ large, or to designated categories of nonprofits such as those involved in health, education, and the arts, are generally matched dollar for dollar—up to $10,000 per employee each year. Some matching provisions are even more generous.

The funds for matching gifts are part of the overall philanthropic budget. Every dollar spent there is a dollar that cannot be used for program grants. Not unnaturally, charitable contributions staff believe that funds directed by them from a central source can enjoy a greater strategic "bang for the buck" than dollars that democratically follow employee choice. On balance, the benefits of the matching-gift program as a complement to and catalyst for employee giving were more than worth any perceived costs.

At AT&T, the rates of employee matching-gift participation were relatively high. That employees voted to support nonprofits with their own funds was a healthy endorsement of the philanthropic function and a leading indicator of a public-spirited company. AT&T participation rates of 4 to 6 percent, though high and costly for a firm whose employees and retirees numbered 387,000 in 1995, was generally greeted with enthusiasm. Of that number, 15,950 people extended 30,203 gifts to arts and education organizations averaging $173 each, for a total of $4,881,782.

Beyond the year-in, year-out standard employee matching-gift program, the AT&T Foundation established some custom-designed versions. For years, the AT&T Foundation offered a match of up to $50,000 to the National Hispanic Scholarship Fund if employees belonging to HISPA contributed or raised at least a comparable sum. HISPA responded with member gifts and the proceeds of an annual community fundraising drive. A special match program was developed to support a named group of environmental organizations. The program was timed to coincide with the annual Earth Day observance and has proven extremely popular.

More recently, the AT&T Foundation has developed a program called AT&T CARES (AT&T Community Awards Recognizing Employee Service). AT&T CARES offers employees the chance to have their voluntary service matched with company cash. Any employee who completes a minimum of 50 hours of volunteer work (or 100 hours for a team of employees) within a year can direct a grant to the nonprofit organization benefiting from that pro bono service of up to $250. (The amount is $500 to $2,500 for teams.) No nonprofit can receive more than $2,500 from AT&T CARES in any single year.

The spirit that infuses all these programs and projects is one of actively seeking the participation of employees. They share in the ownership of the corporate contributions function. If philanthropy were an apartment building, company employees would be housed in neither a rental nor a condominium but in a cooperative. There, too, decisions are widely shared, not closely held.

Encapsulating these efforts to engage employees is, of course, the quality management process. It necessitates a dialogue with business-unit leaders, who are the internal customers for philanthropy. By first eliciting and then attending to their requirements, including those of other senior management and of AT&T Foundation trustees, the cooperation and the provision of supplemental resources needed to get things done was virtually assured.

But aren't the processes of employee engagement also onerous? Weren't too many people involved in the formulation and execution of philanthropic plans? Didn't these multiple forms of employee activity create pressure groups and engender internal advocacy for causes favored by certain employees or by their business units, or from the communities where they lived and worked? How could sound philanthropic judgments be reached amid this corporate cacophony?

The most dangerous place in the world, social commentators have observed, is between an ambitious politician bound and determined to win higher office and a television camera. Surely a close second is explaining to a senior AT&T Bell Labs research scientist and loyal university alumnus why his alma mater should not receive yet another grant on top of the many already extended or pledged in recent years. Contending for high honors in peril must be uttering a firm, unwavering "no" to an insistent AT&T sales executive who is on the verge of closing a major business deal with a nonprofit organization and would like foundation staff to approve its pending grant request right away. Equally dangerous is telling a senior officer, not exactly accustomed to receiving declinations, that his favorite charity falls outside the charter of the company's philanthropy.

A few words of caution are in order here: Do not open the door to employee involvement if you want to avoid being on the receiving end of negative opinion, or if you aren't comfortable with resolving conflict. Most often, business colleagues will yield in the face of decisions based on sound processes, solid guidelines, a body of precedent, and a fair articulation of business interest and philanthropic need. Even the staunchest advocates of favorite causes appreciate that finite resources compel hard choices. If the philanthropist across the table or on the phone demonstrates an understanding of the business and a mastery of how nonprofits and foundations work, the likelihood of continued protest is slim.

Such conversations and explanations take time, of course. There were days when I wondered whether building an enthusiastic constituency for philanthropy all across a Fortune 10 company was achievable. There were weeks when I envied colleagues in other companies who needed only the approval of the chairman and a handful of other senior colleagues to execute programs.

But if your aim is to sustain an enduring corporate commitment to community inside the company and throughout its workforce, if you want to direct energy and supplemental resources to consensus-blessed causes, and if you desire to foster appreciation for the Third Sector among the next generation of senior management, there is no shortcut. Besides, what really makes corporate philanthropy special is the marriage of philanthropic funds; cash and in-kind resources; and creative, determined, impassioned businesspeople. Put simply, participation nurtures commitment. The benefits far outweigh the costs.

Putting It All Together

When a Fortune 1000 company decides in earnest to focus on a social concern and marshals powerful resources spread throughout the firm, sparks can fly, minds can change, lives can improve. The grand-slam home run is at least as rare in the realm of corporate social responsibility as it is in baseball. No other philanthropic source can have such a powerful impact on a national issue as a company intent on making a difference. But doing so isn't easy. The experience of AT&T shows how one candidate for that bases-loaded, game-winning slug into the corporate bleachers made the attempt.

Beginning in the late 1980s, AT&T undertook to integrate its grantmaking, its personnel policies and practices, and its influence on public policy—all with a view to strengthening families and children.

The company targeted the myriad problems associated with teenage pregnancy and parenting for its philanthropy. Here's why.

Every year in America, 1 million teens become pregnant. Three quarters of teen mothers have a second child within two years. More than 50 percent of teen mothers don't graduate from high school, and teen fathers are 40 percent less likely to graduate than their peers.

Most of these adolescent mothers are poor, and many are on welfare. All have limited prospects for a healthy, independent life. Because they often fail to obtain adequate prenatal care, their infants are much more likely than are children of older parents to have birth defects, health problems, or learning disabilities. In short, unwed teenage parents and their offspring are at high risk of dropping out of school, of being unemployed, of staying on public assistance, and of failing to become productive members of society. Any successful efforts to help these young people and their children benefit the economy and the nation at large.

The AT&T Foundation funded a five-year, ten-city initiative designed to keep pregnant teenagers in school, provide pre- and postnatal care, train young mothers on how to nurture their infants, and help high-school graduates acquire business skills and good jobs. Cooperating nonprofits in Atlanta, Chicago, Los Angeles, Washington, D.C., Dallas, Oakland, Detroit, Denver, and in Plainfield and Newark, New Jersey, received funding to provide such services. AT&T employees volunteered as mentors, administrators, and counselors. Local managers, together with foundation officials, worked with the nonprofits to create a consortium of donors to support each site.

The company's decision to take the lead in addressing such acute social problems was unusual. Corporations generally remain aloof from the problems afflicting the poor, the welfare recipient, and the ghetto resident. Tackling tough social issues identified as important by organizations ranging from the Business Roundtable to the Children's Defense Fund, and from the Committee on Economic Development to the Manpower Research & Demonstration Corporation, was viewed as quite unrelated to advancing the company's business interest. AT&T stood to gain little from the outcome, save the knowledge that lives had been somewhat bettered and communities somewhat improved. On the motivational spectrum of idealism and self-interest, most of AT&T's philanthropy fell in the middle. Strengthening poor and vulnerable families veered to the purely altruistic.

In terms of human resource policies affecting AT&T's own, the focus was on enabling employees to better balance workplace requirements with the needs of their children and their parents. Those needs were changing owing to dramatically altered demographics from which the AT&T workforce was hardly exempt.

For example, one in every five American children live in a female-headed household. Fewer than 10 percent live in two-parent families where only one parent works outside the home. Half of America's kids under the age of five are cared for by someone other than a mother or a father.

AT&T people, like other Americans, were facing the multifaceted consequences of the dual-career family, the impact of divorce, the possible resistance to geographic relocation from a spouse or children, and the struggle to find quality day care for kids and quality long-term care for aging and infirm parents. The company recognized that such changes in the dynamics of the American family have profound consequences for the morale and productivity of its employees, too. Firms that keep pace with them will have a special claim on employee loyalty and will earn a reputation for caring about their welfare. Along with philanthropic efforts to strengthen poor families, AT&T undertook a similar program for its own. It included these components:

- The creation of two funds, totaling $10 million over six years, to support expanding quality child and elder care in communities where AT&T people live and work. The funds are supplemented by nationwide information and referral services to help employees locate and evaluate options for their own families.

- A one-year leave, with guaranteed reinstatement to a comparable job, for parents of natural and adopted children and for employees needing to care for parents.

- Employees can take up to two paid days off per year in two-hour increments to satisfy family needs, such as attending parent-teacher conferences, checking in on a sick child or parent, or getting to that critical ball game or theater production in which their youngster prominently figures.

- A company initiative enabling employees to set aside up to $5,000 pre-tax for child and elder care.

- Encouragement of telecommuting for all those with jobs that allow for periodic work at home, subject to supervisory approval.

These benefits were available not only to management but also to all employees. Indeed, some benefits were collectively bargained and built into precedent-setting union contracts with the Communication Workers of America and the International Brotherhood of Electrical Workers. They proved extraordinarily popular with employees.

The child and elder care funds are worth some elaboration. They functioned jointly as a specialized in-house foundation with employees as the only eligible applicants. They make requests for funding support on behalf of schools and community nonprofits. Selected union leaders and AT&T senior executives acted as trustees responsible for final grant decisions.

In six years, the funds added child care capacity around the country for nearly thirteen thousand children in pre-school, school-age, and family day care. They improved care for another twenty-four thousand children by financing the purchase of equipment, supplies, curriculum, and facilities. They provided grants for training more than 8,000 child care providers. Over the same period, the funds added services for more than seven thousand senior adults, improved services for more than five hundred, and trained 730 elder-care providers. Overall, more than forty thousand AT&T people benefited from these two funds or from using the company's child and elder care referral service.

The third part of this exercise of corporate social responsibility entailed influencing public policy. During my tenure at the foundation, I contended that sound corporate philanthropy and family-friendly employee practices were necessary but not sufficient elements of a comprehensive program. Given the centrality of public policy and public resource allocation to such critical matters as preventing low-weight births, prenatal care, welfare reform, day care, and quality education, a company that cared about these issues couldn't remain on the sidelines of government deliberations. In making the case inside AT&T for taking a stand on issues tangential to concrete business interests, I brought to the company's attention an article by Fred Hechinger, the education editor of the *New York Times*, that was published in *Harvard Business Review*. He noted the failure of companies to advocate in the field of public education the allocation of ample public resources as well as to deploy their own. He could just as well have been writing about the corporation and American families and children:

> [I]n the end, all these corporate ventures (school and business partnerships) will amount to little more than public relations unless the business community abandons its frequently schizophrenic posture; supporting the local schools while simultaneously instructing, or at least permitting, its lobbyists to support cuts in state appropriations. . . . Common sense should show the futility of any corporate policy that gives to the local schools with one hand and yet takes away funds with the other.[3]

AT&T's philanthropic efforts to help strengthen poor families "giveth" to the attempt to resolve a key American social problem. The company decided that its public policy stance should therefore not "taketh away." Rather, through the congressional testimony of its chairman, through op-ed articles, and through an active media relations effort, AT&T would acknowledge the relationship between the state of the American family and the nation's economic and social health. It would affirm the necessity for federal budget deficit reduction that would not be made at the disproportionate expense of the poor nor ignore the need to commit more resources to selected programs for at-risk children and families. Corporate support for welfare reform, day care, and adequate WIC (Women, Infants and Children) program funding were among the specific measures advocated.[4]

Editorial boards and columnists took notice. For example, a *Washington Post* editorial of March 7, 1991, under the headline "Hungry Children and the CEOs," noted the congressional testimony of five corporate chairmen—Robert E. Allen, AT&T; John L. Clendenin, Bell South; James J. Reinier, Honeywell; Robert C. Winters, Prudential Insurance; and William S. Woodside, Sky Chef:

> The general condition of the country's least fortunate children—the one-fifth whose families have the lowest incomes and the least access to medical care—is not only wretched but clearly getting worse. The traditional social welfare lobbies and their friends in Congress haven't been able to do much about a deteriorating trend over the past decade.
>
> But it's possible that the rising concern among business leaders can make a difference in social politics.

One child advocate, William Harris, the founder of the Boston-based nonprofit group KIDS-PAC, spoke for many in expressing delight that such formidable new recruits were supporting full funding for WIC: "When those gorillas start to sing everybody listens, and that's terrific."[5]

By combining such public policy advocacy with targeted philanthropic assistance to organizations that enjoy the best track record for helping to avert teenage pregnancies, prevent low-weight births, and break the cycle of welfare dependency for adolescent mothers, AT&T helped replace despair with hope. By taking the family's needs seriously where those needs are said to begin—at home—*and* in government circles *and* philanthropically, AT&T sought to ameliorate one of the nation's most serious social problems.

Integrating the resources of any large organization demands that boundaries be crossed in persuading colleagues of the value of a joint effort. More often than not, the task of doing so is an exhausting, daunting, uphill exercise. Corporate departments, like public relations, human resources, government relations, law, sales, and marketing, tend to be jealous of their prerogatives, certain of their ground, wary of strangers, and offended by trespassers. These are natural and understandable proclivities. But they militate strongly against cooperation across organizational lines and professional disciplines.

To experience a company as more than the sum of its parts requires leadership at multiple levels of the firm. To prevail is to overcome the lopsided odds of inertia and parochialism—sure-fire symptoms of any bureaucracy.

But on those occasions when corporate rowers are persuaded to pull together, destinations that seemed out of reach suddenly come into view. The attempt to integrate company resources in the service of a philanthropically inspired program is worth the struggle. Success releases all kinds of positive energy.

So don't confine public service to philanthropic funds alone. Pick your spots and seek broader impact within and outside the company. The payoff can be extraordinary.

How such elements of philanthropy as governance, employee engagement, and the search for synergy help shape programs benefiting both nonprofits and the sponsoring company is worth examination. The marriage of art and commerce is one good source of illumination.

PART TWO

The Workings of Corporate Philanthropy

4

Corporate Medicis:
The Marriage of Art and Commerce

There was a kind lady called Gregory
Said, "Come to me, poets in beggary."
    But found her imprudence
    When thousands of students
Cried, "all, we are all in that category."

—JAMES JOYCE
a limerick written to his patron, Lady Gregory

THE CLAIMS ON ANY CORPORATION'S PHILANTHROPIC BUDGET are always greater than the funds available. As the federal government continues to reduce its budget in fields of concern to nonprofits, and as state and local counterparts manage competing priorities in the context of straitened financial prospects, the pressure on companies to fill the vacuum will escalate. In such critical areas as health, social welfare, education, day care, substance abuse, and job training, the case for more corporate help will be advanced frequently and urgently.

These representations merit respect. But companies would do well to consider using a portion of their resources to strengthen or initiate a charitable and marketing program in support of the arts in America and in other locales around the world where they choose to operate.

The performing and visual arts continue to enjoy enormous popularity. It is manifested in the growth of arts organizations and ensembles, in new buildings to house events and objects, in expanding audiences, and in the economic impact of enlarged arts activity.

Numbers Count

For companies eager to reach target markets of businesses, consumers, and influential individuals, numbers count. The figures substantiating an unprecedented rise in the arts are impressive:

- There are one thousand two hundred professional symphony orchestras in the United States. According to the American Symphony Orchestra League, they enjoyed a total paid audience of 31 million people in the 1994–95 season.

- The Theater Communications Group notes that the four hundred nonprofit theaters in America presented about sixty thousand performances of nearly three thousand productions before an audience of over 200 million people in the 1993–94 season. There were a total of but fifty-six such theaters in 1971.

- Dance America reports that since 1965, the number of ballet, modern, and ethnic professional dance companies has grown from 37 to 450 in 1992, enjoying an aggregate audience of 25 million people.

- The American Association of Museums records that in 1991, museums in the United States employed ninety-one thousand people and attracted some 700 million visitors on the strength of an aggregate annual operating budget of around $5 billion.

- *Live from Lincoln Center* and *Live from the Met* are weekly nationwide, public-television broadcasts that annually reach 100 million Americans. In any two-year period, a comparable number listen to the Metropolitan Opera on radio.[1]

These specific examples add up to impressive aggregates. For example, in 1992, America's nonprofit arts institutions employed 1.3 million people, garnered about $8.2 billion in total revenue, yielded $37 billion of economic activity, and returned $3.4 billion to the federal treasury in taxes.[2] For example, today Americans spend roughly two and a half times more money patronizing arts events than they do attending sports events. In 1970 the sums spent on both areas of activity were about equal.[3]

The collective weight of these figures—audience size, employment, annual expenditures, economic impact, growth in number of organizations, burgeoning of tourism—is difficult for a company to ignore from either a sales or a philanthropic perspective. Little wonder, then, that John Naisbitt and Patricia Aburdine cited a veritable renaissance in the arts as one of but ten global *megatrends,* the driving societal forces that are shaping lives in the developed countries.[4]

These measures of extensive involvement in the arts are confirmed by polling data collected by Louis Harris for seven consecutive years under the auspices of the American Council for the Arts and the National Assembly of Local Arts Agencies. The Harris poll documents how wide ranging is Americans' participation in the arts and how much they believe that government support is indispensable.[5]

As regards attendance, fully 86 percent of those surveyed report having bought a ticket to one or more arts events in 1995. The percentage level of attendance for specific art forms are quite high: 50 percent for theater; 49 percent for a popular musical performance; 47 percent for a science, natural history, or history museum; 44 percent for art museums and galleries; 30 percent for opera or musical theater; and 21 percent for dance—ballet, modern, folk, ethnic, jazz, or tap.

As to public funding for the arts, 79 percent of Americans believe that federal, state, and local support is important. In fact, substantial majorities of those polled would be willing to be taxed an additional $5 (61 vs. 37 percent) or $13 (56 vs. 43 percent) annually to provide the federal government the support it needs to assist the arts. Harris concludes that the results of his polling demonstrate clearly that American's support for the arts "is strong and runs deep. Claims that backing for federal assistance to the arts has sharply eroded are not borne out by the facts."[6]

Yet another indication of the breadth of appeal of the arts to Americans is the increase in employee matching-gift programs among the nation's corporations. According to the National Clearing House of Corporate Matching Gift Information, in 1995, of the 1,005 companies surveyed, about half matched gifts to arts organizations as compared to 32 percent for civic organizations, 33 percent for social service organizations, and 33 percent for environmental organizations.

AT&T's experience with the arts and matching gifts confirms their popularity. Since 1989, anywhere from between twelve thousand and fifteen thousand gifts were matched annually, and spending averaged around $1.2 million each year. That so many employees and retirees participate says much about the support arts organizations enjoy and about the loyalty they engender.

Resounding votes of confidence in the arts are most recently apparent in the extraordinary number and size of institutional fundraising campaigns. Whether for purposes of capital construction or endowment, arts organizations from coast to coast are formulating and executing huge gift drives, to remarkable success.[7]

In New York City, the Metropolitan Museum of Art has already raised $240 million of a three-year $300 million goal established in 1994. Notably, sixty separate donors pledged $1 million or more to this drive. Delighted with such early success, the Met will upgrade its goal perhaps by as much as $150 million.

The Museum of Modern Art opened a $450 million drive in 1997 with $125 million already raised. The Jewish Museum solicited $52 million in a five-year campaign extending from 1988 to 1993; the Whitney Museum collected $34 million of its $45 million goal in 1995 and 1996. Carnegie Hall met its $75 million goal in two and a half years, and the New York Philharmonic satisfied its $40 million objective between 1991 and 1993. The New York Public Library launched its $430 million campaign in the winter of 1997, having already received commitments of $300 million of that record-breaking sum. Still others, like the Brooklyn Academy of Music, the New York City Opera, and the American Museum of Natural History, have announced fundraising drives larger by far than they have ever undertaken.

The former corporation counsel of the City of New York, Frederick A. O. Schwarz Jr., captured the exuberant spirit of ambitious artistic institutions and of their magnanimous benefactors:

> We've entered a period of institutional excitement comparable only to that which occurred after the Civil War until World War I when several of the city's great civic and cultural institutions were built. We are on the verge of another huge leap in the city's cultural life, a new renaissance.[8]

A privately funded artistic revival is also occurring in Chicago, where, as in New York's Times Square, many historic abandoned theaters are being reclaimed and restored. Several hundred million dollars will be spent to revitalize Chicago's Theater Row. From 1995 to 1997, more than $275 million was raised in special campaigns for just four arts organizations: the Chicago Symphony, the Lyric Opera, the Art Institute of Chicago, and the new Museum of Contemporary Art.[9]

The Dallas Museum of Art has announced its largest capital drive ever. In San Francisco, more than $300 million was raised to erect two award-winning buildings, one for the San Francisco Museum of Contemporary Art and the other for a public library. Ground will soon be broken in Los Angeles to construct the most expensive concert hall ever built in America—Disney Hall. The hall and its associated facilities will require raising some $350 million. And so it goes. Hardly a major metropolitan area in the country can be named where comparable artistic fundraising efforts are not completed, announced, or well on their way to realization.

For corporations, all these numbers, taken together, translate into impressive and impressionable markets receptive to everything from conveying general brand messages to point-of-purchase sale. They represent important manifestations of civic pride with which to associate, the better to improve a reputation for good corporate citizenship. They constitute major outlets for the expenditure of time and treasure by employees and their families. And they offer many opportunities for constructive engagement, to the distinct advantage of both the contributing firm and their partner arts organization.

To be sure, the arts are important to companies as a means of reaching large numbers of consumers and business executives. But quantity alone—however consequential the data—hardly tells the full story.

Qualitative Factors

Support of the arts helps identify a company with important sources of civic pride. It keeps executives in touch with some of the key "movers and shakes" in a given community.

The duties of elected and appointed officials frequently bring them to the artistic centers located in their neighborhoods. Any firm lobbying them during the workday would find it useful to informally mix and mingle under circumstances where the corporation represented supports a politician's favored charity. The same observation applies to that portion of the business community represented on an art center's board and counted among its patrons and benefactors. To a salesman at a firm noted for giving to the arts, prospects abound. Latin-American, Asian-American, African-American and many other ethnic groups proudly portray their heritage through artists devoted to its expression. To align a company with specific target markets and with employees of common descent, support for Ballet Hispanico and Museo del Barrio, or the Asia Society and the Japan Society, for example, or the Alvin Ailey Dance

Company and the Crossroads Theater goes a long way. Existing and potential customers and segments of a company's workforce will rarely fail to take notice.

The arts lend themselves to employee involvement and benefit. A few initiatives from a company is all that's necessary to set employee participation in motion. Whenever employees of benefactor companies enjoy the benefits of a matching-gift program, or special ticket-reservation privileges, or discounts, or free museum admission, or displays of fine and performing art at their work sites, then the connection between what the firm accomplishes in its philanthropy and worker benefits become readily apparent.

Entertaining customers at arts events is a natural, especially in an environment in which the host firm is a valued contributor. Memorable evenings at the opera or theater or dance or symphony can help catalyze and strengthen customer relationships.

The appeal of the arts to critical constituencies such as elected and appointed officials, employees, and customers can translate into business advantage. From a purely philanthropic point of view, the arts are an attractive field to support. One needn't have a full-fledged program or nothing at all. Approaching support of the arts from the vantage point of other driving charitable concerns is often very sensible.

For funders with a substantial philanthropic program in education, for example, it may be worthwhile to consider the arts a natural extension of it at the elementary, secondary, or college level.

For funders whose priority is employment and economic development, it may be practical to consider such burgeoning fields as television, film, video, and multimedia for training and placing entry-level workers and attracting investment. They are among the areas in the arts growing far faster than the American economy as a whole.

For firms heavily involved with the philanthropic support of science and of high technology, it should be noted that some of the most innovative teaching being done today before impressively large student bodies is found in this country's science museums.

For banks, commercial real estate, or insurance firms whose philanthropy emphasizes community development, it should be recalled how much the arts have contributed all across the country to increased employment, economic activity, and commercial traffic in selected neighborhoods. The result of artistic development is rarely other than more security and higher property values for the surrounding community. It is entirely appropriate for arts support to be considered an extension or an adjunct to a grants program centered on strengthening communities.

Finally, for all businesses, there are few if any programs outside the arts that offer as much opportunity for public recognition in the form of live events, media coverage, and celebrity endorsements. To support the arts well carries with it many opportunities for publicity and for marketing the firm's brand.

An International Accent: Aiding the Arts Abroad

All the philanthropic advantages of corporate support for the arts apply outside the United States and then some. The premium on such assistance for American corporations operating overseas is rooted in the pride that the people of so many nations take in the cultural and artistic accomplishments of both the present and the past. In associating publicly with a main ingredient of the identity of a country in which a firm now does— or wishes to do—business, its sophistication is demonstrated. By appreciating the cultural accomplishments of other nations, executives find a common medium of expression with their counterparts abroad.

Painting, dance, music, literature, and film lend insight into the character of foreign partners and customers. Tell a Frenchwoman to meet you at Musée d'Orsay, suggest to an Argentine that on your next trip you'd like nothing so much as listening to a concert at the Teatro Colón in Buenos Aires, demonstrate to an Englishman (or Irishman) familiarity with what's on at The National Theatre or The Almeida (the Gate or the Abbey), and tell a Russian of your plans to visit the Bolshoi, the Pushkin, and the Hermitage, and you are viewed less as a foreigner and more as an aspiring compatriot.

The relative importance of the arts and culture in Europe as compared to America is manifest in the allocation of tax dollars. Nearly all the nations in Europe routinely spend five to fifteen times per capita the amount spent by the United States. In 1987 total public-sector arts expenditure per capita was $4 in the United States, $14 in the United Kingdom, $41 in the Netherlands, $43 in France, $48 in West Germany, and $55 in Sweden. Compare the funding for Italy's Ministry of Cultural Assets, which possessed an annual budget of $1.2 billion in 1994, to the combined expenditure of the National Endowment for the Arts, the National Endowment for the Humanities, and the Institute of Museum Services, which totaled some $375 million in the same year.[10] These order of magnitude differences have grown even sharper as American support for the arts at the national level was drastically cut in the period 1992–97.

But even such comparisons of national government expenditures vastly understate the disparity of total government support for arts and culture. In many European countries, regional, provincial, and municipal appropriations for the arts are huge. Berlin alone spent 1.1 billion marks ($800 million) in fiscal year 1995, or 2.6 percent of its municipal budget, on the arts and culture—a sum amounting to $225 for each of its 3.5 million residents. The new Guggenheim Museum in Bilbao, Spain, is being paid for largely by the Basque region; Barcelona's new Contemporary Art Museum is supported by the Barcelona and Catalan governments. In Great Britain, a portion of the proceeds of the National Lottery is directed to the nation's arts institutions, sums that are transforming their future. In its first year of operation, 5 percent of the National Lottery's revenues or $400 million was allocated to the arts. That's roughly four times the 1997 budget of America's National Endowment for the Arts.[11]

These forms of public support for the arts drawn from tax revenues are largely uncontroversial. They are applauded as reflections of national pride and illustrations of national achievement. Indeed, recognition of their importance can be readily measured by attendance and expenditures. The world's most popular attraction, as revealed by the number of visitors, is not the Eiffel Tower, the Taj Mahal, the Kremlin, or the Statue of Liberty. It is the Centre Georges Pompidou, one of France's many modern art museums, boasting 8 million visitors annually. In Great Britain, the arts are a $20 billion industry. No less than 30 percent of the total foreign earnings generated by tourists in England is attributable to the arts.[12]

These numbers reveal how seriously the arts are taken beyond American shores. They also uncover a pathway to doing business and making deals. Here's why: Almost anywhere one travels—Asia, Latin America, and Europe—great stock is placed in personal relationships as a basis for making a business commitment. Virtually everywhere, executives seek to develop a strong sense of trust in their counterparts in other countries and want assurance that a business prospect is truly interested in becoming a serious customer, partner, or supplier in the context of a relationship of mutual respect.

When Americans bring to such encounters a curiosity about and a zest for a country's arts and culture, business counterparts are impressed. An acquaintance with important works of fine, literary, and performing art makes it easier to understand overseas business practices and concerns and provides an excellent subject for conversation. Unfortunately, Americans are often regarded as lacking fluency in languages other than English and familiarity with foreign customs and protocol. They are thought to neglect the importance of strengthening personal relationships with business partners. These impressions can be partly overcome by an expressed and informed interest in a country's history and culture, however. Doing so with the help of one's company and its philanthropy offers a distinct competitive advantage.

Increasingly, corporations using the medium of the arts in quest of good citizenship or sound marketing or exercising influence are able to push through the open door of financial need, even overseas.

A global convergence of forces is slowly but perceptibly gathering strength. In America, calls for the restoration of public support for the arts have become more frequent. After all, increased admission fees and ticket prices, greater corporate and foundation support, and more individual donations can go only so far. At the same time, in Europe and elsewhere around the world, pressures to reduce government expenditures are mounting—an indicator that excessive dependence by arts institutions on public support is unhealthy. Many foreign museums, theaters, orchestras, opera and dance companies are therefore striving to diversify their sources of revenue. They are not only after more earned income but also what for many is an unprecedented quest for corporate, foundation, and individual donations.

In the search for resources, corporate support is becoming no less prized outside than inside the United States.

The Potential of Corporate Support to the Arts: Does It Get Any Better Than This?

If corporations can enjoy so many advantages from a philanthropic and marketing association with the arts, surely the converse is true as well.

No other partner can do so much in so many ways for an arts organization as a committed American company. Beyond providing cash grants, a company can also help persuade others—sister firms, foundations, suppliers, like-minded partners—to join the cause. A helpful practice is to invite colleagues to performances, openings, and meetings to become acquainted with a given arts grantee. A company can respond affirmatively to invitations to galas, dinners, anniversary celebrations, sports events, theater parties, and other fundraisers. Or it can provide in-kind donations—products and services, use of facility space, technical assistance, and executive loan.

It can match the cash contributions of its own employees to an arts organization and communicate to them news of arts events and programming. It can purchase tickets to arts events and hold corporate meetings in arts spaces. It can advertise on radio and television, in newspapers and magazines, and on billboards and buses about an association with an arts organization or arts event, thereby promoting the bona fides of both the firm and its cultural partner. It can name a given venue as the beneficiary of a marketing campaign, cause-related or otherwise.

From what other single source of assistance can so much be possible?

What's more, a major company's support matters to other donors. It carries an important imprimatur, suggesting that the tests of quality, efficiency, and effectiveness were passed with flying colors. All respected firms are expected to have conducted such due diligence before awarding substantial help to any grantee.

The Need of the Arts for More Private Philanthropic Support

Private philanthropic support, in general, and corporate assistance in any and all of its forms, most particularly, are especially welcomed by arts organizations. The need is starkly apparent because private giving figures far more prominently in the economy of the arts than tends to be the case for other nonprofits. Overall, about 15 percent of total nonprofit revenue derives from private contributions. For the arts, the range is between 35 and 40 percent.

This dependence is exacerbated further by first, the diminution of government support of the arts, and second, the inability to raise ticket prices.

In the 1970s and 1980s all levels of government were in a position to provide substantial public support for the arts. Assistance grew quickly in those decades. But that trend has abated or been reversed in most areas of the country.

Given the dual pressures of balancing the budget and cutting taxes, it was inevitable that appropriations to the arts would be adversely affected. In 1995 public support was estimated to total about $1.1 billion: $162 million from the National Endowment for the Arts; $265 million from state revenue, and $650 million from city and county governments. Major reductions have already occurred from this base level. For example, in fiscal year 1996, the NEA budget was reduced by $62.9 million to $99.5 million. This represented a huge cut of 40 percent, the largest by far in its history.

Even though the share of arts income attributable to government—some 12 percent—is already much lower than health (35 percent), private higher education (18 percent), and social services (54 percent), that proportion is expected to decline even more in the years ahead.[13]

So much for the lessened role of government. Partly in anticipation of this reality, arts institutions joined other nonprofits in very significantly increasing earned income throughout the Reagan, Bush, and Clinton administrations. Ticket prices, museum admission fees, subscription charges, and membership dues all rose at rates well in excess of inflation for some fifteen years. As a result, most arts institutions judge themselves to be at or very near the ceiling of what they can charge the paying public to see dance or theater, listen to a concert, or attend art exhibitions. There may still be room to increase attendance rates, but there's not much flexibility at all to raise prices.

With government support dwindling and earned income no longer as significant a source of budgetary relief, attention turns more than ever to the prospects for private philanthropic support.

Although there have been fluctuations within each donor segment (foundations, corporations, and individuals), arts and culture have fared well over the past three decades. Very significant growth marked each decade beginning in 1964, not only for the total amount received but also for an enlarging share of the total philanthropic pie: for 1964, $2.3 billion and a 3.2 percent share; for 1974, $4 billion and a 4.5 percent share; for 1984, $7.1 billion and a 6.5 percent share; and for 1996, $10.92 billion and an overall 7.1 percent share.[14] This consistent trend shows the sustaining appeal of the arts in the face of significant competition from such other spheres of activity as religion, education, and health and human services.

More specifically, the corporate component of that growth has been particularly impressive. In 1964 it is estimated that only 5 percent or less of the country's corporate contributions were allocated to the arts, or a total of about $16–$21 million. By 1977 corporate contributions to the arts had grown fivefold to $100 million, representing 6.5 percent of corporate giving. In 1996 a Business Committee for the Arts (BCA) study suggested that companies had in the prior year given $875 million in cash to the arts, for about 12 percent of their total gifts. It observed that about 35 percent of all U.S. businesses offered cash donations to arts organizations. And it noted that the $875 million was up 59 percent over the $518 million figure of two years earlier, in 1993, when it last conducted a comparable survey.[15]

No solid figures exist for the cash value of all of the in-kind support generated by America's companies. BCA conservatively estimates it at 20 percent of the cash total. So add $175 million (or 20 percent of the $875 million) to the grand total of what corporations give to the arts, nationwide. The final figure comes to well over a billion dollars and may already exceed all support from government—a major milestone in the relatively brief history of the American corporation as arts Medici.

Two other features of corporate support for the arts as reported by BCA are especially worth noting. They are leading indicators of a promising future.

First, in 1995 roughly two thirds of all corporate support for the arts came from small- and medium-sized businesses with revenues in the $1–$25 million range. The potential growth of support in this corporate segment is very encouraging. Many nonprofit organizations—those in the arts included—spent an inadequate amount of time soliciting from this huge donor pool. Its members are readily accessible in towns and cities everywhere.

Second, in-kind support is growing at an even faster rate than cash. For large companies, this trend suggests that the ways to tap business support extend well beyond ordinary philanthropy—to marketing, advertising, public relations, and human resource (matching gift) expenditures. Many firms are looking not just for grantees but for partners and allies sympathetic to business needs and able to help satisfy them. It is no accident that firms are increasingly talking not about contributing funds but of *underwriting* projects and *sponsoring* events and organizations.

The confluence of nonprofit need and benefit and the advancement of business interests is what sustains corporate giving in any field of endeavor, the arts included. Where these areas of mutual advantage are identified and how they serve both companies and their artistic partners are matters of keen interest. For those committed to the marriage of art and commerce, opportunities are abundant. Lingering at a few of the destinations in the odyssey of one firm's experiences with the arts helps to explain why this union will long endure.

The Arts, Public Health, and Public Television: Support That Matters

From 1984, when the AT&T Foundation was formed, until 1996, when I left the company, AT&T's underwriting, sponsorship, and philanthropic support for the arts and public television were significant. With the possible exception of Philip Morris, no firm has allocated more funds to the arts than AT&T, nor has any been more consistent in treating the arts and public television as a priority. In the performing and visual arts alone, the company estimates that more than $150 million has been spent in those twelve years for foundation grants, corporate cash contributions, advertising, marketing and sales expenses, and sponsorship.

AT&T's high level of involvement in the arts has enhanced the business in many ways. The AT&T brand has been imbued with a more youthful, technologically appealing, and contemporary coloring. Employees have shown great pride in participating in artistic institutions they care about, including those that reflect their particular heritage. Indeed, the enthusiasm of minority employees throughout the company has been unmatched by any other philanthropic program. African-American, Latin-American and Asian-American workers, to cite but three groups, are among the strongest cheerleaders for company support of the arts.

Externally, AT&T's arts profile has facilitated access to appreciative public officials, community leaders, and customers. It has been a source of continuing visibility and contributed importantly to the company's reputation as a good corporate citizen. And it has provided outlets for employee voluntarism, offering leadership development to dozens upon dozens of AT&T executives who serve on the boards of directors of artistic organizations.

A belief that animated the expenditure of funds and of employee effort during those years was that first-class artists, the institutions that nurtured them and their audiences would all benefit. To convert that belief into a reality, AT&T based its philanthropic contribution to the arts on a distinct point of view:

> It stood for the support of new work created by living artists devoted principally to the fields of dance, theater, music, and performance and visual art.

> It favored lowering the barriers to entry of new talent and new organizations. As such, it acted affirmatively to identify high-quality minority and female artists and organizations that gave their work a featured place in their seasons.

> It supported artists in whom foundation program officers reposed great confidence and in organizations driven by a desire to identify and cultivate the gifted.

In advancing these priorities, AT&T did not shy away from the possibility of controversy when the arts became the target of those who took deep offense from something that made its way to a book or a canvas or a stage. Indeed, as a company dedicated to the advancement of communications, AT&T treasured the freedoms of expression and assembly. It took special care to support them when challenged and to value them in its work. Protagonists of the First Amendment cannot help but court debate and elicit protest on occasion.

In looking back on how these convictions manifested themselves in specific programs of value to the firm and to its partner nonprofits, I find many examples that could be cited. The following five case studies depict the various forms of public good and private gain that a corporate philanthropic commitment to the arts can foster.

THE MCNEIL-LEHER NEWS HOUR

In 1982 Charles L. Brown, the chairman of AT&T, at the recommendation of Edward M. Block, senior vice president of public relations, pledged long-term financial support for what became the *McNeil-Lehrer*

News Hour. The program was to be sponsored by the Corporation for Public Broadcasting and aired through syndication on public television stations throughout the nation. In venturing into virgin territory, Brown was taking a bold step. At the time, no other company—indeed, no other source of private philanthropy—vied for the privilege.

The company's public-service motivation is simply to help inform the American people by supporting a high-quality news program, one that would spend the uninterrupted time necessary to illuminate and debate key public issues. By serving as an alternative to the news sound bites of commercial stations, public television could cover complicated stories at a length and in a depth that for-profit network news would never countenance. *McNeil-Lehrer* would invite experts to explain the dynamics at work behind the headlines. The program would cover all sides of an issue and would bring distinction to television journalism.

Over the ensuing decade and a half, the contrast between *McNeil-Lehrer*'s consistent, spacious, reliable, and serious treatment of public concerns and the limitations of commercial network news and associated programming grew starker. Some critics, the journalist James Fallows among them, expressed disdain for the sensationalism and trivialization of the news as represented by such programs as CNN's *Crossfire* and *Capital Gang* and NBC's *The McLaughlin Group*. On those shows and others like them, high decibel levels and provocation drive out any hope for a calm, informed exchange of views.[16]

By any measure—audience growth, critical reception, prizes awarded, longevity on the air—Robert McNeil and Jim Lehrer and their associates offered a first-class alternative to commercial news and public policy talk shows. That Lehrer was selected to moderate the presidential debates in 1992 and 1996 was another sign of the respect and popular acceptance accorded the national evening news as presented by public television. And Robert McNeil's decision to retire, which left his partner as the *News Hour*'s solo anchor, has not adversely affected the program's quality or the size of its audience.

None of this could have been accomplished, the producers will say, without long-term, no-strings-attached support. AT&T was the sole underwriter of the *News Hour* for more than a decade. When AT&T decided to move on to other activities, McNeil and Lehrer were informed four years in advance. This transition period was arranged to allow ample time to secure substitute sponsorship. Indeed, for AT&T, its stewardship as the originating sponsor embraced the obligation to help find successor underwriters. The company did so with pleasure and a profound sense of responsibility. Having been present at its creation, AT&T wanted *McNeil-Lehrer* and its progeny to thrive, long after the company had left the scene.

It's fair to note that AT&T's sponsorship would be judged today by most observers to have been enlightened and in the public interest. It certainly was consequential for public television. At its peak, AT&T spent anywhere from $8 million to $14 million annually to help finance the program and to provide the wherewithal for its advertising and promotion. For years, AT&T's support of *McNeil-Lehrer* represented about 20 percent of the dollar value of all corporate underwriting of all public television programming in America. In all, Chairman Brown's commitment, which was blessed by his successors, James Olson and Robert E. Allen, totaled in excess of $90 million.

Money well spent, most informed commentators would venture to say—now. But then, there were doubters, naysayers, and gadflies galore.

Would such sponsorship eventually clutter the public television airways with excessive, intrusive commercial messages? Would a cost of the acceptance of such corporate support be a loss of independence in the exercise of unfettered news and editorial judgment? Wouldn't private sponsorship prove unreliable compared with public sector funding? Time has answered these perceptive questions definitively: No. No. No.

There has not been so much as a hint of concern that corporate sponsorship tainted *McNeil-Lehrer* decision making in any way. The precedent of benevolent, arms-length sponsorship set by AT&T has been maintained by its successors, corporations as varied as ADM, the CIT Group, and Pepsico. Corporate support has proven far more dependable than either government funds or, for that matter, private foundation assistance. And exactly sixty seconds of inoffensive mention of the identity of program underwriters precedes sixty minutes of uninterrupted news and analysis. No more, no less. The time allotted to crediting the sponsor has not expanded at all.

Only curmudgeons could grouse. That observation applies as much to AT&T insiders as to critics of corporations or of philanthropy. For the firm's destiny was in many respects tethered to executive, legislative, regulatory, and judicial action. To be closely associated with the most watched and admired public affairs program of Beltway aficionados was an asset.

Furthering AT&T's reputation for good citizenship with that influential target audience was an important objective. No one was heard to doubt that long-term sponsorship of the *McNeil-Lehrer News Hour* helped in large measure to realize it.

AIDS TREATMENT AND PREVENTION

The proclivity of AT&T to support causes that have wide public approval but were once controversial found another manifestation soon after divestiture. In 1985, AT&T agreed to be the sole corporate underwriter of a fundraising concert, the proceeds from which would support the treatment and prevention of AIDS. At the time, institutions that associated themselves with projects addressing this affliction were widely accused of lending legitimacy to promiscuous lifestyles and of endangering the sanctity of traditional relationships.

Given AT&T's huge share of the American consumer long-distance marketplace, almost any public matter on which it was seen to take a stand prompted protest. So when AT&T underwrote the expenses of "A Dance for Life," a benefit evening to raise funds for AIDS research, the negative letters far outweighed notes of approval.

The company explained that its action was not intended to express a political perspective or to approve a lifestyle preference. The only purpose was to acknowledge the existence of a dreadful, communicable disease and to help galvanize support to prevent it, detect it, treat it, and find a cure for it. Advocates of the cause of AIDS report that few other companies spoke out as clearly and unequivocally and as early with their support as did AT&T in financing "A Dance for Life." To do so, from AT&T's perspective, made sense for the public and for the company.

A decade later, one really has to wonder what the fuss was about. AIDS research and prevention is a popular cause supported by many firms. It is a source of some satisfaction that AT&T's early and lonely sponsorship, followed up by constant year-in, year-out assistance, helped others to rally round.

MODERN DANCE AND BALLET

The lifeblood of virtually all dance companies is touring. Few ballet troupes and modern dance ensembles enjoy audiences large enough to sustain more than a three- to four-week fall/winter and/or spring/summer run in their hometown base of operations. How to fill out the calendar before and after such stints to afford to pay full-time dancers and to finance adequate rehearsal time preoccupies every managing and artistic director. Arranging a season of performances requires reaching booking agreements with performing arts centers and presenting organizations. Usually, the host presenter pays the company a flat fee, markets and publicizes the events, and hopes that the combination of box-office proceeds and philanthropic support will keep deficits to a tolerable minimum.

For many years, dance touring programs sponsored by the National Endowment for the Arts and state arts councils helped to reduce financial risks and provide incentives to performing arts centers to include dance ensembles in their schedules. Because these programs subsidized traveling ensembles, dance companies could afford to charge out-of-town venues somewhat lower fees. Concurrently, philanthropic support to the centers themselves helped to pay those fees.

Beginning in the 1980s, this pattern of government assistance broke down. Dance touring support dwindled, then virtually disappeared. Performing arts center support declined severely. The net result was a severe reduction in touring activity. That, in turn, decreased rehearsal time significantly, posing major obstacles to maintaining high performance standards.

For a full decade, AT&T filled the gap in support. The withdrawal of government funding for dance tours threatened in particular the nation's smaller, newer, and promising but less proven companies. The AT&T Dance Tour favored these Davids of the dance: Trisha Brown Company, Twyla Tharp Dance, Wim Vandekayerbus of Belgium, Mark Morris Dance Company, Hubbard Street Dance Company, Margaret Jenkins Dance Company, Ballet Hispanico, Dallas Black Dance, Ballet British Columbia, Alvin Ailey Repertory Ensemble, David Gordon Pick-Up Company, Dance Theatre of Harlem, Eiko and Koma, and Urban Bush Women. For $35,000 to $50,000, each of these dance troupes added anywhere from fifteen to sixty performances to their itineraries around the country, filling their dance cards to the delight of audiences that otherwise wouldn't have seen them. The grants helped ensure that the artists in the winning companies worked year round.

In every printed program at every dance site, AT&T was credited as sponsor. Anywhere from twelve to thirty tickets were set aside for AT&T employees and their guests, among them customers, business partners, and key government leaders. In their eyes, the company shone.

This was bread-and-butter philanthropy. The meal was served to some of the country's smaller, hungrier, and needier dance troupes. By favoring the underdog and providing opportunities to female and minority choreographers whenever possible, AT&T advanced quality and innovation. In no place did the plasma of grant funds enter so quickly and beneficially the bloodstream of artistic activity as in AT&T's Dance Tour.

AT&T ONSTAGE

Consistent with the goal of supporting new work by established artists and assisting emerging artists of high promise, the AT&T Foundation and the company's advertising department have conducted a program called AT&T OnStage for more than a decade. It provides grants of $30,000–$75,000 to the winners of an annual competition among invited theaters. Since 1985, anywhere from fifty-eight to ninety-one theaters have been asked to apply for the support of new plays or musicals never before performed on stage. Usually, half of those invited become applicants in any given year.

An advisory committee of distinguished experts in the theater are retained to assist in selecting the winners. They read all scripts and applications; rank and rate them; and debate the merits of each at meetings. Their only instructions are to choose for premiere showing a dramatic or musical work destined for mainstage production that is of the highest quality. In making their choice, the panel is expected to give special consideration to submissions by women and minority artists.

Because the advisory panel is composed of fellow artists of distinction and because only 5 to 10 percent of those who apply receive a grant each year, an AT&T OnStage award is especially coveted. To have one's script judged promising enough to be underwritten by such figures as the theater producers Harold Prince and Cora Cahan, the director and choreographer Graciela Daniele, and Jonathan Kent, artistic director of the Almeida Theatre, all of whom have served as advisory panelists in the past decade, is deemed an honor in itself. So, too, is emerging victorious from a competitive process that attracts the best regional theaters in America.

Because AT&T OnStage operates by invitation only, the applicant theater pool includes only those from communities where AT&T has a major presence.

Because the generous production grant awards are complemented by advertising and promotional support of comparable size and by

$5,000 grants to the playwright, translator, and/or composer, the time and effort required to apply is warranted.

Because AT&T OnStage is into its second decade of existence, it has developed a well-deserved reputation for consistency and dependability. No other firm anywhere in the world has placed a higher priority on supporting the production of new plays and new theater artists. It is a program of which artistic directors and producers are well aware.

Because winning plays receive promotional assistance from AT&T, including extensive advertising, the chances of attracting an audience sufficient to extend a performance run and even of acquiring the financial support to move from a nonprofit venue to Broadway improve inordinately.

And because this competition has been so well received in the United States and because AT&T is a global communications provider, beginning in 1992, theaters in England, Canada, and South Africa have been invited to compete.

Eleven years after its founding, AT&T OnStage can proudly cite having supported four productions honored with Tony nominations and awards. In the 1991 nominated category for best musical was the 1990 AT&T OnStage winner, *Once on This Island*, with book by Lynn Ahrens and music by Stephen Flaherty, produced by Playwrights Horizon. In the nominated category for best dramatic play in 1996 was the 1994 AT&T OnStage winner *Seven Guitars*, written by August Wilson and produced by Chicago's Goodman Theatre. As to award winners, the 1988 OnStage production of *The Grapes of Wrath*, by John Steinbeck, adapted by Frank Galati, and produced by the Steppenwolf Company, received a Tony for best play in 1990. That honor was also bestowed in 1995 on AT&T OnStage winner *Love! Valour! Compassion!* written by Terence McNally and produced by the Manhattan Theatre Club.

AT&T has also helped the works of other established theater figures find their way to the stage: Derek Walcott, Steve Tesich, Harold Prince, Robert Brustein, and Graciela Daniele. Just as important, it has consistently assisted hardly known, emerging talent to find able and willing producers, enthusiastic audiences, and critics who care.[17]

In recent years this competitive award process has opened up to overseas applicants. No other corporate grant process does so, possibly because crossing territorial boundaries is complicated. It requires a special outreach effort and technical assistance to theater groups unacquainted with applying to corporate grant-making programs in America. The program expansion began in 1992. Already, London's Almeida Theatre and the Canadian Opera Company have each won an AT&T OnStage Award twice, while one each has been received by the National Theatre and by the Royal Shakespeare Company.

Global in dimension, high quality by aspiration, new by definition, generous and vigorous by intention, sought after by reputation, and dependable in its longevity, AT&T OnStage adds luster to the corporation's record of supporting new work and assisting promising as well as proven artists. Concomitantly, advantages to the firm's reputation and stature accrue naturally. These range from customer entertainment to employee engagement, from the favorable notice of politicians and community leaders to the good will generated by program credits and other forms of corporate recognition, and from associating AT&T's brand with the innovative to assisting civic renewal.

AT&T NEW ART/NEW VISIONS

The success of AT&T OnStage emboldened the AT&T Foundation staff to create a comparably innovative program for the support of visual art, AT&T New Art/New Visions. This initiative provides grants for the exhibition and acquisition of recently created work by living artists and for audience development through related education activities. As with AT&T OnStage, the pool of applicants is predetermined by the company. Invitations for each of the two grant rounds held to date were extended to some fifty American museums. A panel of experts assists in judging applicants.

The program was shaped at its inception in such a way as to encourage applications from outside the United States. In 1995, museums in Canada, Brazil, Mexico, the Netherlands, Spain, France, Poland, and the United Kingdom competed for support.

Part of what drew an unusual level of attention to New Arts/New Visions was AT&T's enthusiasm for supporting the three major functions of any museum as applied to the advancement of contemporary work—exhibition, acquisition, and education. As with AT&T OnStage, New Arts/New Visions asked nonprofits to apply for support related to the core of their artistic mission. Having to address all three elements of an holistic effort to portray an artist's work fostered an exciting level of collaboration within the departments of each applying museum and stim-

ulated unconventional approaches to featuring new work. And in contributing to the museum's purchase of one or more pieces in the artist's
show for its permanent collection on a cost-matching arrangement,
AT&T tended a unique offer bound to gain notice. No other commercial
firm has ever contributed funds for museums to purchase contemporary
art.

New Art/New Visions operates on a biennial cycle. The grants for
exhibition and education range from $32,500 to $60,000 and, for art
purchase, from $5,000 to $15,000. Often, promotional assistance and
advertising funded out of AT&T's operations supplemented these sums.
In spending about $1.2 million to aid twenty-four exhibition, education,
and acquisition programs, or roughly $600,000 annually, AT&T enjoyed
a philanthropic bargain. The common theme driving the grants program;
its direct relevance to the museum's mission; the excitement generated by
a thoughtfully developed, well-judged creative competition; and the
stated desire to support young institutions and unknown artists at least as
much as the new work of established artists in "household name" venues
all contributed to gratifying levels of interest and impact.

The winners in 1992–93 demonstrate the extraordinary geographic,
programmatic, and organizational mix of New Art/New Vision partici-
pants. Two dozen innovative visual arts centers—ranging from New
York's El Museo del Barrio and the Museo du Arte Moderna in Rio de
Janeiro, Brazil, to the Wexner Center for the Arts in Columbus, Ohio,
and Museo Nacional, Centro de Arte Reina Sophia in Madrid, Spain—
were associated with this tailor-made program.[18]

By interesting curators as much as managers and museum educa-
tors, as well as development directors, New Art/New Visions struck a
responsive chord. Publicity and word of mouth were widespread and
extremely favorable, triggered not only by the original announcement of
the program and the subsequent rounds of grant awards but also by the
opening of each exhibit. The associated educational activities held at each
museum and news of the subsequent purchase of work as permanent
additions to the collection also added to the positive reactions.

What's more, because the work shown was often created by female,
minority, or otherwise rarely exhibited artists, human interest feature stories proliferated. Even veteran museum professionals were enthusiastic

enough about New Art/New Visions to accept and seek opportunities to publicize its merits and the virtues of the benefactor company.

MANY OTHER PROJECTS attesting to the diversity and vitality of AT&T's philanthropic ventures in the arts might have been cited here for their favorable impact on the field and on the company.

One is AT&T American Encore, a program directed to orchestras demonstrating a commitment to American music and especially to playing pieces that had been premiered but were rarely, if ever again, performed. The light shed by American Encore on twentieth-century U.S. composers helped to cure a general condition of benign neglect among the orchestral establishment.

Another is AT&T NEAT (New Experiments in Art and Technology), a program conceived as an incentive to introduce the work of artists into science and children's museums. In promoting the multifaceted relationship between art and science and between artists and scientists, NEAT encourages the exploration of new frontiers.

How to make a difference with the modest resources of large institutions with huge audiences like orchestras and science and children's museums was the challenge to the inventors of both NEAT and American Encore. These programs carve out an identifiable and increasingly recognized AT&T niche. They have enjoyed an influence far out of proportion to grant dollars spent.

In listening carefully to the expressed needs of artists and the institutions that care most about them, patterns emerged. In determining the forces driving AT&T's business interests, themes began to take shape. Blending these requirements into homegrown programs and initiatives became a mark of philanthropic professionalism in the arts and elsewhere at AT&T.

But the AT&T Foundation staff and their corporate colleagues also left plenty of room to respond, one on one, to theaters, museums, dance troupes, opera companies, music ensembles, and performing arts centers. Requests by the thousands were received each quarter. Importance was placed on the sensitivity and speed with which these were treated. How helpful staff could be in assisting solicitors whose priorities didn't quite mesh with those of AT&T, or who were otherwise ineligible for support, was a professional challenge taken seriously. After all, the beneficiaries of AT&T support and the disappointed have one quality in common: They are either customers or the company would like them to become customers. AT&T never forgot that marketplace imperative.

All these examples of the marriage of art and commerce depend on the judgment, taste, and experience of the philanthropic staff. They must be selected for knowledge of the field and for their capacity to shape initiatives that matter. Those qualities of mind function best in an environment that supports risk-taking and encourages new ideas. The AT&T Foundation sought to recruit thoughtful, discerning professionals, alert at once to developments in the arts and in the business of the firm that employed them. The senior management and the trustees of the foundation provided ample resources to support good work and were second to none in a growing company cadre of admirers.

Behind enlightened corporate arts patronage are gifted staff. They are the indispensable modern Medicis possessed of the courage, energy, and discipline to mark new philanthropic pathways with AT&T signage. They and their colleagues allow companies to justifiably lay claim to play an important role in the practice of contemporary American philanthropy.

5

Epithets and Episodes:
When Politics and Corporate Philanthropy Meet

Great ideas, it is said, come into the world as gently as doves. Perhaps, then, if we listen attentively, we shall hear, amid the uproar of empires and nations, a faint flutter of wings, the gentle stirring of life and hope.

—ALBERT CAMUS
from the lecture "Creating Dangerously"

Those are my principles. And, if you don't like them, fear not. I have others.

—MARK TWAIN

DURING MY ASSOCIATION WITH AT&T and its foundation, there emerged three significant challenges to philanthropy. Each was serious and important. Each taught lessons worth recalling. But the central arguments animating all of them were fatally flawed.

The first questioned the legitimacy of philanthropy as a corporate activity. It proceeded from the premise that corporations have no franchise to be involved in charitable matters. This principled contention, articulated most cogently and insistently by the economist Milton Friedman, still finds adherents in the corridors of companies and in university lecture halls. Firms should relentlessly seek to maximize profits, according to this view. Shareowners are free to spend the enhanced value of their holdings and their dividends on selected charities. But the company itself shouldn't be distracted from its overriding mission by tangential concerns like charitable donations.[1]

The second challenge emanated from the extreme ideological right. Its proponents do not necessarily see a conflict in principle between corporate philanthropy and maximizing profits or between a commitment to good corporate citizenship and increasing shareowner value. The quarrel for the right is not so much with the theory animating corporate charitable contributions as with its contemporary practice. In essence, corporations generally stand accused of failing to understand their own interests. It is said that they financially assist their adversaries, offering handsome grants to nonprofits that oppose or disdain the free enterprise system and that support excessive taxation and regulation. "How can such uses of corporate funds be justified?" these critics ask. From the ideological right, the debate turns not on the question of whether there is a place for philanthropy in the life of modern business but on the purported overwhelmingly liberal bias of their benefactions.[2]

The third challenge emerged somewhat surprisingly from the left wing of American politics. It came in reaction to the AT&T Foundation's decision not to renew a grant to Planned Parenthood after having provided that organization with a quarter century of continuous support. In 1991 that decision unleashed a furious and public rhetorical assault. The company was suddenly cast as an opponent of choice, at the mercy of right-wing Christian Coalition zealots, a renegade abandoning a worthy organization in a time of great need.[3]

Each of these assaults on the cogency of corporate philanthropy is worth understanding, especially for those who believe the charitable enterprise of corporations should flourish. AT&T is hardly alone in being accused, by turns, of unjustifiably donating finite corporate resources to the detriment of profit-seeking, of misunderstanding business interests into the bargain by aiding nonprofits that allegedly aim to undermine free enterprise, and of abandoning principle at any sign of strong protest, however misguided.

Corporations so characterized should pay heed. When politics and philanthropy mix, the combination is highly combustible.

A Critique from a Corporate Insider

Corporate charity exists so that CEOs can collect awards, plaques and honors, so that they can sit on a dais and be adored. But that is not what the shareholder is paying them a million bucks a year—plus stock options and bonuses—to do.

Show me a chief executive who's on five boards and who lends his or her name, prestige, and time to 15 community activities, and I'll show you a company that's underperforming. A chief executive is paid to run the company. *That's* the CEO's job. Corporations become woefully inadequate when CEOs think they are great social messiahs.

—ALBERT J. DUNLAP
Mean Business: How I Save Bad Companies and Make Good Companies Great.[4]

It is deceptively easy to dismiss Al Dunlap, the former CEO of Sunbeam, and his critique of corporate philanthropy. It appears that he can advance his case only by engaging in hyperbole. In fact, many CEOs from companies with sizable contribution programs resist being honored at fundraising luncheons and dinners. They don't like the spotlight, nor are they convinced they merit the plaudits. They prefer to see their companies contribute to the welfare of the community each day and to enjoy a good night's sleep rather than a long evening out.

Nor does one need to serve on five boards or lend one's name and time to fifteen community activities to advance the well being of important Third Sector institutions or causes. But even by Dunlap's own exaggerated standard, he should be reminded of the example set by Lou Gerstner, Roberto Goizueta, and Walter Shipley. It would be difficult indeed to demonstrate that under their leadership IBM, Coca-Cola, and Chemical Bank (now Chase-Manhattan) have underperformed. To the contrary, Wall Street is as pleased with the financial returns as philanthropic Main Street is with these firms' charitable contributions record.

This is empty rhetoric. What's more, in his sweeping accusations about CEOs believing that they are great social messiahs, Dunlap mentions no names.

It would be reasonable for Dunlap or anyone else to set forth the pragmatic view that a firm's community service activity should be proportionate to its interests and its resources. Community relations and charitable contribution programs should be executed in a way that doesn't detract from but rather contributes to earning a profit. For Dunlap, however, philanthropy literally has no place in a business enterprise:

If you're in business, you're in business for one thing—to make money. You must do everything fiducial, legal and moral to achieve that goal. And making excellent products that are expertly marketed is the primary way of making money.

Executives who run their businesses to support social causes—such as Ben and Jerry's or The Body Shop—would never get my investment dollars. They funnel a portion of profits into things like saving the whales or Greenpeace. That is not the essence of business. If you want to support a social cause, if you have other agendas, join Rotary International.[5]

Here Dunlap has erected straw men to knock down. Neither Ben Cohen nor Anita Roddick, founders of Ben and Jerry's and The Body Shop, respectively, have been heard to say that they run their businesses *in order* to support social causes. What they *have* maintained is that there is no inconsistency between building well-run, profitable companies *and,* beyond generating quarterly earnings, discharging their social responsibilities. Nor does any responsible business executive claim that corporate contributions are the essence of what a business does. Dunlap offers no evidence, not even a single example to substantiate this contention.

While he is hardly persuasive, Dunlap's case is stronger than its articulation in *Mean Business.* I will compose his side of the argument more compellingly.

It *is* tough to advance a robust philanthropic program when a company consistently fails to earn a profit or when it otherwise dashes the expectations of investors. Defending substantial charitable contributions activity in the face of persistent employee layoffs and other expense reductions *is* a daunting task. At certain periods in a firm's history, the task of addressing broader societal obligations and opportunities must give way to the basics of earning a profit. Just as individuals who experience financial setbacks or hard times are less likely to put as much emphasis on the needs of others as when fortunes are favorable, so too with business enterprises. Even when individual donors and corporations have intentionally set aside assets in philanthropic funds precisely to tap them in a bad earnings period, spending during such intervals is usually sparing and reluctant.

It is obvious that a business corporation is organized to advance the interests of shareowners and that significant marketplace constraints restrain the corporate pursuit of noneconomic objectives:

> Competitive conditions usually restrict the decisions by which a corporation is operated to two main channels. One is directed to keeping the corporation's costs low, so that its goods and services will be priced com-

petitively; the other is directed toward keeping the corporation's resources concentrated on developing products for which demand is likely to be high at a profitable price.[6]

So warn, the Yale economist Paul W. MacAvoy and the corporate lawyer Ira Millstein. For them, philanthropic activity should be prudent and affordable, consuming neither excessive cash nor inordinate executive time. Of course. But soon their sound argument, grounded in classical economic principles, starts to weaken:

> The competitive market place for goods and services generally does not distinguish between companies whose social performance is good and those whose performance is bad. It searches out the best product or service at the lowest cost, so that socially concerned companies that experience higher costs as a result of their effort, may sacrifice market position to their less socially concerned competitors.[7]

But suppose the costs expended by socially concerned companies are only slightly higher than those of their socially indifferent competitors, leading to only barely perceptible, inconsequential price differentials. Or suppose a company's brand reputation allows it with impunity to charge a little more for its product or service. Suppose further that the business benefits of such expenditures—nowhere mentioned by MacAvoy or Millstein—reduced, equaled, or outweighed the costs.

If corporate philanthropy helps a firm recruit smarter, more highly motivated employees from college campuses or provides more privileged access to pathbreaking research from university laboratories, don't such advantages find their place somewhere on the scale of economic competitiveness? If corporate philanthropy helps to make a company more aware of the risks of environmental litigation or protest or the possibilities of penetrating new markets, shouldn't such a contribution to business advancement be acknowledged? And presume for a moment that a solid record of philanthropy tangibly improves a company's reputation as a good citizen and wins for it the favor of public officials and other influentials. Then where in the calculus of costs and benefits do such attributes receive recognition?

As corporate philanthropists increasingly take into account the interests of their businesses in dispensing grants, costs are correspondingly offset by realized marketplace benefits. Few critics of corporate philanthropy consider carefully those benefits, whereas many exaggerate its costs.

To the constraint that competition imposes on the size and scale of a company's philanthropy should be added another: business is not government nor is it an individual citizen. Critics of corporate philanthropy often claim that the profit-maximizing employer already contributes mightily to societal advancement twice over, even if no contributions program exists. First, the corporation is a taxpayer. Second, its employees pay taxes on their incomes. The more each earns, the greater the proceeds to help fund social programs in accordance with the democratic process.

> Let's assume that a corporation creates $5 billion worth of value and that its shareholders all sell their stock. If the tax on that increased capital is 30 percent, that's $1.5 billion the shareholders would give to government. Much of that money would go to social causes. Isn't it better for $1.5 billion to go to social causes in that manner than for a corporation to waste its time and resources trying to duplicate the purpose of other agencies.[8]

Apart from Dunlap's contention that corporate philanthropy is all pain and no gain and that its exertions would not be different from or complementary to but would duplicate those of government, the basic point is on target. Corporations and employees as taxpayers are essential to the economic well-being of communities where their people live and work. How significant a business is as a taxpayer depends, of course, on its economic performance.

Peter Drucker has it right in more ways than one when he characterizes earning a profit as the first responsibility of a business. Economic performance is the sine qua non of free enterprise. It is definitely the first but not the only obligation of a firm. It is utterly necessary but by no means entirely sufficient to discharge a company's social responsibility.

Altough cautions and reservations of critics may be well founded, they are raised less often now that corporate philanthropy has gained acceptance as a conventional business activity. Today, hardly a Fortune 1000 company can be found without a substantial charitable contributions program. Eight and one-half billion dollars in cash and more than $1 billion in kind was contributed by for-profits to Third Sector organizations in 1996—a tribute to the widespread acceptance of philanthropy in business.

More than forty years ago, the Supreme Court of New Jersey established the precedent for the widespread adoption of philanthropy as a valid corporate function. The court responded to a shareowner's suit against A. P. Smith Manufacturing Company for giving $1,000 to Princeton University. The court ruled against the plaintiff, finding that philanthropy was fully permissible as a legitimate part of the corporate enterprise.

Memorably, the court opined that far from being questionable, corporate philanthropy might well be a condition of public responsibility. In these words *Smith* v. *Barlow* forecast the growth of corporate contributions and offered an expansive explanation for the broader role to be played by companies in society:

> When the wealth of the nation was primarily in the hands of individuals, they discharged their responsibilities as citizens by donating freely for charitable purposes. With the transfer of wealth to corporate hands and the imposition of heavy burden of individual taxation, they have been unable to keep pace with the increased philanthropic needs. They have therefore, with justification, turned to corporations to assume the modern obligations of good citizenship in the same manner as humans do.[9]

Few critics and commentators who carry any intellectual weight quarrel with the citizenship obligations of the modern company in the manner of Al Dunlap. But various opinion sources do take issue with companies for *how* they discharge these obligations and for the alleged ideological bias displayed in doing so.

Political Ideology vs. Business Practice

The most consistent and comprehensive annual review of corporate philanthropy is prepared by a nonprofit educational organization, the Capital Research Center (CRC). Founded to study critical issues in philanthropy, the CRC has issued *Patterns of Corporate Philanthropy*[10] annually since 1987. This study positions the recipients of corporate philanthropy on an ideological spectrum based on an eight-point scale: 1 (radical left), 2 (left), 3 (liberal), 4 (center-left), 5 (center), 6 (center-right), 7 (conservative), and 8 (classical liberal). It then rates and ranks corporations ideologically, taking into account the political bent of the recipients and the amount of support they receive. Generous donations to many groups on the right side of the spectrum merits a high grade. Broad contributions to nonprofits on the left of the political universe warrants a low mark.

These grades are meant only to characterize corporate giving to nonprofits focused on public affairs. *Patterns* is not interested in evaluating corporate giving in the areas of health, education, cultural, or social services. It focuses exclusively on corporate philanthropic assistance to advocacy groups endeavoring to influence public policy. Such groups cover a broad range of domestic, foreign policy, and national defense issues. *Patterns* organizes them into eight categories: national security/foreign policy, energy/environment/natural resources, regulation/taxation/trade, minorities, women/family, education, philanthropy, and legal. Of course, some advocacy groups cover ground in more than one specialized field; these are classified as multi-issue.

The outcome of the analysis is straightforward. For example, in the 1993 edition of *Patterns,* 226 nonprofit organizations and 825 corporations are profiled. Each received a rating for its political orientation, accompanied by a description of its work.

The results left the authors of *Patterns* discouraged, perplexed, outraged, and stunned. Consider just a few selections from the 1993 summary commentary:

> It may come as a surprise to some to learn that Corporate America is NOT inherently conservative and does NOT carry the banner for free markets, private property and private contracts.
>
> The view that Corporate America champions the cause of laissez-faire capitalism and free market individualism and responsibility is an outdated Marxist fiction. However, Lenin's boast that the Capitalists would prepare for their own suicide has never been more appropriate than in contemporary Corporate America.
>
> The grades received by this year's sample must discourage any citizen who favors private initiative over collective coercion, individual responsibility over public compulsion, and a free market rather than a regimented economic and social system.[11]

If these characterizations aptly summarize the realities in 1993, it can hardly be said that the situation has improved much over time. For in 1988, *Patterns* found that more than two thirds of the grants by the Forbes 250 corporations in 1986 and 58 percent of total grant dollars went to left-of-center organizations. Two years later, the 1990 edition of *Patterns* reports an almost identical finding: "The most generously funded left-of-center recipients again received over twice as much as their counterparts on the right. . . . Overall, 15 of the highest funded groups are left of center, and seven are right of center."[12]

Now, fast forward to 1995. The state of affairs had deteriorated even further, moving from (very) bad to (very) worse. In the 1989 *Patterns,* for every dollar of contributions that had gone to organizations favoring free enterprise, $1.87 was directed toward groups that worked against free market and economic growth. In 1993, the first full year of the Clinton administration, that ratio had moved alarmingly, to wit, from $1.87 to $4.07.

That may be why a note of frustration and exasperation crept into the alarmist wording of the subtitles of the reports of Capital Research authors:

Patterns of Corporate Philanthropy: The Suicidal Impulse (1990)

Patterns of Corporate Philanthropy: Funding False Compassion (1991)

Patterns of Corporate Philanthropy: The Progressive Deception (1992)

The authors seem to be asking several questions: Why do corporations continually feed the hand that bites them? Why does a situation too true to be good fail to improve over time? Why are logical admonitions to companies to act in their own self-interest so persistently ignored?

The answers can be captured in two critiques. First, *Patterns of Corporate Philanthropy* uses a flawed methodology that in turn leads to drawing false conclusions from the data. Corporations do not lean as nearly to the left as CRC staffers and *their* philanthropic supporters would have the public believe. Second, by seeing the country only in combative ideological terms, the *Patterns* authors fail to discern many competing and complementary corporate interests. In a Manichean world of friends and enemies, allies and adversaries, the choices between black and white are stark. One's advantage is easy to identify. In the far more complex real world of global competition, shades of gray emerge. Decisions are neither easily nor helpfully depicted in the political language of pro or con.

Each of these explanations implies the seeming paradox of American corporations that apparently cannot or will not behave rationally when engaged in philanthropy—but appearances may be deceptive.

The cogency of the CRC's analysis depends on the validity of its classification of the political bent of nonprofits. And that classification is entirely subjective, not submitted for independent review or evaluation.

Hence the reports and their conclusions are virtually predetermined. As Peter Frumkin, a leading CRC critic, notes:

> CRC ultimately gives grades to each corporation for its philanthropy, based on the ideological orientation of its grant recipients.
>
> Instead of relying on experts or a survey of nonprofit professionals, the ratings are based only on the impressions of CRC staff. CRC's failure to set up an independent system of control allows many questionable classifications to taint the findings of the report. The following organizations, for example, are placed on the left of the American political spectrum: The American Cancer Society, the National Geographic Society, the Council for the Advancement and Support of Education, the Audubon Society, the Council on Foreign Relations and the American Heart Association.[13]

Some 70 percent of the three hundred recipient organizations mentioned in the report are classified as liberal, which means that corporations are guilty of supporting the left. The CRC, Frumkin concludes, loads the dice.

The second major methodological flaw in *Patterns* is that it selects a far too narrow sample of Forbes 250 corporation grants. By focusing only on grants for advocacy and policy work, CRC characterizes the whole by looking at just *5–7 percent* of what these corporations annually spend philanthropically. Moreover, CRC classifies as advocacy grants any sums sent to a nonprofit with a general advocacy mission, even if the programs supported have nothing to do with the public affairs work of the recipient organization.

Beyond the glaring deficiencies of CRC's research procedures, its staff reveals little tolerance for corporate support of any group it labels liberal.

Obviously, an organization like the Children's Defense Fund (CDF), which supports national health insurance, expansion of Head Start, and an increase in the minimum wage, could not possibly advance corporate interests. How, then, can such companies as Bristol-Meyers, Squibb, DuPont, Merck, Ætna, Dayton-Hudson, J. P. Morgan, Citicorp, Fannie Mae, and AT&T support CDF?

For one thing, not all companies hold the same positions. Many believe that in raising the minimum wage, there's no harm done to the country at large, let alone to shareowners. Some see the expansion of Head Start as a sound investment in a child's ability to learn and to contribute productively to the nation's economy. Some are concerned that 40 million Americans have no medical insurance in a nation that spends more money on health care per capita by far than any other country in the world. From such vantage points, the positions of CDF are not necessarily inconsistent with sound public policy or corporate interest.

But suppose that one or more such stands of CDF did vary from a corporation's own lobbying position. Companies support politicians on both sides of the aisle with political action committee (PAC) dollars, even though many do not always vote on the floor of the House and Senate in the way they would prefer. They do so to secure access to corporate views by members of Congress, to influence legislators on future votes, to learn why others disagree, and to gauge the strength of the opposition. The same is true of philanthropy. Grant support for CDF does not mean a company agrees with all of its public policy views. Indeed, cash contributions may well have nothing to do with any of them but may instead be directed to the assistance of direct service programs. What donors do accomplish is that they put their company in touch with a body of opinion and a set of influential individuals.

CRC asks how Exxon (not to mention Alcoa, Chrysler, Ford, General Electric, General Motors, Phillips Petroleum, Texaco and Weyerhauser) can support the Environmental Law Institute (ELI), "which advocates strong regulations and litigates against corporations that 'harm' the environment."[14] Maybe these firms believe that common ground between ELI and their interests can be found. Maybe these firms do not oppose the regulation of and litigation against companies that conduct themselves irresponsibly on environmental matters. And maybe these firms can learn something from activist groups that reflect the views of "environmentalists," a label most Americans, in fact, view favorably.

Just as AT&T could support the conservative Manhattan Institute without subscribing to all the social welfare views of its senior fellow Charles Murray, as depicted in his book *On Losing Ground*,[15] it can assist the Brookings Institution without identifying with any, let alone all, of its studies.

CRC would establish firm "are you for 'em or against 'em litmus tests" in a fast-changing world where pro and con are hardly permanent and hardly apply equally to all issues. CRC would sooner accuse a company of feckless, neglectful, or unwitting conduct than acknowledge that its definition of business interest may be short term, incomplete, or just plain flat-out wrong.

Businesspeople are pragmatic. They are practical; they deal with the world as it is, not how they would wish it to be. Nor do they worship ideological idols. So even when House Majority Leader Richard K. Armey used his congressional stationery to write to eighty-two CEOs whose companies received "failing grades" for their philanthropy, citing *Patterns* as his source, little changed. Armey's claim that the companies' philanthropy confirms that "big business is firmly behind the welfare state" was widely dismissed as false and reckless. And his use of House stationery was cited formally as an abuse of House rules.[16]

That Majority Leader Armey could be moved to influence the content of corporate philanthropy is a potent symbol of the attempt to have charitable contributions become another instrument of ideological warfare. There's no evidence that such high-level representations are yet working, but not for want of trying.

CRC's staff continue to take mainstream corporate philanthropy to task. The *Wall Street Journal's* editorial pages reflect the views they espouse. Right-wing talk radio programs offer CRC staff ample air time. News and business magazine coverage of each year's release of *Patterns* also helped ensure that this broad-scale critique reached some senior executives at AT&T, including the chairman. It occasioned healthy questions about whether there was an ideological tilt to AT&T Foundation grantmaking and whether its trustees represented the full range of political and social perspectives. The company also asked whether the process was balanced, and the outcomes biased?

So extreme was the criticism and so easy were the rebuttals that few at AT&T took seriously the annual assault by CRC. Harsh in judgment, partisan in tone, flawed in methodology, and sweeping in the companies it indicted, the critique implicit in *Patterns* was dismissed in many corporate quarters as little more than the work of dyspeptic ideologues. Their impact is hardly discernible to most corporate insiders.

The Right to Say No: Public Advocacy of Private Agendas

If the far right grouped AT&T with other companies as being much too supportive of left-wing causes, one major incident with a liberal organization could hardly be so characterized. AT&T was quite alone in being on the receiving end of withering criticism from the Planned Parenthood Federation of America.[17] What prompted Planned Parenthood to call

AT&T a "corporate coward" in a four-page press release, in full-page advertisements placed in the *New York Times, USA Today,* the *Los Angeles Times, The Investment Banker,* and the *Newark Star-Ledger,* and on CBS's *This Morning* and NBC's *The Today Show?* Why, after twenty-five consecutive years of support, a record probably unmatched by any other company, was AT&T treated this way?

The events leading up to the crisis began with a letter I wrote on March 12, 1990, to Faye Wattleton, the president of Planned Parenthood, to inform her that the AT&T Foundation trustees had decided to provide philanthropic support no longer. I explained that over the prior year, AT&T's grant assistance to Planned Parenthood had given rise to an unprecedented number of expressions of concern from employees, customers, suppliers, and shareowners. Essentially, these groups had come to believe that by virtue of assisting Planned Parenthood, AT&T was financing advocacy for abortion rights, if not abortions themselves.

AT&T had done no such thing, of course. Its most recent grant to Planned Parenthood was part of a philanthropic initiative designed to strengthen families. By helping teenage parents to raise their children to become independent adults and to avoid unwanted pregnancies, AT&T hoped to help address one of America's most serious social problems. Few companies ventured into this area of societal need at all. For AT&T, the initiative encompassed dozens of grants totaling $6 million between 1988 and 1990.

Under Wattleton's leadership, Planned Parenthood had become publicly identified as a leader in the pro-choice movement. She was deeply engaged in highly visible political activity to support issues relating to reproductive freedom, holding press conferences, appearing on radio talk shows, and giving television interviews. Philanthropic supporters of Planned Parenthood became associated in the public mind with what the nonprofit thought most important and spoke most often about.

The reproductive freedom of women was a cause I personally supported and Wattleton an advocate I personally admired. I also found the conduct of some of the opponents of choice utterly reprehensible; for example, the campaign to intimidate physicians psychologically and physically so that they would withdraw from working in Planned Parenthood clinics was despicable. And, the arson, the bombs, and the bomb threats directed at those same sites were outrageous and contemptible acts.

But my personal beliefs couldn't govern the position taken by a firm of 350,000 employees and 3 million shareowners. As a publicly held company, AT&T neither took a corporate position on the highly personal issue of abortion nor did it want to be perceived as doing so. Planned Parenthood was free to change its priorities, to allow its health and education programs to be overshadowed by lobbying and litigation in the general public's mind. What it could not fairly expect was that its donors would necessarily agree.

Although AT&T was not consulted or informed by Planned Parenthood about a basic shift in the organization's priorities and public image, the company needed to consider the consequences. AT&T business leaders asked why the company should be the target of protests because a grant recipient took contentious stands on matters unrelated to our corporate philanthropic assistance. My letter to Ms. Wattleton maintained:

> As your emphasis on abortion advocacy has grown, our support for Planned Parenthood's education programs has become impossible to separate from Planned Parenthood's advocacy activity. The public identification of Planned Parenthood with rights to abortion may be desirable given your organization's purposes. For AT&T, such an association is misleading and unintended.[18]

Earlier, in December 1989, I had called Wattleton to tell her that the sudden public association of Planned Parenthood with strident, pro-choice advocacy was generating substantial protest to at least one corporate donor, AT&T. Some of the protest was organized by the Christian Action Council. But other customers and employees who did not necessarily take a stand on the issue of abortion, one way or another, were also troubled by what appeared to be AT&T's departure from a neutral position. Her response was to rail at the tactics and motivations of her opponents. Oddly, she offered to ask her constituency to contact AT&T with written expressions of support for its assistance so as to "neutralize" that opposition.

I declined the offer. Did she think AT&T was a government, I wondered? The company doesn't hold elections. The objective of its philanthropy is not to anger shareowners or customers or to see whether advocates of choice outnumber opponents of abortion. AT&T welcomed business from all quarters. To see good customers defect to competitors because a corporate contribution decision identified AT&T with a cause the customers did not espouse, rather than with a program they did support, made no sense. To a politician, any election won with more than 55 percent of the vote can be considered a landslide, an overwhelming mandate. To a business executive, incurring the anger or disappointment of a substantial minority of one's customers over a matter outside AT&T's mission was counterproductive in the extreme.

Embattled as she was, Wattleton evinced little interest in the implications to firms like AT&T of the stands taken by Planned Parenthood. Some of her trustees were concerned about the consequences, but their views hardly won the day. One hopes that they at least received a respectful hearing.

My telephone call was intended as a friendly early warning that Planned Parenthood might need to look elsewhere in the future for a donor to replace AT&T's $50,000 of grant assistance directed to teen mothers. By providing early notice, a funding source offers a grantee time to adjust—a sound, considerate philanthropic practice. After twenty-five years of support, parting in a spirit of mutual respect seemed not unreasonable.

Neither during that telephone call, nor at any other time in the ensuing controversy, did Wattleton express concern about the lost funds. The teen mothers' program was never in jeopardy for want of AT&T support. Rather, our possible step in not renewing the grant was viewed by Ms. Wattleton as a body blow to the cause of choice and the political success of Planned Parenthood, just as our support for a program of Planned Parenthood had been viewed by the opponents of abortion as a corporate vote for unrestricted reproductive freedom.

I reported to the trustees that the AT&T Foundation was caught between two embattled parties, both of which were comfortable with politicizing philanthropy. I noted that Planned Parenthood was unlikely to greet in silence any decision to decline future support.

Thus, after a quarter century of consistent association with Planned Parenthood, it fell to me to inform Wattleton formally and in writing of a decision thoroughly discussed by foundation trustees and reviewed methodically with the leaders of AT&T's businesses. In anticipating from Planned Parenthood something other than a thank-you for two and a half decades of stalwart support, I demonstrated a remarkable gift for understatement. I certainly didn't expect Planned Parenthood to run a full-page advertisement in major newspapers around the country.

In large bold-type its headline read "Caving In to Extremists, AT&T Hangs Up on Planned Parenthood." Here's a small sample of what Planned Parenthood chose to say as a prelude to asking the reader to complete two coupons, one addressed to Robert E. Allen, Chairman and CEO, urging him to reverse course and renew philanthropic support, and the other requesting a charitable contribution from the reader:

> The saddest part of this shameful episode is that AT&T's action has only made abortions more likely.
>
> Indeed, in a panic to distance itself from Planned Parenthood, AT&T has sent a message that education and family planning—the only safe and sure ways to reduce abortion—are unworthy of support.
>
> That's precisely what the anti-choice extremists want. To see their threats succeed. To silence discussion. And, take away all our choices, one by one.[19]

A variation on the ad's theme was sent in the form of a letter to the six hundred thousand members and supporters of Planned Parenthood:

> AT&T, a major American concern, has been brought to its knees by a fringe group, and has allowed fanatics to dictate its corporate policy. . . . We did not think that AT&T would cave in to a threatened boycott by a small minority, and turn its back on these programs.[20]

The member letter and Planned Parenthood's press release, like the advertisement, called on the pro-choice public to write protest letters to AT&T's chairman, Robert E. Allen, and to contribute funds to Planned Parenthood.

Those closely associated with AT&T's philanthropy, including employees and business colleagues, were surprised and deeply disappointed with the ads and letters. The company didn't cave into a campaign of the Christian Action Coalition, nor had it left vulnerable teenagers at risk. Nothing about AT&T's commitment to education and social services for young parents had changed at all. Indeed, its financial support of this cause, rarely assisted by other companies, was the most generous in America.

What had changed, radically, was Planned Parenthood. A respected nonprofit health, education, and social service organization, which AT&T had historically supported, had also become a deeply political organization. Shortly before the imbroglio with AT&T, Planned Parent-hood had threatened a consumer boycott of Idaho potatoes if the gover-nor, Cecil Andrus, did not veto an abortion-restricting bill that had just passed its state legislature. And by early April, Planned Parenthood had formed a political action committee. All of this it was free to do.

But adding high-profile advocacy on controversial issues that are deeply personal in nature to low-key service delivery makes for a volatile mixture. It was Planned Parenthood's relatively new course of political action and the negative reactions of employees and shareowners that pre-cipitated AT&T's decision. To castigate AT&T for buckling under to the interests of a small fringe pressure group seemed extreme.

But Wattleton was a strong leader who dominated the organization. In her opinion, AT&T had foolishly not accepted the invitation to set in motion a letter-writing campaign to convince shareowners and senior management to maintain support of Planned Parenthood. Wattleton told me in a phone conversation that AT&T needed to understand that it was being manipulated by "pro-criminalists, right-wing zealots." The com-pany had not only informed Planned Parenthood of its intention to sus-pend assistance but by letter had also let those who had corresponded regularly with AT&T know of its decision. That the Christian Action Coalition, in turn, informed its supporters of AT&T's action, and that the company fully briefed its own employees, infuriated Ms. Wattleton. She claimed in a conversation with me that the matter was now "public" and that she was compelled to reciprocate in kind.

Public? Nine days after I sent the letter to Ms. Wattleton, a newspa-per article had appeared that mentioned AT&T's decision in a round-up story devoted to several so-called right-to-life victories. The *Washington Times* carried the story on March 21, 1990, on page C3. The public nature of this dispute was exaggerated by Wattleton. To call private com-munications and the most minor, inconspicuous news coverage "public" seemed a mere pretext for lashing out at AT&T.

The first casualty of a calculated ideological campaign is truth. For a few weeks, newspaper interest in the story was apparently generated by the advertisements and Wattleton's television appearances. Some accepted wholesale Planned Parenthood's version of events.

A *Boston Globe* column, headlined "AT&T Scarlet Letter," con-cluded that "AT&T now stands for Abortion, Timidity and Teeming mil-lions more unplanned babies." And Gannett's Westchester newspaper editorialized that "AT&T is being vilified, perhaps deservedly for kow-towing to blackmail and surrendering to small-scale terrorism, for surren-dering to commercial fear." Raymond Coffey of the *Chicago Sun-Times* took the opposite position: "What obliges a company, or anyone else to take sides in or help fund someone else's war?" The *Baltimore Sun's* Jon Talton found fault on both sides: "The board can be blamed for allowing an activist group to influence its decision. . . . The true reason for the anti-AT&T ads was propaganda mileage."

AT&T recognized that a continuing public controversy was in nobody's interest. Consequently, the company refrained from rebutting Planned Parenthood's advertisement with ads of its own. It responded to media requests dutifully and factually but engaged in no activist efforts to generate news.

As the date of AT&T's 1990 annual meeting in Los Angeles approached, Planned Parenthood attempted to mobilize supporters through ads and a letter to members that generated thousands of responses expressing opposition to the company's decision. By a roughly three-to-one margin, right-wing groups wrote in approval. At the annual meeting, AT&T's chairman fielded questions about a proposed share-owner resolution that would have prohibited support for any organiza-tion involved with abortion. Company directors recommended *against* the proposal.

AT&T endeavored to remain neutral on the subject of abortion. Support for the resolution would compromise that neutrality. Moreover, the resolution, if passed, might well have precluded AT&T from support-ing hospitals that performed abortions or social service agencies that counseled pregnant mothers. It might even have prohibited AT&T from offering to employees medical insurance that covered abortion. The reso-lution was defeated by more than 90 percent of the votes cast.

At AT&T's annual meeting a year later, Planned Parenthood arranged for another shareowner proposal on the subject of abortion to be put to a vote. This one called for the foundation to restore Planned Parent-hood funding. Despite the efforts of Elizabeth Holtzman, then Comptrol-ler of the city of New York, to organize her city government colleagues around the country to vote the AT&T shares in their retirement funds in favor of the resolution, it, too, was overwhelmingly defeated.

And in April 1992, Faye Wattleton resigned her post as Planned Parenthood's president. By any measure, her fourteen-year tenure was distinguished. She left the organization fiscally and programmatically much stronger and the cause of every woman having the fundamental right to choose whether to have a child well defended. My view remains that the unnecessarily provocative and public controversy with AT&T was not one of her finest moments.

Wattleton was succeeded by Pamela Maraldo, who assumed the post after a decade of service as president of the National League of Nursing. Her tenure was brief, lasting from November 1992 to the early spring of 1996. In June of that year, Gloria Feldt was appointed to the CEO's job. Neither individual has become a household name. Each has kept a low public profile. Planned Parenthood is no longer at the ramparts in pro-choice political battles. Emphasis appears to have returned to its historic health, counseling, and education mission, as reflected in the advertising placed in newspapers in mid-1997.

Under the headline "Planned Parenthood helped me make the right choice for me," three women are quoted thanking Planned Parenthood for its services. One expresses gratitude for pre-natal and post-natal care. Another appreciates receiving facts about contraception and abstaining from sex. A third welcomes a broad range of counseling services. The sub-head reads. "Health Care. Education. Counseling. That's what we do at Planned Parenthood."[21]

That mission is hardly a minor one. Planned Parenthood's 167 not-for-profit affiliates operate 922 clinics in forty-nine states and the District of Columbia, serving close to 5 million Americans annually.

In reflecting on this contentious episode, six lessons emerge that may be of enduring value.

First, unlike individuals and private foundations, publicly held companies have many constituencies and shareholders. Their needs and views need to be taken into account on any number of matters, philanthropy included. But even sophisticated professionals who have never worked at a for-profit company can fail to appreciate this condition of business conduct. For example, Alan Pifer, the former president of the Carnegie Corporation, was moved to write in a letter addressed to me that in discontinuing support for Planned Parenthood, AT&T had "caved in to outside pressure." This was my reply:

> I'm mystified by how you distinguish between listening to the views of a company's stakeholders and "caving in to outside pressure." It's not at all

apparent to me in what sense the view of an AT&T shareowner, or an employee, or a customer is "outside." Outside of what?

Perhaps the Carnegie Corporation could reach decisions in relative isolation from the views of others. But I think it is unfair and inaccurate to castigate a firm for allowing expressions of opinion—such as your own—to influence our thinking.[22]

No rejoinder from Pifer reached AT&T's mailroom.

Second, those employed by an organization, must have the discipline to distinguish between personal predilections and institutional interests. I personally admired the stand Planned Parenthood had taken on reproductive choice. The campaign of opposition and intimidation sustained by elements of the religious right needed to be confronted, and Wattleton warmed to that challenge.

But in my capacity as a representative of a Fortune 10 publicly held corporation, I had to consider the views of valued employees, customers, suppliers, partners, and shareowners who disagreed strongly with Planned Parenthood's stand. Still others were offended by the tactics and the rhetoric. One hardly needed to be a right-wing zealot to fall into either camp. AT&T was obligated to take those views into account in its decision making.

Third, the inevitable result of public assaults on the behavior and motivations of companies, like that of Planned Parenthood about AT&T, is to chill corporate social involvement. Whether the pressures are brought from the strident and self-righteous right or left, the message to firms is identical: shun controversy; take no risks; keep your head down.

Planned Parenthood never enjoyed a large component of corporate financial support. It amounted to 1–2 percent of a budget of about $45 million. But after witnessing the attacks on AT&T, no corporation could possibly grant Planned Parenthood funds without concern that should it change its course or its priorities, a public excoriation might well be in store.

For Planned Parenthood, the direct result of its public display of disapproval has been to keep companies from offering support.

For AT&T and other firms, it is clear that the price of engagement in social philanthropy will be harsh criticism from some activist groups. AT&T was prepared to pay that price. Its early funding of AIDS prevention measures was not universally acclaimed. Its assistance to some artistic institutions that sponsored controversial work sparked protest. Being a benefactor of the NOW Legal Defense and Education Fund and the Children's Defense Fund drew fire. AT&T's philanthropy was no stranger to criticism, but most companies find that price too high.

Fourth, passionate single-issue groups have dramatically changed America's social environment. They value ends over means and do not brook compromise. Many use sophisticated marketing and advertising methods to advance their agenda. Being caught in the rhetorical crossfire over choice and abortion brought home how hyperbolic and impassioned are groups on both sides of the issues. Sadly, anger, namecalling, and incivility dominated debates. Respect for truth, tolerance for the views of others, and a search for common ground were not easy to find.

Fifth, it is important to involve the senior management of the company in major decisions about philanthropic direction or about potentially controversial matters. The thorough discussion that the disengagement of AT&T from Planned Parenthood received inside the firm stood all in good stead when the subject became public. For AT&T's senior officers and foundation trustees, disentangling the company from identification with what had become a highly political, hyperactive, single-issue advocacy on the part of Planned Parenthood was a matter of principle. In taking a firm stand, the company was well able to weather the name-calling and misrepresentations that followed.

Sixth, building a record for enlightened social investments and progressive philanthropy pays dividends, especially in times of strife. In detailed surveys and focus groups devoted to other purposes like sales and marketing, AT&T inquired after any damage to corporate reputation that might have ensued from the Planned Parenthood episode. Little could be found. Only a handful of customers lodged protests by leaving AT&T. That they then switched to competitors, *none of whom* ever supported Planned Parenthood with charitable donations, was an irony that escaped the attention of few of my AT&T colleagues.

Some customers have very long memories and can't forgive the company. But most of those still aware of the controversy also think of AT&T as a good firm that cares about the welfare of the communities in which it conducts business. As such, it should be given the benefit of the doubt, or at least pardoned for a mistake. That buffer zone of tolerance and good will is precisely what a generous philanthropic record cultivates among a company's attentive public.

6

Corporate Philanthropy Comes of Age

Nothing is possible without men; nothing is lasting without institutions.

—JEAN MONNET
Memoirs, 1978

There is nothing more difficult to take in hand, more perilous to conduct, or more uncertain in its success, than to take the lead in the introduction of a new order of things.

—NICCOLO MACHIAVELLI
The Prince, 1532

THE FUTURE OF CORPORATE PHILANTHROPY is inextricably associated in the minds of most observers with the question of whether it will grow in real terms. Philanthropy in America directs precious pools of private capital to nonprofit institutions and causes in an effort to advance the public good. Given the recent reality of stable or declining federal, state, and local support in most fields of concern to nonprofits, however, the size of those funds is a matter of major import. Growth is healthy; the status quo is stagnation. Reductions in donations indicate that the whole enterprise of philanthropy is out of favor.

Three generalizations have proved extraordinarily accurate as indicators of whether sources of charitable gifts will grow or diminish over time. For individuals, the size of charitable gifts has been highly correlated to levels of after-tax income. As Americans increase their discretionary income, the propensity to be more generous philanthropically grows as well, so long as prevailing charitable tax deductions are held constant. For private foundations, grant payouts go up when stock market returns are buoyant; they decline with stock market downturns. Although this "rule" has always been at play, it gained even greater power following the passage of the 1969 Tax Reform Act, which requires that no less than 5 percent of the earnings on a prior year's fund assets be donated to 501(c)(3) organizations in each subsequent year. And for corporations, giving levels have historically been closely associated with earnings. This pattern has persisted ever since statistics have been compiled by the Conference Board—until 1987, that is. After that date, something else happened. Unaccountably, while earnings rose, contributions fell.[1]

Danger Signals and Skeptics

From 1964 through 1987, corporate philanthropy grew every year in inflation-adjusted dollars from a base of $3.35 billion to a high-water mark of $7.49 billion. But in the period 1987–94, corporate cash giving declined in constant dollars by 20 percent, from $7.49 billion to $6.11 billion, averaging a 2.8 percent loss per year.

The plot thickens with the recognition that over that same seven-year period corporate after-tax earnings doubled and the Dow Jones Industrial Average increased by 102 percent. In these years, particularly 1990 through 1994, American productivity rose markedly; the U.S. budget deficit declined substantially; job growth of 10 million surpassed that of Japan, Western Europe, and Latin America combined; unemployment stayed well below 6 percent; and American national competitiveness, as compared with that of France, Germany, and Japan, among other nations, improved significantly.

In contrast, during that same 1987–94 period, individual giving in inflation-adjusted terms moved from $123.13 billion to $129.88 billion. In only two of those seven years did individual philanthropy decline, whereas in the other five years corporate philanthropy failed to keep pace with inflation in five of those seven years.[2]

Other data may be cited to advance the case that the corporate giving track record is disappointing and that corporations can and should do more to increase charitable contributions:

- Between 1986 and 1996 corporate profits nearly tripled, whereas corporate contributions increased by only 70 percent, from $5 billion to $8.5 billion.

- Translating the corporate contributions statistics for the 1986–96 decade into pre-tax net income (PTNI) percentage figures reveals a drop of more than 50 percent, from 2.36 percent in 1986 to 1.33 percent in 1996.

- Only 25 percent of all U.S. companies claim any charitable tax deductions and only 10 percent declare contributions of more than a nominal sum. Moreover, according to the Conference Board, 27 percent of all corporate giving emanates from fewer than four hundred companies.[3]

Such evidence suggests a corporate philanthropic downshifting that should not be ignored and does not bode well for the future. For if company benefactions have declined in real terms when the overall economy and earnings have been buoyant, then reductions in giving may be severe when the American economy next experiences a recession. There are those who believe that this gloomy picture is precisely what the future holds.

They assert that corporations are under relentless, unprecedented pressure to improve earnings. As a consequence, all "non-essential" expenditures are scrutinized with great care, with philanthropy falling more often than not into the category subject to cuts. The higher demands on operational performance also find CEOs and their senior executives possessed of neither the time nor the inclination to use the company as an instrument of social improvement.

They also contend that little more should be asked of them if companies pay their fair share of taxes; produce goods and services that are safe, beneficial, and competitively priced; treat employees fairly and the environment respectfully; and generate anticipated profit levels consistently.

Moreover, they claim that the "golden era" of corporate philanthropy, when CEOs like Reg Jones of General Electric, Irving Shapiro of DuPont, and David Rockefeller of Chase Manhattan Bank articulated an impassioned rationale for a firm's social responsibility, is long gone. For them and like-minded colleagues, corporate philanthropy was an article of faith rather than a pragmatic business tool. In its place is a "show me the immediate business benefit" demand that casts an often impossible-to-meet burden of persuasion on in-house advocates of philanthropy. The situation calls to mind lines from a Paul Simon song, "Proof": "Faith . . . faith is an island in the setting sun. Proof . . . proof is the bottom line for everyone."[4] For skeptics and naysayers, the glass of corporate philanthropy is half empty and losing liquid.

The Half-Full Glass

Another school of thought is optimistic about the prospects for corporate philanthropy. It interprets the evidence about the present situation more favorably and it contends that the future is bright. This body of opinion takes comfort from data that show corporate giving growing in 1995 by 7.5 percent to $7.9 billion, at a rate roughly double the size of inflation in that year. The figures for 1996 were equally encouraging: Corporate cash donations rose another 7.6 percent, or 2.5 times the rate of inflation, to $8.5 billion.[5]

The 1987–94 unprecedented real dollar decline in philanthropy, even in the face of rising earnings, can be explained, the optimists argue. The cause wasn't a clear and deliberate diminution of the function or a lowering of the corporation's civic commitment. Rather, the culprit was large-scale reductions in employee head counts throughout the period. Ironically, such employee reductions have been no small cause of that very earnings improvement and associated stock value appreciation. But few companies that cut their employee ranks severely, no matter how high their earnings, are inclined to concurrently raise contribution budgets. And in the seven-year period under examination, employee cutbacks swept through corporate America at unprecedented post–World War II levels.

From 1990 through 1995, 17.4 million Americans lost their jobs involuntarily, according to the U.S. Labor Department.[6] In the first few years of the 1990s (1990–93), one out of every twelve Americans, or 9 million, were laid off. Subsequently, employee layoffs slowed somewhat. Although the size of employee cuts had begun to diminish, displacement remained high, leading to commensurately high levels of job insecurity. Even a rapidly growing economy could not assuage workforce anxiety, both white collar and blue.

So enormous was the criticism that massive corporate downsizings received, particularly during the Republican presidential primaries in the winter of 1996, that they are now viewed more skeptically. It is widely believed that too many companies cut back their staffing levels too far to maintain adequate customer service and to find new sources of revenue.

Lowering costs is not seen as a sustainable way to consistently post healthy corporate earnings. Security analysts look increasingly to "top-line growth" before recommending an investment in a firm's common stock. If huge employee cutbacks are not to characterize the conduct of corporate America as much in the future as in the past, then a major obstacle to the growth of corporate philanthropy will have been removed.

The optimists' oracle maintains that to make too much of the recent cash figures is also mistaken because they capture only what is labeled as philanthropic funds. But the fastest-growing corporate resources destined for nonprofit coffers emanate from other sources:

> Observers in the field of corporate philanthropy have noted that corporate social responsibility has assumed a new face in recent years. Traditional corporate giving is driven by philanthropy staff and executive officers interested in contributing to a range of charitable causes. This model of corporate support is being supplanted by more strategic, *less statistically observable* programs housed in marketing and public relations departments and overseen by corporate financial officers. This redefinition does not mean that corporate support is diminished, but rather, that increasingly it is falling outside the realm described by contributions data.[7]

Giving USA, the definitive annual report on American philanthropy published since 1954 by the American Association of Fundraising Counsel (AAFRC) Trust for Philanthropy, offers a description of the problem that is right on target. It is not just sources of company cash outside philanthropy budgets that the data fail to capture; they do not record product and equipment gifts, or advertising underwriting, or executive loan and other forms of corporate volunteer assistance. These types of contributions, together with cash from outside traditional philanthropic channels, are estimated to have grown annually in the double digits for at least a decade. Noncash gifts to nonprofit organizations are now thought to total at least 25 percent of corporate cash giving. In sum, the tools for measuring corporate support of nonprofits are being outdated by multiple sources of financial assistance that corporations are alleged not to be embracing. In essence, corporate philanthropy is increasingly being cast into a larger mold, one that takes fuller advantage of the broad range of business interests, concerns, and resources.

It is no accident that perhaps the fastest-growing national business association in America is Business for Social Responsibility (BSR). Founded in 1992, it has grown to include more than one thousand member companies and affiliates. Consider in the excerpt that follows how broadly BSR defines its mission. Note that although philanthropy is an integral part of any description of corporate social responsibility, it is not mentioned explicitly:

> BRS is a membership association for companies of all sizes and sectors.
>
> BSR's mission is to help its member companies achieve long-term commercial success by implementing policies and practices that honor high ethical standards and meet their responsibilities to all who are impacted by their decisions. . . .
>
> BSR helps companies prosper in ways that contribute to a healthier, more sustainable economy and a more just society.[8]

That BSR's board of directors represents the full spectrum of firms—large and small, publicly and privately held—and includes Fannie-Mae, Reebok, Hasbro, Phillips Van Heusen, WalMart, and Polaroid along with Shorebank Corporation, Just Desserts, and Graham Contracting, Inc., is an indication of its wide appeal.

Another example of how a company's social contributions may be viewed with the aid of a telescope rather than a microscope was the President's Summit for America's Future, held in Philadelphia in early May 1997 and chaired by General Colin Powell. The summit constituted a broad-based appeal to America's businesses to galvanize their resources to assist disadvantaged children. Launched with the help of President Clinton and former presidents Ford, Carter, and Bush, it is noteworthy that most of the many very substantial corporate commitments responding to this call to action have not found their way into cash philanthropic figures. Instead, they involve executive loan, employee volunteers, equipment gifts, advertising, and cause-related marketing expenditures.

What may well be occuring, then, is not the downgrading of corporate philanthropy but the spread of its influence articulated in nontraditional, unconventional terms. Corporate citizenship fully embraces but isn't confined to giving ample sums of money away. Nor should the size of cash philanthropic budgets be the sole measure of what constitutes good corporate citizenship.

Those gloomy about corporate philanthropy, classically defined as duly recorded cash contributions, probably make too much of the drop in giving as a percentage of PTNI. The percentage reductions are due far more to the sustained excellent earnings experience of American firms since 1992 than to any marked or prolonged reduction in cash giving. Ironically, should American corporations experience sudden earning reversals and fare poorly, pre-tax net percentage figures would commensurately jump without a single additional dollar finding its way to a needy nonprofit.

Indeed, if some credence is given to large employee layoffs as a cause of temporary downward blips in charitable contributions, than the recent bounce back in business giving is hardly surprising. In 1991, the median corporate contributions per employee was $202, whereas by 1996 that figure had increased by roughly 50 percent to $306.

Focusing only on PTNI leaves one nervous about the state of corporate philanthropy, but including in the calculus of judgment the recent rise in both absolute levels of cash giving and contributions per employee offers a more balanced picture. Factoring in the myriad forms of cash and in-kind support for nonprofits moves the observer into positive territory.

For philanthropic cheerleaders, not only is the glass of corporate philanthropy more than half full, but new pitchers are being set before nonprofits that go largely unrecorded by conventional methods. Count me in the upbeat camp.

Philanthropy Debunked: Right and Left

Extreme right-wingers attack philanthropy as a dangerous distraction from the profit-making mission of corporations. Extreme left-wingers trivialize philanthropy as inconsequential compared to the importance of government resources and edicts. Yet corporate philanthropy continues to flourish, decade after decade. Still, less radical conservatives and liberals offer a critique worth attention.

Forty years ago, the economist Milton Friedman railed at the notion of corporate social responsibility in such books as *Capitalism and Freedom:*

> Few trends could so thoroughly undermine the very foundations of our free society as the acceptance by corporate officials of a social responsibility other than to make as much money for their shareholders as possible.[9]

Friedman is not without contemporary sympathizers. In a *Wall Street Journal* article of July 15, 1996, aptly titled "Corporate America,

Mind Your Own Business," Herbert Stein, the former chairman of the Council of Economic Advisors under Presidents Nixon and Ford, noted somewhat less unequivocally:

> Efficiency in maximizing the nation's product, as that product is valued in markets, is not the only objective of life. But it is the one private corporations are best qualified to serve. . . . To rely on the corporation's responsibility to solve major social problems—other than the problem of how to put our people and other resources to work most efficiently—would be a wasteful diversion from their most important function.

If conservatives such as Friedman and Stein fret about the possibility of companies straying from their raison d'être, some liberals assert the improbability that corporations will act beneficently for very long. Here's what the liberal economist Robert Kuttner had to say in an article for the July–August 1996 issue of *The American Prospect:*

> It would be very nice if we could infer from the logic of the market that "it's just good business" for corporations to invest in worker training, provide decent health care, not lay off faithful employees, support communities, devise "family-friendly" workplaces, and make sure contract workers in wretched corners of the Third World are treated with human dignity, but these are self-defeating dreams. Indeed, the more intensely competitive the commercial environment becomes—the more it reflects market principles—the less likely are corporations to behave humanely. Corporations can add value, but citizens must add values. For the most part, the business sector needs to be dragged kicking and screaming into a social contract. To pretend otherwise is to unilaterally disarm.[10]

Neither Friedman nor Stein on the right nor Kuttner on the left can readily explain or discount the rise of corporate philanthropy. To the surprise and consternation of conservatives, the sky has not fallen on such firms as GE, IBM, P&G, Coca-Cola, and Dayton Hudson, who take their corporate social responsibilities no less seriously than their profit-maximizing obligations. Indeed, the growth and visibility of corporate contributions as evidenced by the creation of hundreds of asset-based foundations in the Fortune 1000 has hardly engendered a murmur of shareowner protest. Unlike Friedman and Stein, some investors do not see a conflict between doing good and doing well. For them, advancing charitable endeavors or, for that matter, engaging in other exercises of corporate social responsibility like purchasing from minority contractors, or exceeding legal requirements in pursuing sound environmental practices, or offering child care and elder care assistance to employees, are fully compatible with solid financial performance.

To further test the apparent predisposition to corporate social responsibility in the general public, AT&T asked a wide sample of Americans in 1991 the following question:

Which of the following statements better describes your feelings?

A. I think businesses such as AT&T have a responsibility to society beyond just making a profit. Business has a role to play in solving social problems and contributing to our society and culture.

B. I think business should stick to business. It should not be spending its money on social programs, but rather invest this money in its own R&D or its own employees, returning it to stockholders or simply lowering prices.

Overwhelmingly, by a three-to-one margin, the public endorsed the first position over the second.[11] Why, then, one wonders, are the views of Friedman and Stein seemingly out of touch with America's shareowners and citizens? Their arguments appear not to have stood the test of time.

Although liberals may disagree, there is plenty of evidence that corporations behave humanely without government edict. The citizens Kuttner calls on to add values do precisely that—and not just in the voting booth but in the workplace as well. Kuttner's view that competitive conditions signal a race to the bottom of social responsibility is profoundly cynical. It leaves unexplained the phenomenon of growth in the philanthropic enterprise. It also ignores the good faith efforts to exceed the minimal conduct expected of law-abiding firms.

What CEOs Think about Philanthropy

Behind the significant growth in corporate giving is the support of CEOs. In a 1982 study conducted by the Daniel Yankelovich Group for the Council on Foundations, 225 CEOs and 100 senior officers of the Fortune 1000, medium-size companies ($50 million to $100 million of annual revenue), and smaller companies ($25 million to $49 million

annual revenue) were interviewed about their views on corporate philanthropy.[12] Overall, they expressed strong support for corporate contributions and acknowledged their substantial involvement in this activity.

In 1988 these conclusions were reviewed in another Yankelovich
study, which found that CEO commitment remained strong: "Motivated
by personal principles, a sense of ethics and company tradition, the overwhelming majority of CEOs are firm in their resolve to continue corporate giving programs." This pulse-taking revealed that CEOs are
increasingly sensitive to growing pressures to cut business expenses. To
sustain strong giving programs will therefore require finding better ways
to align corporate interest and societal need.[13]

Such interview results come as no small source of solace to those
convinced that mergers and acquisitions, low earnings in some sectors,
and the changing generational guard among CEOs would combine to
diminish the commitment to corporate philanthropy. There is little evidence to sustain such a concern.

In 1994 a study was conducted of a generous sample of Silicon
Valley companies to determine whether relatively young high technology
hardware and software firms, bereft of deeply rooted philanthropic
tradition, are also committed to philanthropy. The results are gratifying
to those who root for a strong corporate role in the exercise of social
responsibility:

> The study concludes that community involvement of Silicon Valley com-
> panies is more extensive than thought. Forty-three companies reported
> worldwide contributions of $329 million and $29 million in local contri-
> butions.
>
> The Conference Board [has] calculated that large U.S. companies con-
> tributed $226 per employee worldwide in 1992; in Silicon Valley, worldwide
> contributions for comparably sized companies were $229 per employee.[14]

Such support for philanthropy from newer firms often headed by
CEOs under forty-five years of age demonstrates how compelling are
societal needs and charitable motivations and rationales.

Summits on Education and Employee Welfare

In 1996 two major meetings of many of the nation's CEOs confirmed the
ready acceptance of an important role for the corporation as a social actor.

In March, the nation's governors and more than 100 CEOs gathered in Palisades, New York, for an education summit. Louis Gerstner, IBM's chairman, cited various statistics to describe the weak state of America's educational system: more than 80 percent of American eighth graders cannot calculate fractions accurately; 40 percent of fourth graders cannot tell northeast from northwest on a map; 60 percent of the students entering the California university system require remedial courses in math and science; and one in five adults doesn't know how to use a road map. He estimated that poor literacy alone costs American business $25 billion to $30 billion a year in lost productivity.

The meeting, addressed by President Clinton, confirmed a growing consensus that educational standards need to be set much higher, met more consistently, and become more uniform across the country. Toward this end, a commission of corporate executives and governors was appointed to recommend standards, a system of accountability to see that they are satisfied, and a timetable for implementation.

In May, the president convened the White House Conference on Corporate Social Responsibility. Its purpose was to provide a forum for thirteen chief executives whose firms are acknowledged to be model places of employment to share their best practices with others and to stimulate discussion about obstacles to their widespread emulation. The president's challenge to the conferees and, by extension, to all American companies, was embodied in a paper appealing to businesses to pay attention to employee needs by:

1. creating and maintaining family-friendly work places that allow workers to be productive and caring, responsible family members;

2. providing economic security that a living wage, health care and pension benefits can give;

3. investing in employees through education and training for new skills and advancement;

4. partnering with employees so that they have a voice in the workplace and share the burdens and benefits of good and bad times;

5. providing safe and secure workplaces that protect the health and safety of employees through management commitment and employee involvement.

The guidelines met with widespread general acceptance.

At both events corporate executives participated willingly and enthusiastically from the perspective of their firms' business interests. U.S.-based companies are dependent on the quality of America's educational system for the basic skills of their workforce. As corporate taxpayers, they benefit from higher levels of student performance in the nation's public schools. As employers, they need entry-level employees more fluent in math and reading, more possessed of general knowledge, and better equipped to learn new skills. As global competitors, they are eager to see American children move up in international ratings and rankings on basic proficiency exams compared with their counterparts in Europe and Asia.

The CEOs at the two meetings are aware that the past decade of unprecedented layoffs and downsizings has weakened employee commitment to the firm. They appreciate how important are the knowledge and skills of their workforces, for they possess no more powerful competitive weapons. How to refashion strong bonds to employees while improving earnings and productivity to expected levels is a major challenge common to all.

But there's more at stake than advancing corporate interests. Participating chief executives are also cognizant of how society benefits overall from poised and educationally well-prepared high school graduates and from reduced job insecurity in the country's workforce. Indeed, as parents and citizens, these CEOs should welcome improvements on both counts. Also noteworthy is that the chief executives participating in these meetings harbor few illusions about the limitations on the role their companies can play.

The primary and secondary schools of this country are part of complex bureaucratic systems that spend hundreds of billions of dollars, embrace dozens of well-organized interest groups, and comprise many overlapping governmental jurisdictions. Corporations pay taxes, grant funds and equipment, donate talent, and exercise leadership to foster improvement. These are no small contributions, but even when added together they leave corporations no more than helpful supporters of progressive change. They are no substitute for intelligent educational policies, well-run and well-equipped schools, soundly trained and highly motivated principals and teachers, strong parental guidance of children, high educational standards, and accountability for results.

Similarly, CEOs recognize that the highly competitive environments in which they operate preclude them from engaging in no-layoff pledges or veering too far from market norms in salaries and fringe benefits. What they can do is framed in no small measure by the macroeconomics of the national and global economy and by the microeconomics of their industrial or service sector.

In sum, these two cases of corporate involvement in social issues can be characterized as business-centered, realistic, and measured. They are modulated based on the issues at hand. But they are also conditioned by major changes in the boardrooms of corporate America.

Heavy Lies the Head That Wears the Crown

In recent years, CEOs have been held more strictly accountable by their boards of directors and by institutional shareowners for corporate performance. This trend has reached even into the staid precincts of the Fortune 50. John Akers of IBM, James Robinson of American Express, Roger Smith of General Motors, and Myres Miles of Philip Morris are among those who were forced to resign because on their watch the performance of such leading American firms did not measure up to investor expectations. The general lesson is hardly lost on their surviving CEO colleagues. To avoid a similar fate, they must achieve demonstrable increases in shareowner value.

Under such circumstances, the concerns of Friedman and Stern that, under the banner of corporate social responsibility, companies will stray from their primary obligations to shareowners seem badly misplaced. Equally suspect is the claim that company efforts, because they are measured and partial, amount to little. Tell that to university administrators who raised more than $2 billion in cash contributions alone from corporations, or 13 percent of the total of $12.75 billion of giving to higher education in 1995. Or explain to arts managers the insignificance of $700 million of corporate cash philanthropy. Both sets of institutions benefit as well from many other forms of corporate assistance and cooperation even as less support is likely to emanate from federal, state, and local governments.

Robert C. Goizueta, chairman of Coca-Cola Company from 1981 until his recent death in 1997, captured this combination of idealism and hard-headed practicality:

> Society has always placed its most demanding expectations on its sturdiest institutions. We have known for a long time that business must do good for business to do well. The healthier the social environment in which business operates, the better the environment for business and vice versa. There are plenty of examples of business doing the *right thing* for their communities because they know it is *the best thing* for their own long-term success.[15]

Such assertions came from a CEO whose firm's annual net income per share in the 1990s grew by an average of 18 percent and whose total market value increased by $27 billion to $93 billion from 1994 to year-end 1995 alone. As such, Mr. Goizueta could hardly stand accused of having been some "woolly-headed" CEO engaged in philanthropic flights of fancy. Nor could the vast majority of his colleagues be fairly accused of such conduct.

Many signs point to a favorable climate for corporate philanthropy: the aggregate data on corporate cash gifts, the faster-paced growth of equipment and in-kind support, CEO survey results on attitudes toward giving, good corporate earnings for Silicon Valley firms, and high-profile national conferences on education and employee welfare. Two additional sources of stimulation can help ensure that corporate philanthropy remains a vibrant area of growth and innovation.

The Protagonists of Philanthropy: Donors and Donees

The first source of stimulation emanates from the corporate professionals who direct the philanthropic activities of their firms. Their productivity and creativity in practicing philanthropy is indispensable to its perception by insiders. To add value to such company activities as marketing, sales, research and development, recruiting, education and training, customer and employee satisfaction, executive development, and governmental relations while strengthening carefully selected nonprofit institutions and causes is to increase support for philanthropy. The more the areas of overlap between business interest and societal need are identified and exploited, the greater the likelihood that corporate philanthropy will flourish, isolated dissenters notwithstanding.

The second source is the professionals and volunteers who are effective in asking for support. The demand side of the equation counts for much in the calculus of decision about how philanthropy and kindred efforts like cause-related marketing will fare. The more frequent, intelligent, persuasive, and focused the solicitations, the more likely senior corporate executives will come to appreciate overall charitable needs. A company has many front doors. The more that well-informed solicitors knock, the more doors will open, with helpful resources at the ready.

For the powers that be in most companies, philanthropy is what philanthropy does, not what it professes. To corporate senior officers, the picture of a benefactor's role is often painted in the concrete examples conveyed by friends, business associates, family members, colleagues, and customers. They present a social need, portray corporate obligation as opportunity, and suggest philanthropy as the avenue to resolution. Multiply those case examples, and a collage of activities emerges impressive in their diversity and energy. Peer influences are powerful.

As the resourcefulness, versatility, and professionalism of those who solicit grow, so too will the net impression that the welfare of nonprofit institutions matters. Out of just such perceptions, corporate contributions to the Third Sector blossom and convictions about the indispensable role of philanthropy crystallize.

Philanthropy Flourishes: The Telecommunications Profile

If the prognosis for corporate philanthropy is generally healthy, the story of telecommunications charitable giving since the breakup of the Bell system is one of uninterrupted growth. Breaking up may be hard to do, but in AT&T's case, philanthropy is viewed as indispensable to establishing an independent corporate identity, one committed closely to the communities in which customers are served.

In 1983, the last year that AT&T, Bell Laboratories, Western Electric, and all of the local telephone companies reported their contributions collectively as one Bell System, $73 million was dispensed to nonprofit organizations. Seven years later, in 1990, the RBOCs alone enjoyed charitable cash budgets of $122.4 million. AT&T's giving registered at $35.9 million, for a total of $158.3 million. That increase of 127 percent since 1983 represented more than triple the overall growth in giving for corporations during the same period, or roughly 41 percent.

Three years later, in 1993, philanthropic budgets of the component parts of what had been the Bell System continued to expand at a healthy clip. The RBOCs—Ameritech, Bell South, NYNEX, SBC, Bell Atlantic, Pacific Telesis, and U.S. West—were themselves giving away $151.3 million in cash alone. AT&T's philanthropy that year came to $41 million. The components parts, when aggregated, moved to $192.3 million in 1993 from $158.3 million in 1990 for a 21 percent increase, or an average of seven percent annually. In contrast, during 1990–93, corporate philanthropy generally grew at less than three percent annually, or at roughly one half the rate of the increase in the telecommunications industry.

A comparable phenomenon appeared to be at work when AT&T split into three parts, a process whimsically called "trivestiture." By the beginning of 1997, three free-standing, publicly held companies had emerged from one. The first is Lucent Technologies, a manufacturer and installer of switches, transmission equipment, software, wireless gear, and silicon chips for sale worldwide, and the new owner of Bell Laboratories. Its revenue approximated $24 billion.

The second is NCR, a computer firm serving principally the business community, with about 65 percent of its $6 billion in revenue derived from outside the United States.

The third is AT&T, the long-distance provider that also offers local calling, Internet access, and wireless service, garnering revenue in the $50 billion range.

In 1995, the cash philanthropy of AT&T totaled $43.2 million. In September 1995, trivestiture was announced. Much of the business of 1996 was to prepare for the trivestiture, and philanthropy was no exception. In anticipation of the 1997 formation of three independent, separately funded philanthropic programs—one each for AT&T, Lucent, and NCR—a total of $62 million of cash philanthropy was authorized to be spent. In other words, $18.8 million more in charitable contributions was distributed in 1996 over 1995, for a whopping 43.5 percent increase.

AT&T's 1996 cash philanthropy of $62 million, an all-time post-divestiture high, is impressive. Adding in the best comparable data for the same year for the RBOCs and other carriers paints a positive philanthropic picture (see Table 6-1).

The total comes to a very healthy $239.4 million, with little sign of diminution ahead as all of these carriers prepare for the onset of competition in each of their respective marketplaces.

Indeed, for 1997, AT&T alone enjoyed a cash philanthropic budget of $64 million, Lucent of $22 million, and NCR of $3 million—for a

TABLE 6-1. The Telcos: A Philanthropic Profile

Company	Total 1996 Cash Contributions
Ameritech	24.5 million
AT&T	62 million
Bell Atlantic	17 million
Bell South	21.5 million
NYNEX	19.5 million
Pacific Telesis	9.5 million
SBC	26 million
USWest	25.4 million
GTE	24.5 million
MCI	4.6 million
SPRINT	4.9 million

SOURCE: Data has been derived from the published annual business or philanthropic reports of the companies cited and, whenever necessary, from telephone interviews with corporate philanthropic staff.

total of $89 million—a 30 percent increase over the 1996 total and more than double the 1995 total.[16]

Doing the math reveals a very impressive continuous rise in giving for the telecommunications industry. Although mergers and acquisitions most often result in a new, larger entity with fewer philanthropic resources than its component parts had possessed, corporate spin-offs are regularly accompanied by growth in charitable contributions. From a philanthropic perspective, breaking up may be hard to do but it's not unpleasant. It's a growth business!

Post-Trivestiture Giving: The Why and Wherefores

All the reasons for maintaining and sustaining a corporate giving program apply to the newly formed, independent companies emerging from divestitures and kindred break-ups. In the fields of telecommunications and information movement and management, distinctive factors have catapulted philanthropy to new highs. Companies housed in these adjacent industries are so rivalrous, and deregulation so thoroughgoing, that new major market entrants are competing with every passing quarter.

As AT&T enters the $100 billion local calling business, it must establish itself as a "hometown" firm. Competing with the RBOCs that have enjoyed a virtual local market monopoly for the twelve years since the 1984 Bell System breakup means that AT&T must once again establish a new identity. It must win friends and influence people in many new places and increase significantly interaction with state and local governments, including, of course, public service commissions. It must motivate employees to care about the company's character and reputation for community commitment. To help achieve those objectives, among others, it will need to use philanthropy as an avenue to the influential Third Sector.

Lucent's competitors are also numerous, powerful, and well entrenched. NEC, Northern Telecom, Alcatel, Siemens, Ericsson, Panasonic, Nokia, and Motorola number among them. All are much stronger outside their home national markets than is Lucent. Of Lucent's $24 billion of 1996 revenue, less than 20 percent came from outside the United States. In explaining to all its current and potential customers around the world what Lucent is about and what it stands for, philanthropy has a role to play.

Its generous and discriminating use will send a message that Lucent seeks to do business by investing in countries and communities and not merely by extracting profits, that it cares for the quality of life in the places where customers live and work, and that it will extend itself by charitable and other related means to be of assistance.

NCR's future philanthropy draws on a century-old tradition of close connection to communities not unlike Lucent's immediate progenitor, the Western Electric Company. Buffeted by radical personnel reductions, the exiting of major lines of business, the failed six-year dalliance with AT&T as its parent company, and no fewer than four CEOs during the period 1991–97, NCR will need some time before it can give philanthropy a significant role in its radically reconfigured operational plans. But the roots of corporate philanthropy run very deep at NCR, and they are planted in the fertile soil of civic-mindedness.

So the sun shines on philanthropy, post-trivestiture. Amply funded, professionally staffed, and ably supported by senior management, the historically strong philanthropic enterprise of the Bell System and its post-divestiture programs are being honored as AT&T breaks up again. Indeed, the order of magnitude increase in budgeted donations for 1996 and 1997 not only paid respect to corporate heritage but also offered homage to the resilient value and adaptability of this quintessentially American habit.

PART THREE

The Beneficiaries of Corporate Philanthropy—The Secrets and Rewards of Asking Well

7

Disclosing Trade Secrets:
Strategies and Tactics for Successful Fundraising

Most people buy not because they believe, but because the salesman believes.

—BEN FELDMAN

In the first place, I advise you to apply to all those you know will give you something, next to those whom you are uncertain whether they will give you anything or not and show them the list of those who have given and lastly, do not neglect those whom you are sure will give nothing, for in some of them, you will be mistaken.

—BENJAMIN FRANKLIN

Treat donors gently, respond thoughtfully to their requests, and let them know that they are very important people, because they are.

—*Rosso on Fundraising,* p. 57.

A CORPORATION CAN BE AN ESPECIALLY INTIMIDATING, mysterious, and uninviting donor.

To be sure, the trend over the past several decades has been for corporations to publicly disclose the eligibility requirements of their formal, structured philanthropic programs. Corporate philanthropic reports and grant guidelines, for example, are widely available. Up-to-date information for grantseekers is increasingly appearing on corporate Internet sites and on pre-recorded voice mail messages responding to the most frequently asked questions. Industry periodicals, like the *Chronicle of*

Philanthropy and the *Chronicle of Higher Education* and newsletters like *Corporate Philanthropy Report* disclose the activities of business donors.

Still, the process by which decisions are reached is often unclear. One reason is that opportunities for face-to-face discussions with grant-making staff, particularly for newcomers, are few and far between, and specific feedback on a proposal's weaknesses and limitations is rarely forthcoming. Moreover, as a general rule, the clarity of grant guidelines for formal corporate grantmaking fades when one inquires about discretionary cash contribution budgets. Similarly obscure are the rules that guide other decisions: on corporate memberships, benefit dinners, auctions, sports tournaments and other fundraisers, sponsorships, underwriting, cause-related marketing, the use of advertising and customer entertainment funds, donations of equipment, products, and services, and executive loan. These potential sources of assistance are even more difficult to apply for in an orderly way. As a result, one cannot assume that a case will be judged on its merits.

The frustration of fundraisers with this state of affairs is understandable. So, too, is the plight of corporate philanthropists. Most are overwhelmed by the daunting number of applicants for finite funds, a burden compounded by the many other demands on their time and attention. To add insult to injury, the contributions staff of most companies (never comparable in number to their private foundation counterparts) has been cut severely in the past decade.[1]

Those still active in the field are spending more time than ever trying to understand the swiftly changing priorities of the business that employs them. Determining the philanthropic implications of major alterations in a company's business is no mean task. Here are just some of the major transformations AT&T experienced from 1984 through 1996:

1. Reduced its workforce by 100,000 people from roughly 375,000 to 275,000.

2. Spent $7.2 billion on the purchase of NCR, a computer company headquartered in Dayton, Ohio, with fifty-two thousand employees, more than half of whom lived and worked outside the United States.

3. Moved from an almost totally domestic U.S. company to become a multinational firm with fifty thousand employees de-

ployed overseas and 25 percent of its $80 billion of revenue generated offshore.

4. Launched a credit card business that, five years after its creation, became the second most widely held card in America.

5. Purchased McCaw Cellular Communications, Inc., headquartered in Redmond, Washington, at a cost of $11.5 billion (and an assumption of $5.56 billion of debt), which brought to AT&T in 1994 the country's largest provider of wireless communication services, $3 billion of incremental revenue, and about five thousand new employees.

6. Announced an intent to divide into three parts: NCR, Lucent Technologies, and AT&T.

7. Witnessed passage of the Telecommunications Act of 1996, which promised to accelerate and intensify competition from many domestic and foreign companies in voice and data communications.

8. Experienced three different CEOs and many other changes at senior management levels, as the company reconfigured its constituent organizations and executives left of their own accord or were forced to leave.

These developments posed major challenges to important components of the business and therefore to the then-existing philanthropic program. They altered the geographic locations of AT&T's partners, suppliers, and customers inside the United States and around the world; philanthropy was accordingly recast. They radically changed the firm's brand identity. They called for major modifications in research and development priorities and personnel recruitment needs. These "mega corporate events" also swiftly changed the expectations of senior executives for what philanthropy might accomplish and increased the demand on available charitable resources. Under the circumstances, identifying a specific return on company charitable investments was regarded as de rigueur.

Such transformations, while perhaps different in degree, were hardly different in kind from those affecting many other industries. The philanthropic colleagues of AT&T—contributions managers in such fields as banking, drugs, health care, airlines, investments, and autos, to name but a few—were also digesting the impact of acquisitions, spin-offs, downsizings, globalization, restructuring, and senior management shifts. Major changes in many businesses had picked up in velocity throughout the eighties and nineties. To serve one's company well, attention to them had to be paid, and the more, the better.

Contributions staff everywhere are not only spending more time in the business to understand it better, they are also investing a lot of energy in forming relationships with line and staff colleagues, the better to work productively with government relations, human resources, public relations, and sales and marketing counterparts. Indeed, these colleagues increasingly are viewed as key customers or clients of philanthropists. Their levels of satisfaction are an important measure of the effectiveness of the contributions enterprise.

A third source of demand on the time of grants staff is processing internal business. Staff must interpret grant guidelines to business colleagues and give advice on their philanthropic involvement. They must also prepare executives for encounters with would-be grantees and for participation on nonprofit boards or in community events.

Another major chunk of time is devoted to planning "by invitation only" grant projects. In such endeavors only a pre-selected group of non-profits from a given field (e.g., higher education) is invited to compete for a specific purpose (e.g., develop new curriculum in manufacturing engineering at universities from which AT&T recruits students). Such inner-directed endeavors increasingly carve out significant resources and substantive fields for targeted treatment.

For a would-be grantee, the obstacles may seem overwhelming. In seeking corporate funds, you've got a lot of company. The targets of your attention feel understaffed and overworked. The needs of their businesses are demanding that more and more time be spent internally. And no small portion of that energy is devoted to narrowing the focus of grant-making, prescribing with greater precision what firms wish to accomplish, and frequently pre-identifying those nonprofit organizations most likely to be successful.

All of this paints a picture of high barriers to entry for newcomers and tough challenges to penetrating the inner circle of grantees. But in the advice that follows, I hope to improve the odds of success significantly. If you as a grant seeker begin to see your challenge through the eyes of the would-be donor and act accordingly, good things will start to happen.

Do Your Homework

Little so impresses corporate grantmakers as nonprofit staff who study grant guidelines, printed annual reports, and other prepared contributions literature. Such documents address elementary questions: Is the organization or cause eligible for funding? Are there programs and projects that the nonprofit is operating or contemplating that fall into areas of corporate interest? What does the track record of the company's grants reveal about the probabilities of support?

What companies are about philanthropically can also be gleaned from the publications of the Foundation Center, periodicals like *Foundation News* and *Corporate Philanthropy Report*, and relevant meetings of service organizations like the Council on Foundations and regional associations of grantmakers.

Because a corporate grantmaker seeks to have the philanthropic function advance business interests, learning about major developments inside the firm and the industry of which it is a part pays handsome dividends. To become schooled in such trends, the corporation's annual report and any of these publications are a good place to start: *Business Week, Fortune, Forbes, Barrons,* the *Wall Street Journal* and the *Harvard Business Review.*

The fundraiser who appreciates not only the nonprofit's need but also the interests of the company being solicited wields a significant advantage over the competition. If you can help a firm to identify how your needs complement its interests, then you number in rare company. You will likely be well received because corporate executives are naturally impressed by nonprofit professionals conversant with business challenges. To enjoy that status requires both empathy and time-consuming preparation. There are no shortcuts.

Seeking a Personal Contact

Soundly developed, cogently argued, and well-informed proposals are important. They put you in contention for grant support. But many more such applications are received each year than it is possible for any corporation to fund. Your chances for success are much greater if you have met with the grantmaker, responded to questions, concerns, and curiosities, and stated your case for support face to face.

Such meetings are often resisted. The ever-present mountain of proposals and pile of telephone messages threaten to overwhelm the reduced staff available to respond. Meetings with applicants compete with many other priorities for the expenditure of scarce time. Besides, being invited to meet with a donor is often interpreted as tantamount to a firm expression of interest, possibly even support. But premature pressures to act favorably are usually avidly resisted by corporate philanthropists.

Nevertheless most corporate contributions managers know that their value to the company diminishes the more isolated they become from the needs of nonprofits and the executives who best articulate them. However busy they may be, *some* grantees and new applicants will be given audiences. Your challenge is to be among them.

To improve the odds, find out all you can about the contribution managers. What is their educational and professional background? Where do they live? What subjects interest them most? To whom in the firm do they report? The answers to these questions cannot only be garnered from corporate contribution guidelines, newsletters, and annual reports, they can also be acquired from your network of experienced development colleagues. Whatever the source, such information will help reveal whether anyone on your board or staff or among volunteers, contributors, or consumers knows these particular contribution managers and is in a position to encourage a meeting or otherwise favorably influence the disposition of your request.

In any event, it is prudent to inventory all the significant relationships between your nonprofit's extended family and the companies from which you'll be seeking support. Are there executives in a given firm who are friends, neighbors, fellow congregants, club members, or school parents of those close to your favorite nonprofit? They can be very helpful. So can board members, volunteers, clients, or contributors whose range of contacts and influence are valuable assets.

When any such nonprofit constituents feel comfortable in mentioning to the contributions executive that they are aware of your application and think well of it, or that they believe a meeting with you is worthwhile, you have won a leg up on the competition. Of the many proposals always under consideration, some stand out by virtue of tactful and informed expressions of support from within the firm.

Indeed, building advocates within the company to speak well of your cause is very much worth the effort for more reasons than favorably impressing the contributions executive. For in the measure that cash and in-kind resources can be found behind many doors in a given firm, acquiring a wide range of corporate friendships among line and staff business-people is smart fundraising. Often on their own authority, they can decide to contribute funds from marketing or sales or entertainment budgets, or to authorize some advertising, equipment, gifts, and executive loan.

Most nonprofits bemoan the complexity and the ambiguity of how resources potentially helpful to them are scattered far and wide throughout a given corporation. The sophisticated delight in such decentralization and devolution of authority. They ask early and often for assistance from all those in a position to provide it or influence a decision-making process favorably. Tidiness is not a virtue in abundant supply in most companies. Err on the side of entrepreneurship, resourcefulness, and aggressiveness in cultivating corporate contacts. The effort is likely to be admired. Far more often than not, overreaching will be excused. When in doubt, seek forgiveness, not permission. Any reasonable excesses flowing from an all-out fundraising program are likely to be pardoned. Restraint is rarely rewarded.

Count Employee Beneficiaries, Engage Employee Voluntarism

The more corporate insiders who know of a nonprofit, the more who are favorably disposed to it and advocate on its behalf, the better. Well-targeted efforts to seek the advice of corporate executives and to elicit their involvement pay off in many ways. Presumably, direct benefits flow from any pro bono projects taken on by corporate employees and volunteers. But positive engagement in the life of an organization also begets a pride and a broader commitment to its welfare.

That is why, to take the university as an example, it is critical to possess such information as how many graduates work for a given company, how many of its employees offered the school a matchable donation, how many children of current employees are matriculating, and how much total philanthropic support has been received from the firm. Hospitals should master similar information about current and former patients, social service organizations about their clients, community centers and environmental organizations about their members, and performing arts ensembles about their audiences.

When the display of a corporate ID card allows for free or reduced admission to a museum or a discounted seat at a concert, when a non-profit chooses to publicly acknowledge the assistance of a company at an event, in the media, or through advertising, and when a corporate senior executive is invited to serve on a board of trustees, a firm's loyalty is solidified.

What companies can provide to charitable organizations is reasonably well known and sought after. That nonprofits have it within their power to strengthen bonds with companies is somewhat less appreciated. The more each party understands about existing and potential overlapping interests, activities, and people, the broader the common ground of mutual benefit on which they can walk.

From Bottom-Up to Top-Down: Gaining Access to Corporate VIPs

A complementary approach to identifying and reaching managers inside companies associated with your organization is, first, to analyze the organization chart of the firms you wish to solicit. Then identify the chairman or chief executive officer and all those who report directly to that position. Next, ask your colleagues, trustees, and substantial contributors who knows whom among them well enough to set up a meeting, or request the purchase of a corporate table at the next fundraiser, or solicit an in-kind gift, or arrange an introduction to the corporation's contributions director or foundation president.

In some firms where philanthropy still isn't professionalized, or where the professionals are less than fully respected, securing access to senior executives through friends, customers, business or social peers and persuading them of the merits of your cause wins the day. Essentially, funding decisions are made by senior management and are carried out by others who may be called philanthropists but serve a purely administrative function.

Even in firms that respect the expertise of contributions staff, securing an audience with a corporation's most senior executives hardly hurts one's case. During my tenure at the AT&T Foundation, few grantseekers were disposed to go to the chairman directly. But who could deny the attractiveness of a person-to-person appeal from Paul Newman, Elie Wiesel, or David Rockefeller on behalf, respectively, of the Actor's Studio, the

Holocaust Museum in Washington, D.C., and the Center for Inter-American Relations? These exceptions proved the rule. In each case, philanthropic staff were present at the meeting and were subsequently asked for a recommendation on the merits. In order, the responses were no, no, and yes. All were accepted.

Still, few of life's endeavors depend more for their success on who knows whom well than does successful fundraising. A powerful board matters, particularly when its members are moved to action. Influential clients and contributors help, especially when they are highly motivated to come to your side. Expressions of support for a nonprofit's request from a firm's major customers or suppliers are rarely ignored.

So peruse that address book, thumb through that Rolodex; consult the college yearbook, the country club membership roster, and the directory of church congregants. Encourage all the friends and allies of your nonprofit to do the same. Such resources are too often neglected. Put them to work. Unlock their value. Ask others for help.

Breaking Through the Clutter: Ideas That Sing

Capturing the favorable attention of busy, influential people isn't easy, as anyone selling a product or a service quickly discovers. The company salesperson, the advertising agency copywriter, the local merchant, and the politician share common challenges with the fundraiser. How to gain access to the prospective donor (purchaser, consumer or voter). How to arrest the attention of a potential benefactor long enough to allow you to make your pitch; how to advance the merits not just to increase awareness and understanding but to yield positive action.

Breaking through the clutter of messages in a donor's crowded life to distinguish sharply the claims of your favorite nonprofit from all others is an exciting challenge. Meeting it may entail gaining access to the potential benefactor in a special way or encountering one another under especially favorable circumstances. It might involve the benevolent intervention of a third party well known to or admired by the identified prospect. It may embrace methods of presenting your case that are tailored to a potential benefactor.

Much of good fundraising is intimately related to matters of form, technique, timing, and craft. Putting them all in the service of a potential donor defines top-notch solicitation. But there are times in the life of an organization when what it wishes to accomplish, the animating idea itself, is so compelling that a carefully targeted prospective contributor's attention will be arrested at first hearing. Use such vital passages in the life of your institution to emphasize substance over form, steak over sizzle, and ends over means.

What follows are four superlative examples of ideas so galvanizing that they appeal to large audiences of appreciative donors. They virtually sell themselves to interested parties.

LISC (Local Initiative Support Corporation)[2] approaches potential supporters by highlighting the large and growing need for affordable housing in the country's inner cities and suburbs. Neither the federal, state, or local government nor the private sector is likely—on its own—to even begin to address it seriously. To seize the challenge, LISC proposed creating a set of national and city-based partnerships.

Corporations and banks can invest in funding consortia by using federal tax credits for building low-income housing. State and local governments can appropriate housing funds from their existing operating or capital budgets. They can also seek supplemental resources by issuing long-term bonds. Private foundations and the philanthropic arms of for-profit firms can provide grants to the many building costs and "soft" services (job training, counseling, education, leadership development, day care, transportation) that make communities work. And all parties can lend assistance to the agents for housing construction and the stewards of the buildings that result—local CDCs (community development corporations). LISC invites broad and diverse participation in the support of its constituent chapters by cannily appealing to the distinct interests of targeted institutions.

Since its founding in 1979, LISC has raised more than $3.1 billion in donations, investments, and below-market loans from about 1,900 corporations and foundations to bolster CDC activities in over 50 cities. This investment has been supplemented by $3.8 billion raised locally by the CDCs themselves. All concerned parties appeal both to philanthropists and to investors by highlighting the social needs they address, together with the advantages of using low-income housing tax credits to reduce corporate federal income taxes.

The results? As of year-end 1997, more than 1,500 CDCs have built or rehabilitated 80,000 affordable homes and apartments and created 10.3 million square feet of commercial and industrial space. What is just as important, LISC has helped to strengthen CDCs as indispensable instruments of community renewal and neighborhood transformation.

Identifying an important social need. Providing an analysis that concludes current methods of satisfying it are woefully inadequate. Formulating an alternative approach, one that is affordable, fundable, and, in every other respect, viable. Leaving potential investors confident that a nonprofit solicitor and its partners can deliver the goods. Possessing the ability to describe the whys and wherefores of what one is about concisely, simply, and movingly. These are the attributes of an idea that sings. LISC has one. So does Teach America.

The nation's public schools, particularly those located in poor neighborhoods, are in need of energetic, committed, and able teachers. Too many graduates are from certification programs that leave them ill prepared to cope with the conditions in inner-city elementary and secondary schools. As a result, more than half the teachers who begin work in urban settings drop out and leave the profession in less than five years. If the quantity and quality of teacher supply is now wanting, demographic trends suggest even greater demand from a cohort of youngsters from nine to eighteen that will grow by 30 percent in the next decade.[3]

The large and still-growing gap between supply and demand is addressed by Teach America.[4] Its founder, Wendy Kopp, conceived of an alternative to the standard and expensive year-long certification programs, so many of which are failing adequately to prepare teachers. Instead, she proposed that college graduates who successfully apply to Teach America with a willingness to accept inner-city school assignments be allowed to spend four months in a specially designed preparatory program. By studying intensively with their peers, who are all destined for similar assignments, and by plowing into a curriculum developed with attention to the causes of high teacher dropout rates, new sources of teaching talent could be tapped. Most particularly, liberal arts college graduates, many of whom would never have considered teaching in public schools, are attracted to this four-month, peer-supported experience. And when they arrive at pre-designated schools, a mentor and a principal are there with a welcome, as is a nationwide support network of contemporaries and Teach America graduates.

In the past seven years, more than three thousand college graduates have been assigned as teachers to elementary and secondary schools in thirty geographic areas, including locales as different as New York City, the Mississippi Delta, and South Central Los Angeles. Coping with some of the toughest urban and rural conditions and with very challenging youngsters isn't easy. Teach America has experienced problems in balancing the need for rapid growth with the ability to sustain itself managerially. But the compelling rationale for having bright, well-educated, and enthusiastic college graduates address the educational deficits of disadvantaged children remains indisputable. It propels Teach America.

An idea that sings. BAM (Brooklyn Academy of Music) has one.[5] BAM's idea is the Next Wave Festival, whose purpose is to bring avant garde art to its large performing spaces where new audiences—younger, more diverse, possessed of unconventional appetites—and New York's leading critics could be found. Identifying and nurturing promising, but relatively unknown performing artists and ensembles became BAM's forte.

If you recognize names like Laura Dean, Trisha Brown, Bill T. Jones, Susan Marshall, Mark Morris, Pina Bausch, Carol Armitage, Martha Clarke, and Twyla Tharp, then you are aware of important figures in modern dance. Much of these choreographers' work might well never have seen the light of day but for BAM. If the names Philip Glass, Steven Reich, Lucas Foss, or John Adam ring a bell, then welcome to BAM's eclectic musical sensibilities. If performance artists like Laurie Anderson, Meredith Monk, and Robert Wilson are not unfamiliar, credit BAM with some of their notoriety if not their very discovery. For all of these performers and their associated ensembles, BAM offered a welcoming home when no other comparably sized presenting institution in the country would take the necessary artistic and financial risks.

By consistently supporting innovative work, relentlessly promoting it, and aggregating artists and ensembles into the Next Wave Festival format, audiences and donors could flock to a place with a clear and compelling identity. And they have. Over the past decade, moreover, many other mainstream institutions have taken notice. They have welcomed BAM's favored artists and engaged in some home-grown artistic risk-taking.

To round out this quartet of examples, consider the following hypothesis. In large measure, Americans can improve their health by changing their habits, for example, by not smoking; by exercising regularly; and by eating a nutritional balanced diet. Such preventive measures can do more to prolong life, reduce pain, and eliminate billions of dollars of health care costs than any remedial actions.

The way to change the behavior of Americans and move them toward healthier options is to convey consistent messages through the media. Not just through public service advertising but by altering the content of movie and television scripts so that characters buckle up, select a designated driver after drinking, practice safe sex, eat sensibly, and shun smoking.

The Harvard University School of Public Health[6] followed this well-researched line of argument straight to an idea that brought them to the door of the nation's movie and television producers and their screen and scriptwriters seeking the voluntary use of preventive health practices on the part of their characters. The cooperation has been magnificent and the results nothing short of startling.

These four organizations—LISC, Teach America, BAM, and the Harvard School of Public Health—have more in common than attractive ideas. They share in common, uncommon leadership. Paul Grogan, Wendy Kopp, Harvey Lichtenstein and Dean (now Provost) Harvey Feinberg, the respective chief executive officers of these nonprofits, are driven, obsessed professionals. They embody the ideas animating the institutions that house them. They are completely committed to the fullest realization of these ideas. And in their successful propagation, each has overcome major barriers, some institutional, others personal.

For LISC, the daunting challenge is simply stated. Why should the private sector rally to do in partnership with government what the public sector in earlier decades used to accomplish on its own—building an adequate supply of low-income housing?

For Teach America, overcoming the resistance of bureaucrats to an alternative certification program is no mean task. It is compounded when the founder is a twenty-one-year-old Princeton graduate with indomitable energy, admirable resourcefulness, a solid idea, but no institutional track record and no prior professional experience.

For BAM, its physical location, relatively far from the audience it sought to attract and the donors it needed to cultivate, and its artistic orientation, a considerable reach for many patrons, offer the elements of a major struggle.

For the Harvard School of Public Health, the challenge may be expressed this way: Why are nice doctors and nurses traipsing through Hollywood studios and television headquarters? Wouldn't they be better off sticking closer to what they know best—medicine?

These barriers were overcome by the force of a driving idea, one so captivating and engaging that it virtually commanded support of all kinds.

Striving to articulate that compelling idea is an exercise worth all the energy and imagination you and your colleagues can muster. When you have it, no clutter can stand in the way.

The Winning Attitude

The complexity of raising funds from large companies can be very formidable. Don't become overwhelmed by the process of asking. All the guidelines and procedures are but a prelude. The potential corporate donor knows why you've written or sought a meeting; it's not to pass the time of day. Your target of opportunity expects a solicitation, so don't disappoint. Push through the open door.

If the prospect of asking is still daunting, keep who will benefit from an affirmative response to the request for funds uppermost in your mind. It is not for yourself that a grant is sought but because of what can be accomplished for others. By keeping your eyes on the prize—how the lives of beneficiaries will be improved—rather than on yourself as a tremulous solicitor, anxieties should ease.

Moreover, when it comes to institutions like foundations and corporations, think of fundraising as creative matchmaking. Both private and corporate foundations exist to distribute funds to causes and institutions they deem worthy. But determining who receives support isn't easy. First-rate grantees are indispensable if such charitable instrumentalities like foundations are to advance the noble mission for which they were created and for the support of which they are afforded many legal privileges and immunities.

Viewed from this perspective, intelligent efforts to secure contributed income should be welcomed by corporate donors. They have their own interests to advance. They certainly wish to burnish reputations as caring citizens who help to identify and resolve important social problems. Present them with ideas to help realize that objective. Demonstrate that you can deliver the goods. Then you are, in effect, doing philanthropists a favor. There is no reason to be self-effacing or nervous. There is every reason to be energetic and confident.

Finally, don't set the bar so high for what constitutes fundraising success that you are doomed to disappointment and discouragement.

Those who ask for money on behalf of charitable causes often seek a better batting average than the most successful baseball players. In baseball, to consistently average .333 by securing a hit one of every three times at bat is considered world class, most valuable player, all-star eligible, Hall of Fame stuff.

Yet most fundraisers—even professionals—would feel the onset of chills at the prospect of being rejected in two of every three corporate solicitations. They think of fundraising as being more like a multiple-choice exam in college. If you answer one out of every three (or even one out of every two) questions correctly, you've flunked.

To reduce the fear of failure, fundraisers should set goals more like those of the baseball player and less like those of the student. The more times a fundraiser steps up to the corporate plate with a solicitation, particularly face to face, the more likely will there be a record number of hits for a given nonprofit organization. The way to raise money is to multiply the number of recognized peers who solicit for causes they really care about and the potential donor is interested in. Don't err on the side of caution. Properly viewed, requests declined are opportunities to learn. By asking more often and doing so with a sense of humor and a toughness of character, you'll display a winning attitude.

Institutions now considered pillars of the establishment often became so only by dint of the indefatigable effort of their volunteer fundraisers. The Brookings Institution, a much-admired think tank in Washington, D.C., enjoys the largest endowment of any similarly situated organization. And how did this good fortune come to pass?

> He would tackle anyone for money . . . and if you had any that wasn't nailed down, Brookings would likely get it . . . he never let up on a man, and just wore people out.[7]

Such tenacity of belief in the cause and unflagging determination captures the spirit of fundraising at its best. Brookings would have welcomed you into his fraternity of energetic solicitors. It's never too late to join. New members are always welcome.

Practical Guidance: Sins to Avoid and Questions Worth Pondering

As you weigh how to develop or energize a corporate solicitation program, consider the top ten sins to avoid and the ten most important questions to ponder. By not committing grievous mistakes and by responding intelligently to the questions that follow, you'll be well on your way to enlarging the roster of business allies to whom you can look for support of many kinds.

The Corporate Supplicant's Sins: A Top Ten

1. *Failure to do homework.* Study a company's annual report and grant guidelines and identify areas of mutual interest between your nonprofit and each solicited corporation.

2. *Failure to communicate your case clearly, compellingly, and concisely—on paper, electronically, or in person.* Be brief, businesslike, and cogent.

3. *Failure to learn the basics about the current business objectives of your corporate prospects.* Bone up on the latest news about target company aspirations and performance. As a result, a request for support will be better informed and more realistic.

4. *Failure to be aware of the number of occasions your organization asks for support, the number of people who attempt to raise funds and the number of corporate executives who are solicited.* Unless a firm indicates otherwise, there is no set limit on the type and frequency of solicitation, save for the dictates of prudence. But a responsible party should be aware of and comfortable with fundraising practices in general, and those regarding each and every target donor.

5. *Failure to specify the measurable results expected to be attained by a given program or project for which funds are solicited.* Activities and processes are the means. Their description is necessary. But enumerating them is no substitute for clarity about the concrete goals targeted for achievement and susceptible to evaluation.

6. *Failure to keep a corporate benefactor informed between requests for support.* Fundraising is largely about widening the circle of supportive relationships a nonprofit organization can call its own. Find as many ways as feasible to engage key corporate employees in learning about and participating in your nonprofit's work.

Communicating regularly about major institutional developments is indispensable to effective solicitation.

7. *Failure to offer to be helpful to a benefactor company.* A nonprofit can provide many benefits to a firm and its employees: discounts, privileged terms and conditions of access, opportunities to volunteer, public expressions of thanks and displays of corporate recognition, or purchase of company goods and services. All such acts are noticed and appreciated.

8. *Failure to respect the time of corporate executives.* Submitting a grant proposal and pressing for a decision too quickly is a no-no. Seeking telephone or personal contact with corporate officials when answers to questions are readily available in print or electronic form isn't smart. Filing inaccurate, incomplete, or late applications for assistance doesn't win friends.

9. *Failure to demonstrate broad financial support for your organization from those who know it best.* If a nonprofit's board of directors, volunteers, consumers, and foundations specializing in the field it addresses are not generous donors, why should more distant parties become so? Corporations like nonprofits that enjoy a balanced portfolio of donors. Excessive dependence on any single source of funds or even any particular donor market segment (large corporations, big foundations, family foundations, small businesses, wealthy individuals) is unhealthy.

10. *Failure to ask—energetically, entrepreneurially, and intelligently.* Corporate executives believe they can be helpful to institutions, causes, and people in need. Being solicited for support of all kinds comes with the territory. Don't be shy. Don't disappoint. Ask.

The Corporate Fundraiser's Checklist: Questions Worth Pondering

1. Are you consciously trying to avoid committing all of a corporate fundraiser's top ten sins?

2. Before applying for funds, have you done your homework on the interests and concerns of the prospective donor? Are they addressed directly in your proposal? Is that document clear, compelling, and persuasive?

3. Have you expended enough energy and time to identify potential areas of mutual interest between your nonprofit organization and the target grantor?

4. How important is fundraising in your nonprofit organization? Is its standing reflected adequately in the time given by the chief executive, by board members, and by key staff to research and write proposals and to solicit corporate donors? How satisfactory is the range and level of philanthropic support from major donor categories—trustees, large and family foundations, individuals, and small businesses?

5. Are you familiar with business in general and with the businesses of your prospective corporate donors in particular? How many of the following general business publications do you read regularly? The *Wall Street Journal, Fortune, Forbes, Barrons, Business Week, Harvard Business Review.* Do you regularly read the business pages of the *New York Times,* the *Los Angeles Times,* or the *Washington Post*? And how many of the recommended books listed in the bibliography have you read?

6. Roughly $130 billion, or 87 percent of American philanthropy in 1996, came from living individuals or by way of bequests. Foundations gave away about $10 billion, or 7 percent of the total. Corporations distributed $8.5 billion, or 5.6 percent of the total. Do you spend your time raising funds in rough proportion to where the sources of funding are to be found? If not, are there sound reasons to apportion your energy differently?

7. Does the composition of your board of directors reflect the need to give and help acquire funds to support the organization? In particular, does the board have among its members an adequate number of business executives?

8. Have you thought about whether fundraising is more akin to the game of baseball or to a final examination in a college course? In the former, a hit every third time at bat converts you into a most

valuable player, batting .333. In the latter, one right answer out of three yields a failing grade. Consider yourself an athlete wielding a bat rather than a student brandishing a number 2 pencil.

9. Are you stepping up to the plate often enough by soliciting well-researched corporate prospects for grants? What needs to change in your organization to answer affirmatively? Is your nonprofit asking a sufficient number of nonbusiness sources for support? Are enough trustees and volunteers joining professional staff in the solicitation process?

10. How self-aware and self-critical are you about the fundraising methods and techniques employed and the results achieved by your nonprofit organization? Are you endeavoring to accomplish stretch goals, given the distinctive fundraising history and potential of the nonprofit you help lead? When it comes to fundraising, how committed are the staff and board to continuous improvement?

8

A Corporate Philanthropist Meets Established and Aspiring Grantees:
The Most Common and Most Probing Questions

This, then, is held to be the duty of the man of wealth. First, to set an example of modest, unostentatious living, shunning display or extravagance; to provide moderately for the legitimate wants of those dependent upon him; and, after doing so, to consider all surplus revenues which come to him simply as trust funds . . . which he is strictly bound as a matter of duty to administer on the manner which, in his judgment, is best calculated to provide the most beneficial results for the community—the man of wealth thus becoming the mere trustee and agent for his poorer brethren.

—ANDREW CARNEGIE
The Gospel of Wealth, 1889

Noah's principle says: No more credit for predicting rain; credit only for building arks.

—ANONYMOUS

AN OCCUPATIONAL HAZARD OF THOSE ENGAGED in philanthropy is the tendency to become detached from the challenges and concerns of nonprofits, existing grantees, and new applicants.

Philanthropists meet with one another regularly through such organizations as the Council on Foundations, regional associations of grantmakers, groups dedicated to advancing common fields of endeavor (e.g., grantmakers in the arts, health, environment) and in the case of corporations, by the Conference Board's Contributions Council.[1]

Joining such professional associations is important and necessary. Mastering the dynamics of the business of which you are a part and building a network of empathic associates are also indispensable to extending the influence of philanthropy inside a large firm. But neither obligation should be discharged to the exclusion of regular encounters with those who receive corporate philanthropic support and those who aspire to that status.

U.S. Supreme Court Justice Louis Brandeis called sunlight the best disinfectant. And the light shed by the existing and potential beneficiaries of a philanthropic fund can be illuminating in the truths it discloses. Such encounters with representatives of nonprofits raise issues about foundation priorities, policies, and practices difficult to learn about in any other way.

Below are the nine most common and most probing questions that have come my way from the hundreds of audiences I addressed in my years at AT&T. Friendly and adversarial, gentle and caustic, diplomatic and impertinent, all are challenging in their directness and down-to-earth in their authenticity. Such honesty and candor merited nothing less than responses in kind. Those, too, I've endeavored to provide. What's on the mind of fundraisers I've been privileged to meet may well resemble some of your preoccupations and curiosities.

MOST NONPROFITS MOST OFTEN NEED GENERAL OPERATING SUPPORT TO SUSTAIN THEIR BASIC FUNCTIONS. WHY, THEN, ARE INSTITU-TIONAL DONORS—FOUNDATIONS AND CORPORATIONS—SO INTENT ON GIVING PROGRAM AND PROJECT GRANTS? WHY DO THEY RESIST PROVIDING GENERAL ASSISTANCE?

This question gets to the essence of asking for funds and donating them: how to identify the confluence between the professed needs of nonprofits and the interests of benefactors.

Donors are usually attracted to a particular part of an institution's operation, rather than the whole. They are often eager to carve out a niche of specialization, one or more areas of concern and expertise with which the public associates them. In general, they are eager to evaluate the impact of philanthropic support. Serious philanthropists want to know whether their grants make a difference, to whom or what do they matter, and why. None of these donor requirements are satisfied by pro-viding general operating support.

Once having supplied general assistance to a nonprofit, on what plausible grounds can one refuse a second, third, or fourth request? As long as a grantee remains financially and programmatically solvent over the course of a gift's life, success for the donation can be claimed with some justification. General support provides no specific criteria for assessing the impact of assistance. By contrast, aid to identifiable projects offers the donor a pathway to hold a nonprofit accountable for achieving projected results. Upon the expiration of the grant term, anticipated outcomes have been met or exceeded, or shortfalls were encountered. Such solid experiential evidence can become the basis of future grantmaking decisions.

For most institutional donors, the nonprofits selected for support are means to achieve defined ends. Take the field of higher education as an illustration. Universities contribute to the social mobility of poor and working-class students. They are indispensable sources of high technology and biomedical research. They advance the nation's economic competitiveness. They prepare young people for jobs in fields needing well-educated, highly motivated personnel. Support for colleges and universities can be the vehicle for advancing such larger goals. Far less often is it perceived by the institutional donor as a self-justifying end.

By targeting a particular area of nonprofit work for support, the donor acquires a stake in its success and a way to connect to an organization more closely. Project support enables a corporation to conceive methods by which volunteers could be of assistance or equipment gifts of use. It also allows the donor to believe that without its grant assistance, a given activity might not have happened at all, or in as high quality a fashion, or to the benefit of so many people. General support gets lost in the "noise" and the "clutter" of many donors and diffuses help.

There are occasions when support of a nonprofit, even for a large institutional donor, comes very close to being an end in itself. Prudential Insurance, headquartered in Newark, New Jersey, desires to see an ambitious New Jersey Center for the Performing Arts erected downtown. The center's anticipated overall favorable impact on economic development, property values, and neighborhood security motivates the firm to be a leading donor. Boeing and Microsoft, both headquartered in Seattle and its environs, support the University of Washington as an institution from which they hire all kinds of graduates and to which they send hundreds of students annually. In such cases of real or perceived close connections between donor and donee, nonprofits can legitimately aspire to general operating support or contributions to endowment and building fund campaigns.

As a general rule, then, the more intimate the relationship between a nonprofit and its funding targets, the greater the likelihood of general operating support. That's why board members and nonprofit customers (alumni, former patients, subscribers to concerts and theater) are such prime candidates for general assistance. Funding sources rooted in and dedicated to the welfare of specific communities are also solid prospects. Close observers of an organization's performance and those familiar with its needs are far more inclined to consider providing flexible assistance, offering maximum discretion in the use of funds to leaders they know well.

The more distant the relationship—geographically, operationally, experientially—the more a successful nonprofit will appeal to a donor because of what it can specifically accomplish rather than because of its general mission.

The reasons for the strong tendency of large institutional donors to provide program or project support are sound and compelling: grant evaluation is facilitated; helping to achieve a tangible result is gratifying; being publicly identified with making specific things happen advances the donor's visibility and promotes good will. These reasons are tough to overcome. It may not even be worth the necessary investment of time and energy to try.

OKAY, SINCE INSTITUTIONAL DONOR INTERESTS APPEAR SO STRONGLY ALIGNED TO PROVIDING PROJECT GRANTS, WHAT'S YOUR ADVICE TO NONPROFITS THAT ARE NONETHELESS VERY MUCH IN NEED OF GENERAL OPERATING SUPPORT?

First, charity begins at home, and general operating support must start with a nonprofit's board of directors. After all, they hold the institution in trust for service to others. By definition, they should most strongly believe in the organization's overall mission. And it is trustees who should provide willingly the most flexible, no-strings-attached form of financial assistance. Every board chairman or president, together with the chief executive officer, should ask trustees each year to contribute as much general operating support as their means allow.

Second, maximize contributions from individuals. They give about 85 percent of all donations. They are much less likely to insist on specific purposes for their help than are institutions, particularly for gifts of $10,000 or less. For decades, nonprofits that assist in the treatment and prevention of specific diseases have raised funds from tens of thousands of people by direct mail. What helps to sustain the American Heart Association and the American Cancer Society has spread to social action groups, environmental organizations, and public television. The direct mail and telemarketing membership drives of for example, Planned Parenthood, the ACLU, People for the American Way, the Audubon Society, the Environmental Legal Defense Fund, WNET, KQED, and WTOP are techniques that take advantage of the general assistance potential of individual donors.

Such direct mail and telephone solicitations aren't equally effective for all nonprofits. But virtually all can take advantage of special-event fundraising. Gala dances, dinners, luncheons, auctions, concerts, and theater parties, are excellent occasions for raising general operating support. Corporations are as responsive to such affairs as individuals. Most companies set aside separate budgets for sales, marketing, customer entertainment, and community relations. So pitching for support of nonprofit special-event fundraisers does not usually interfere with requests for more formal philanthropic grant assistance. To the contrary, social occasions provide nonprofit trustees and professionals with important opportunities to meet, greet, or strengthen relationships with company executives. Striking up such acquaintances can always help engender a favorable reception for grant applicants.

Fourth, remember that companies often reflect in their giving the values of their employees. Efforts to reach employees of companies with fundraising appeals can be doubly gratifying. Usually, employee gifts are matched dollar for dollar (or more) by the Fortune 1000. Significant support of a nonprofit by corporate employees will not go unnoticed when you request grant support from the company per se. Don't fail to highlight employee use of your services as consumers or support for your programs as patrons, whenever either is present.

Fifth, when applying for corporate project or program grants be sure to allocate general overhead costs to the expenses warranting assistance. Corporate funders are sophisticated enough to know that it takes the time and talent of general managers and the existence of an organizational infrastructure to launch and sustain any innovation. They are aware that projects incur significant management and general costs. Calculate these costs accurately. Allocate ample funds to them. Too often, nonprofits are shy about recovering all the direct and indirect expenses attributable to a fundable endeavor. Forgo any such reticence.

The breadth and diversity of the donors that contributed $150.7 billion to charity in 1996 is enormous. Don't waste time over concerns that certain segments of this benefactor market are disinclined to favorably entertain requests for general operating support. Instead, pursue a balanced portfolio of patrons, many of whom will be prepared to offer flexible assistance. For others, be sure to prepare your project support applications in a way that, if successful, will fully reimburse relevant basic overhead costs.

How can a nonprofit gain access to the informal corporate processes that lead to cash or in-kind support from outside pure philanthropic grant benefits? What's the best way to tap sales, marketing and equipment resources, and to recruit corporate volunteers?

There's no substitute for engaging in two key activities. First, learn all you can about a company's business strategy and determine its implications for community relations in general and for your niche in the Third Sector in particular. Find out who's who inside the firm. Determine the name, rank, and serial number of those responsible for departments that manage assets of potential use to you. Second, identify supporters, friends, and allies of your nonprofit who know those influentials and can introduce them to your work. Spend time acquainting them with your outfit—in person and on-site, in an appealing manner that respects an executive's time and responds to his or her interests.

Such executives and those who know them well might be among your nonprofit's clients or customers. Or they could be neighbors or members of your church or country club. Once you've matched an executive to someone with whom he or she is well acquainted and who admires the work of your nonprofit, the rest is downhill. When the time is ripe, recite some of the unmet needs of the organization that can be satisfied with corporate help. Ask whether that's possible. You'll probably be astonished at the number and generosity of positive responses to such straightforward, face-to-face requests for help from a nonprofit advocate previously unknown to a corporate manager.

If the company's contributions director is both a donor of your nonprofit and well regarded inside the firm, don't hesitate to ask for introductions to colleagues who control resources that aren't strictly philanthropic. The converse is also true. If you or your allies know executives who believe in your cause, ask them for introductions to their colleague, the in-house philanthropist.

In my experience, once having won a company's philanthropic support, nonprofits too often fail to ask for help in broadening the sources of assistance, both from others inside the firm and from like-minded colleagues outside it. You'll be surprised by the generally supportive reactions of insiders to requests for advice and then for help. Although some may feel put upon by such inquiries, most will be flattered that you thought enough of them to ask.

The phrase "nothing ventured, nothing gained" must have been coined by a fundraiser.

Doesn't the mixture of corporate self-interest and philanthropy trouble you? Aren't there risks that a nonprofit will succumb to inappropriate corporate requests motivated by business needs, not charitable concerns?

Corporations are no less likely to think about philanthropy in relationship to their interests than are individuals or private foundations. Responsible corporate executives know that the tax-deductible features of philanthropy allow only for indirect benefits accruing to a donor from a gift. Quid pro quos exacted in exchange for a donation are illegal. But well within the zone of legality and well on the safe side of ethical lapses in judgment, it would be unnatural and objectionable for corporations to ignore their interests in reaching grant decisions.

Consider a high-technology company's philanthropy. Its priorities in higher education are shaped by business imperatives. Grants are given to graduate schools sponsoring research in fields of greatest interest to the company. Grants are also awarded to schools from which it regularly recruits graduates and to which it directs its employees for continuing education. Or grants are advanced to the alma maters of executives. On what grounds are such priorities inappropriate, even if they are driven by corporate self-interest?

Indeed, suppose a high-tech firm like Microsoft or Intel decided to devote a substantial portion of its education philanthropy to musical conservatories or graduate schools of theology. Surely its mystified shareowners would be entitled to an explanation as to what business purposes were served by such untargeted largesse.

As corporations move in their dealings with a nonprofit from a philanthropic to a business relationship, a careful weighing of costs, benefits, and risks is in order. For example, does the cause-related marketing campaign of American Express to end hunger excessively commercialize the charities invoked in huge television, radio, and print advertising campaigns? Or does such a campaign call much-needed attention to a cause unlikely to become widely known without the brand power and resources of a supportive firm like American Express?

Is displaying a brand-new Lexus in the grand foyer of a concert hall as part of an agreement governing sponsorship support for orchestral performances likely to annoy or inconvenience audiences? Is a nonprofit sponsorship by a company that produces a dangerous product (tobacco, firearms), or delivers a deficient or high-priced service (cable television), or is otherwise controversial, an association best avoided?

These are the kinds of questions that nonprofit executives and their trustees must seriously entertain. They are, after all, free to just say no to any strings attached to corporate offers. Or they can suggest to American Express in precisely what media its arts-hunger ads should not run or lead Lexus to the least objectionable location in which to situate the latest car model in the performing arts center.

No one could credibly suggest that because a very few individual donors seek undue influence that the giving of all Americans should be suspect. Corporate dealings with nonprofits require vigilance and hard bargaining as well. Nonprofits should advance their interests and protect those they serve from harm or embarrassment. As a general rule, the vast majority of donors will respect the needs and prerogatives of Third Sector constituents. Articulate them clearly.

LET'S SWITCH THE SUBJECT FROM THE FORM OF CORPORATE SUPPORT TO ITS CONTENT. BY SEARCHING FOR THE INTERSECTION OF THEIR INTERESTS AND SOCIAL NEED, DO COMPANIES PLACE A LOW PRIORITY ON ASSISTING NONPROFITS THAT SERVE POOR PEOPLE? IS THERE A BIAS IN CORPORATE PHILANTHROPY TO SUPPORT CAUSES OF GREATEST CONCERN TO THE MIDDLE AND WORKING CLASS, IN THAT ORDER, RATHER THAN TO THE INDIGENT?

Yes. Yes.

In the measure that the charitable contributions of corporations are closely correlated to business interests and accurately reflect employee preferences, most funding will not find its way to assisting poor people.

Indeed, the same observation applies to individuals and their giving. In a recent study, *Why the Wealthy Give,* Francie Ostrower comes to this important conclusion:

> Philanthropy is as much about the idea that individuals should "do their share" to support the organizations from which they benefit as it is about giving to others. Although instances of giving to support causes used by wealthy donors has been criticized as abuse of philanthropy, such giving is in fact typical, and not only among elites. The recognition that this is true is important not only for understanding philanthropy but also for accurately assessing its capabilities and limitations.[2]

Both corporations and individuals are taxpayers. Acting in that capacity, they assume that the funding necessary to maintain a social safety net to protect the poor is assured. Supplementing that basic public expenditure with philanthropy to support innovative services and replicable demonstration projects is an appropriate task for donors. But massive undertakings like moving poor people from welfare to work, or housing the homeless, or providing health insurance to the medically indigent, requires resources that far exceed what philanthropy can or should provide.

To acknowledge the indispensable responsibility of government to address the needs of the poor is neither to deny nor gainsay the auxiliary role of private philanthropy in general and of corporations in particular. The importance of banks and insurance companies to assisting community development corporations in building and maintaining housing for the poor is widely acknowledged. The dramatic impact of corporate assistance from local and long distance telephone companies and software firms in providing public school access to the Internet is a blessing to thousands of communities. The generous support the television and motion picture industry devotes to the detection and treatment of AIDS has helped to finance discoveries that promise to arrest the advance of the disease in many patients. And the almost universal business aid to hundreds of United Way chapters across the nation helps to sustain important services delivered by thousands of voluntary agencies, from community centers and summer camps to homeless shelters and nursing homes, and from hospitals and family service agencies to hospices, the Salvation Army, and the American Red Cross.

Rather, the distinction between public and private resources is drawn to acknowledge twin realities. The first is a matter of size. In 1996, all of the nation's philanthropy amounted to $150.7 billion. Contrast that figure with the combined spending of federal, state, and local governments estimated to have been $2.5 trillion, or almost seventeen times more.[3] Logic points to the irrefutable conclusion that addressing large-scale social problems in America without ample public resources is an exercise in futility.

The second distinction is a matter of governance. Governments in the United States reach decisions based on a democratic process involving the consent of the voters. Competing claims on public resources are ultimately resolved by compromise between and among elected officials in the executive and legislative branches. At any given time, those decisions reflect the will of the people. By contrast, donors reach decisions by individual volition. Some combination of their own interests and assessment of social needs results in donations. As taxpayers, we may find ourselves supporting with our funds activities we find objectionable. As benefactors, we enjoy the unfettered right and privilege to support whatever institutions, projects, or causes we wish, and to do so willingly and unapologetically.

> Critics of the nature of the recipients of elite donations also suggest that the wealthy corrupt, rather than practice, philanthropy. The wealthy have been criticized for failing to give more to the poor and for favoring causes such as cultural and educational organizations. Such criticism assumes that redistribution is a basic aim of philanthropy and criterion by which it should be measured. . . . This study shows that although wealthy donors believe philanthropic gifts should have a public benefit, they do not equate it with redistribution for the poor. Indeed, they view gifts to hospitals, museums and the broader range of philanthropic institutions as equally legitimate.[4]

In writing about wealthy individual donors, Francie Ostrower, Associate Professor of Sociology at Harvard University, could just as accurately have been characterizing business executives who reach decisions about corporate largesse: "Many donors ardently defend the social values of philanthropy. Yet the way in which they interpret philanthropy allows them to enjoy the sense that they are making a contribution to society while defining social benefit on their own terms."[5]

This highly prized individualism mightily resists efforts to influence giving choices. Those who believe that as government withdraws its tax-based support of the poor, private philanthropy will rush to fill the vacuum are wrong on two counts. One is size: There simply isn't a sufficient level of philanthropy to substitute for rather than complement the expenditure of public resources on major social problems. The second is motivation: What drives philanthropy are millions of individual decisions idiosyncratically inspired, not collective action driven by the power of a centralized commanding authority. In his book *What Charity Can and Cannot Do,* Julian Wolpert puts the matter this way:

1. There is a serious mismatch between the location of charitable resources and needs.

2. There is a mismatch between the kinds of programs that attract charitable donations and the kind that benefit needy people.[6]

It has been estimated that only about 10 to 15 percent of the country's philanthropic support directly helps the poorest Americans. That figure probably holds as true for companies as for private foundations and individuals.

Although there is plenty of room for growth in the proportion of private philanthropy directed to the assistance of the poor, even a substantial increase is unlikely to address any major health, education, or social welfare shortfalls nearly as well as a small percentage increment of the far larger pool of public funds. Advocates for the poor have a compelling case to advance to individuals and corporations in their capacity as donors. The case is even stronger and the stakes much higher when they address individuals and corporations in their capacity as citizen taxpayers.

WHAT GENERAL ADVICE WOULD YOU OFFER TO YOUNG PEOPLE WHO EXPRESS AN INTEREST IN WORKING FOR A PRIVATE OR CORPORATE FOUNDATION?

My overall response is easily contained in a point of view and a question to youthful jobseekers. The point of view: "Not no, but not now." The question: "Are you ready?"

Use the gift of time to test how realistic and informed is your interest in philanthropy. As you benefit from professional and civic experience, consciously weigh whether other lines of endeavor can satisfy some of the needs that manifest themselves in that expression of interest. Invest some years in developing yourself to perform ably in foundation work in the unlikely event that the motivation to become a professional philanthropist remains strong.

The steps to take to prepare yourself are straightforward. Gain some challenging professional experience in government, business, or a nonprofit organization. Acquire or perfect the skills that add value to almost any undertaking—the ability to listen adeptly and to communicate well, orally and in writing; the capacity to work productively with others; fluency in the language of the computer; analytic proficiency and the like.

Develop not just know-how but knowledge. Read widely in the substantive areas that you care most about. Gravitate to experts in those fields—at universities, professional associations, and the workplace—securing introductions from people you already know. Ask questions persistently. Satisfy curiosities daily and meet new people weekly. Consider pursuing your fascination with a subject by studying for an advanced degree.

No matter where you may work, acquaint yourself with the Third Sector by becoming a member of nonprofit organizations that strike your fancy. Perform voluntary service at others that capture your attention. Along the way to building a résumé of professional and civic accomplishment, spin a web of references and associations from which clues and cues to your future can be gathered.

In the meantime, learn more about what philanthropists really do. Those distant from the realities tend to exaggerate the immediacy and impact of giving on nonprofits and the clients they serve. They also tend to understate the routines and frustrations of giving away money for a living. Buried in paperwork and attached umbilically to a telephone, many desk-bound foundation staffers are hardly to be confused with the glamorous portrayals sketched in the minds of many.

Foundation work often just fills a space in the operations of nonprofits. Any single source of funding may be little more than a marginal supporting player in the life of a nonprofit organization or cause. Foundation work brings little speedy gratification. Its investments take the form of grants spent to achieve results measured in years. Foundation work requires some detachment from the day-to-day challenges of applicants. Its professional staff run the risk of distancing themselves from the social problems of the poor and working class as they operate from the protected sanctuaries of well-furnished office quarters.

Reading philanthropically conscious general newspapers and periodicals, and reviewing nonprofit trade publications, like the *Chronicle of Higher Education, Chronicle of Philanthropy,* and *American Benefactor,* will help acquaint the curious with the limitations and constraints as well as the virtues and attractions of foundation work. So will spending time with those who practice philanthropy, showing up where they speak, and reading what they write about themselves in content-laden annual reports.

Also take a few practical matters into account. According to some estimates, there may be as few as three to four thousand philanthropic program officer jobs in the entire country. When vacancies occur, many of those are filled by insiders. Contrast that very small number of posts open to competition with the several million available in the nation's vibrant, sprawling nonprofit sector. The odds are stacked against the job candidate who chooses to ignore the huge employment pool within institutions devoted to health, education, social services, and arts and culture in favor of the relative handful of genuinely contested philanthropic positions. Landing a job in a foundation located geographically where you wish and placed in a situational setting that's appealing is one tall order.

If you have established a solid professional track record, developed an area of expertise, crafted praiseworthy job skills, garnered meaningful Third Sector experience, acquired a more down-to-earth and less overly romanticized view of philanthropy, understand the low probability of success in winning a desirable job, and you *still* wish to proceed, then three final observations come to mind.

First, you really want to be a philanthropist.

Second, you now have the makings of becoming an able one.

Third, and by no means either incidental or accidental, you are no longer quite as young.

SOME OBSERVERS CONTEND THAT FOUNDATIONS AND CORPORATIONS ARE PHILANTHROPICALLY FADDISH, ALTERING THEIR PRIORITIES AND CHANGING THEIR GRANTEES ALL TOO QUICKLY. OTHER INTERESTED PARTIES MAINTAIN THAT FAR FROM BEING "SUMMER SOLDIERS AND

SUNSHINE PATRIOTS," TOO MANY INSTITUTIONAL DONORS ARE PRONE
TO INERTIA, FAVORING A CHARMED CIRCLE OF FORTUNATE BENEFICIA-
RIES AND ERECTING HIGH BARRIERS TO ENTRY FOR ASPIRING NEW-
COMERS. WHICH IS IT? WHOSE VIEW IS CORRECT?

Both and neither. In the aggregate, resources allocated to fields of
interest by corporations change only by small increments over the years.
Dramatic shifts are few and far between.

Consider for example, a recent decade of corporate philanthropy. In
1983, large businesses were estimated by the Conference Board to have
contributed $3.1 billion in cash to nonprofits. By 1993, that figure
roughly doubled to $6.11 billion. Table 8-1 shows how those funds were
distributed by a percentage of the total for each year:[7]

TABLE 8-1. Corporate Cash Funding of Nonprofits,
            1982 and 1993

Field of Endeavor	1982	1993
Health / Human Services	31%	26.3%
Education	40.7%	38.3%
Civic and Community Affairs	11.7%	10.5%
Arts and Culture	11.4%	11.2%

Keeping in mind that small- and medium-size firms may experience
more pronounced shifts in their giving patterns, note how little these
numbers fluctuate between categories for the Fortune 1000. Over the
decade, two notable developments occurred. Giving to environmental
causes and giving to nonprofits working overseas rose sufficiently to register on the philanthropic temperature chart. Otherwise, most changes
occurred only *within* traditional categories of support. Illustratively, by
1994, within the category of education, donations to primary and secondary schools were much higher than had been the case in 1983. Illustratively, in 1994, the proportion of corporate funds in human services
allocated to United Way had shrunk since 1983.

Variations between categories of giving for private foundations over
the same decade were somewhat greater, but not dramatically so. Emerging beneficiary categories of assistance from foundations over the past
decade include environmental, international affairs, and science and technology organizations. That phenomenon aside, the real action and the
most marked change were inside conventional categories of support.

Under such circumstances, institutional philanthropy writ large cannot be fairly accused of jumping from subject to subject or issue to issue. On the other hand, any particular foundation might change its priorities quickly and stand accused of lacking constancy in support of its grantees. Certainly, corporate mergers, acquisitions, spin-offs, downsizings, and facility closures transform overnight a firm's business interests. Is it any surprise that philanthropy aligned to business directions would also change?

Foundations that adhere to a grantee policy of "once on, never off" are relatively rare. Conversely, except for those in a dramatically altered situational setting, very few foundations toss history overboard and proceed with a tabula rasa. Such polar opposite tendencies are extreme and extremely rare. Fortunately, the nation's foundations are diverse enough in their purposes, varied enough in their practices, and rooted enough in their interests, missions, and locales to resist fads and to adapt to change.

All foundations and corporations must do their philanthropic math and explore the implications of the issue at hand by asking: Are we giving our funds excessively to the same old crowd of grantees? Are we adequately sympathetic to fresh appeals from strangers? Do we stay the philanthropic course long enough to make an impact on a field of concern, but not so long as to encounter diminishing returns? Are the challenges that initially gave rise to a given program priority still at work? If so, stick to the knitting. If not, doesn't change beckon?

WHAT HAVE BEEN THE MOST IMPORTANT SOURCES OF PROFESSIONAL SATISFACTION AND DISAPPOINTMENT YOU ENCOUNTERED DURING A DOZEN YEARS OF CLOSE ASSOCIATION WITH CORPORATE PHILANTHROPY?

The question puts one in mind of the proverb, "One gives generously and ends with more. Another stints on doing right and incurs a loss."

From the perspective of what I received, the blessings were abundant. To select from among them isn't easy. But under duress I'd offer that being involved broadly in the exercise of corporate social responsibility put me in touch with some of the nation's most gifted, selfless, driven, and idealistic people. Not a day flew by when I didn't marvel at the rich array of concerns addressed by the Third Sector's constituent organizations, traditional and unconventional, veteran and newborn. Their creativity and resourcefulness, their tenacity and purposefulness, and their problem-solving ingenuity amount to nothing less than one of America's greatest strengths. To be in a position to learn about, let alone support and influence the activities of some of the most important causes of our time, was satisfying beyond measure.

From the perspective of what I could help to contribute, two areas of activity were the most gratifying. The first was stretching the boundaries of what a Fortune 10 company could do to help address a societal problem or seize a community opportunity. The mission was hardly confined to exploring some philanthropic frontiers. It also entailed efforts to orchestrate a huge firm's core resources on behalf of the public. Persuading business colleagues to see value in collaborating on issues of concern to nonprofits brought immense gratification.

The causes ranged widely. From refusing to do business in South Africa to helping prevent the spread of AIDS. From strengthening the nation's universities devoted to the highest quality research of interest to the scientists at Bell Laboratories to reducing the incidence of teenage pregnancies and low-weight babies. From advancing the case for the country's five African-American medical schools to championing the cause of new art and the art of newcomers. From improving the nation's physical environment to helping America strengthen its capacity to compete with other nations in the world economy.

The minds and material resources tapped to advance these causes were to be found in every nook and cranny of the firm. Leadership was recruited from within all business units and from all departments. Hardly a tangible asset that could be of use to charity was willingly neglected. These included the company's art collection; employee volunteerism and cash contributions; used furniture and equipment; state-of-the-art, top-of-the-line products and services; internships and summer jobs; and facility space. Also, real estate; satellites; sales events, premiums, and discounts; company cars, trucks, and planes. All of these were regularly donated, borrowed, or otherwise deployed alongside cash contributions. Together, they were intended to help advance the quality of the communities in which AT&T's people, along with their customers, suppliers, partners, retirees, and shareowners, live and work.

The second rich source of professional fulfillment originated in what might be called philanthropic matchmaking. Sensing a gap on the board of directors of a nonprofit and recommending that it be filled with the right AT&T executive proved to be a special treat. To many of my most senior colleagues, being on the inside of the governance of a university, an orchestra, a social service organization, or a nonprofit think tank was a pleasurable revelation. The opportunity to serve others was seized with energy and enthusiasm by virtually all. For many dozens of executives, the trustee experience with a nonprofit transformed the way they understood an area of social or cultural interest, the way they envisioned what a modern firm should do to be of assistance, and, not least, the way they viewed themselves.

This personal effort to match institutional needs with corporate talent helped to convert business executives to members in good standing of the nonprofit community and to vocal advocates of the Third Sector. It enriched the delighted organizations flexible enough to receive them on their boards. And it changed the lives of seasoned professionals eager to "give something back" to society if someone would but trouble to help them find the ways and means of doing so.

As to disappointments, they were mild by comparison and hardly in the control of AT&T. For example, I wish the company could have more frequently joined forces with other firms and private foundations to collectively tackle common social challenges. The preoccupation of leaders with their own shops and how they fare, combined with the startling indifference of large private foundations to corporations as institutions of power and influence, undermined most attempts to launch sustained collaborations. How many so-called intractable problems might have been resolved or eased but for the general proclivity to "go-it-alone" philanthropy?

I also wish AT&T had experimented more with advances in communications technology to address the specific needs of nonprofits. Beset by vibrant competition on every front and moving rapidly to reorganize the business and deploy its assets, the company never quite assembled and deployed the critical mass of expertise that could consult with select nonprofits on alternative technological approaches to discharging effectively and efficiently their missions. There was plenty of useful voluntary advice and guidance. But it remained too ad hoc, episodic, and inconsistent.

CAN YOU RECALL ANY SPECIAL ENCOUNTERS WITH SOLICITORS OF FUNDS THAT OFFER USEFUL LESSONS TO GRANT SEEKERS?

I vividly remember Elie Wiesel, looking gaunt and fragile, sitting in a chair several sizes too large for his frame, as he visited in May 1984 with the then chairman of AT&T, Charles L. Brown. What brought Wiesel to our corporate headquarters at 550 Madison Avenue was the cause of building a Holocaust Museum in Washington, D.C. He hoped Mr. Brown would agree to chair the capital campaign.

Here is a paraphrase of the first sentences uttered by Mr. Wiesel at that meeting. Even roughly and inadequately rendered, the message of this Nobel Prize winner is arresting enough to stop in his or her tracks even the busiest CEO:

> Mr. Chairman, I am well aware that until January of this year you have been the head of the Bell System, the largest company in the world, possessed of no fewer than 1 million employees and 3 million shareowners, the first firm ever to report earning a billion dollars of profit in a single quarter.
>
> To such a man, attractive proposals of every possible combination must regularly present themselves. But this afternoon I summon the temerity to believe that what brings me to your door may well be singular and unprecedented, even for a business leader like yourself. For I am here to offer you nothing less than a page in history.

I also recall a visit from Beverly Sills, the world-famous diva who at the time was general director of the New York City Opera. What occasioned her sudden request for a meeting was truly an emergency. All the opera company's costumes had been destroyed the week before in a New Jersey warehouse fire. With characteristic poise and conviction, Sills asked for an immediate grant to help restore a costume collection for the opera company. Possessed not only of persuasive skills, Sills also enjoys a boisterous sense of humor. Allowing as how the need was clear and compelling, she made it abundantly clear that leaving my office without a pledge of at least $100,000 was quite out of the question.

And I recall how brilliantly Vartan Gregorian, then president of the New York Public Library, put his argument for a capital campaign that would build underground capacity to house several million books, restore and renovate many of the Forty-second Street and Fifth Avenue location's grand spaces of public accommodation, and completely reconfigure and refurbish Bryant Park. His entrepreneurial energy was infectious and his enthusiasm was utterly irresistible. Even veteran philanthropic types have been known to find themselves swept away by Gregorian's optimism and self-confidence.

A page in history. A costumeless opera. A great but much neglected public library in need of belated attention. What these causes had in common was that they were personified by gifted, driven, not-to-be-denied leaders who knew how to ask unabashedly for financial support. After all the fundraising feasibility studies are concluded and when all of the cost-benefit analyses of funding proposals are conducted, benefactors, as individuals, or as representatives of corporations and foundations, respond to the solicitations of real people.

Do these solicitors advance their cause by the stories they tell and the needs they portray? Do they elicit confidence in their institutions? Will funds granted be spent efficiently and effectively? Can these leaders accomplish what they set out to do?

Institutions have a human face, and the face that matters most is the leader at the top. One must never forget the importance of the CEO and the chairman of the board as fundraisers. When these individuals are articulate and self-possessed, their personal solicitation efforts are often indispensable to successful fundraising campaigns.

Now, in Washington, D.C., stands one of the most moving and most frequently visited museum spaces in the world, the Holocaust Museum. It is an accomplishment of which Mr. Wiesel and his fellow survivors can be very proud.

Now, more than a decade after Beverly Sills finished a successful term of service as New York City Opera's general director to later become the chairman of the board of Lincoln Center, the company thrives—quite handsomely clothed, one might add.

Now, the New York Public Library at Fifth Avenue and Forty-second Street is positively spiffy—above ground, in Bryant Park, and even underground, where books by the millions are safely ensconced. Whatever he subsequently accomplished as president of Brown University and whatever the future may hold in store for his tenure as president of the Carnegie Corporation, Vartan Gregorian lifted the sights of the library and successfully solicited hundreds of foundations, corporations, and individuals. All are the better for the experience.

PART FOUR

The Future of Corporate Philanthropy

9

Forecasting Corporate Philanthropy:
Four Emerging Trends and Unbounded Potential

It is not required of thee to complete the task, but neither art thou free to desist therefrom. . . . He who saves one life, it is as if he has saved the whole world.

—THE TALMUD

If it can be imagined
It can be done.
This is America.
We never say good enough.
We never say die.

—THE CIT GROUP CORPORATE ADVERTISING

THE PROSPECTS FOR CONTINUING GROWTH in American philanthropy are excellent. Expansion in giving is dependent on a healthy economy and the progressive accumulation of assets. In recent years, Americans have benefited from both in very good measure.

Unemployment in the 4–5 percent range. Inflation at around 3 percent. Consumer confidence very strong. The value of common stock more than doubling, with the Dow Jones Industrial Average moving from a low of 3,200 to a high of 9,300 between 1992 and 1998. Fourteen million net new jobs created over the same period. These are some outcomes of America's overall economic performance during the Clinton administration. Indeed, President Clinton's reelection in 1996 was widely attributed to the American people's satisfaction with the state of the economy over the prior four years. The positive momentum carried over into 1997 and 1998, the eighth consecutive year of economic growth. During this period, many Americans enjoyed solid gains in after-tax income and extraordinary improvements in net wealth. Such economic good fortune has always been strongly associated with higher levels of giving by individuals.

The grant sums expended by private foundations are largely a function of asset appreciation. The record of the past few years has been nothing short of superlative. In 1995 and 1996 alone, soaring stock values saw the average foundation portfolio grow at compound annual rates of 17 percent. Indeed, the capital position of the country's foundation assets has never been in better shape. More generous grant payouts year over year are virtually inevitable as long as stock market valuations do not plummet.

The corporate climate is also sunny. American firms continue to report excellent earnings growth and high levels of productivity. Labor costs are being held in check. The benefits of expense cutting and investments in technology are becoming apparent. Output per worker in industry after industry is improving markedly. It is not surprising, then, that investment in the stock of American firms both directly and through mutual funds has been rising to record levels. Senior corporate executives with the authority to reach decisions on the level of contribution to their asset-based foundations and on annual grant payouts have sound reasons for optimism about their personal financial prospects and the outlook for their firms.

By the fourth quarter of 1996, it even appeared that the historically high levels of employee reductions in the Fortune 1000 had run their course, adding to a positive psychology about expending corporate resources to help meet community needs. Moreover, the sharp turn-around in the American economic condition contrasts sharply with relative stagnation in much of Western Europe and Japan. As the economic competitiveness of America improves measurably in field after field—from agriculture to pharmaceuticals, aircraft to automobiles, computers to biotechnology, and telecommunications to transportation—the mood of American business remains upbeat. The apparent ironclad commitment of the Clinton administration and a Republican-controlled Congress to balance the federal budget only adds to the positive state of mind.

If the supply side of American philanthropy from all three of its sources seems strong and vibrant, evidence abounds that the demand side is energetic and purposeful. Since the Reagan era, federal expenditures in almost all the fields of interest to nonprofits have been dramatically reduced. State and local government support of these same areas is generally down as well. One effect of this historic decline in public resources flowing to nonprofits has been to focus attention on raising levels of earned income. Tuition, admission, membership, or ticket costs at most nonprofits has been rising well in excess of inflation for more than fifteen years. The result? In New York City, for example, the $30,000-a-year bill for tuition, room, and board at a private university; the $75 play or concert ticket; or the $2,000 health club membership at the local Y. Such price escalation is meeting strong, if belated, resistance.

The confluence of government budget austerity and constraints on earned income growth is compelling nonprofits to look to philanthropy with a keener eye and a stronger appetite. Corporate, foundation, and individual benefactors are seen as sources that can finance improvements in physical plants, cash positions, endowment size, service provision, and staff and program quality. Sophistication is growing in raising funds not just by grant submission but by other means: direct mail, telefundraising, special events, and face-to-face solicitation. A major trend over the past two decades in the governance of nonprofits has been to increase the size of the board of directors.[1] It has been caused largely by a desire to broaden the number of substantial contributions. More trustees truly committed to the welfare of a nonprofit will also swell the ranks of high-powered volunteer solicitors of funds from external sources. Those trustees require professional support, which is yet another reason why one of the fastest-growing employment areas on the management side of nonprofits is variously called resource development, contributions management, or fundraising. The burgeoning number of want ads for professionals needed to staff this critical function attest to the high level of demand.

At the close of the twentieth century, as one attempts to peer into the future, a constellation of forces suggests that record-breaking increases in philanthropy lie ahead. Among these forces are relatively strong and self-confident sources of supply, and highly motivated and rapidly growing wellsprings of demand. Such a powerful combination suggests that a general renaissance in American philanthropy is about to begin. If so, corporations will play a strong supporting role.

Four themes will characterize the content of business participation in America's philanthropic future. First, the likely emergence of small and mid-size firms as the engines of corporate giving. Second, the use of philanthropy by American companies conducting business abroad as a tool of international expansion and as a symbol of good corporate citizenship. Third, the salutary impact of technological advances on the aspirations and operations of corporate philanthropy. And, finally, the ascendance of the employee as catalyst and stakeholder in the exercise of corporate responsibility.

Small and Mid-Size Firms:
The Engines of Business Philanthropy

An accumulating body of evidence suggests that the fastest-growing segment of philanthropy in the for-profit sector is small and mid-size business. Until recently, this nascent trend had been hard to detect. The principal sources of data on corporate giving—the Council on Financial Aid to Education, the Conference Board, and the Council on Foundations—have been concentrated almost exclusively on companies with at least five hundred employees and $100 million of revenue. Much less is known about the charitable habits of firms with fewer than five hundred employees, even though they account for 53 percent of all paid employment in America, than about the Fortune 500. But research is beginning to reveal how critical the role of smaller firms has become to business giving. Three studies point to their centrality in the years ahead.

One inquiry was devoted to examining small and medium-size business giving habits in the states of Indiana and Oregon.[2] It found that firms with fewer than five hundred employees and $10 million of revenue donate at least as much per employee and as a percentage of net income as do larger firms. The importance of that funding is magnified when one considers that small businesses, already dominant in industries like wholesale trade, retail trade, and construction, are currently the fastest-growing segment of commercial firms in America.

More is known not only about the size of small business philanthropy but also about its composition and character. Smaller firms donate a higher proportion of equipment and service compared to cash than do their larger counterparts. A much larger percentage of employees volunteer their time to charity as well. Only one in five small and mid-size companies that give substantial sums away account for the gifts in a formal contributions budget. Most treat donations as operating expenses or as part of the costs of goods sold.

What factors motivate giving by small and mid-size businesses? "The strongest factors affecting giving by small companies were the personal values of the owner, the condition of the business, social responsibility, public relations and the quality of the organization making the request."[3] In very small firms of 100 employees or fewer, contribution decisions are usually made by the owner. In mid-size firms of 101–500 employees, those decisions are likely to be delegated to a single manager. In firms of more than 500 employees, those choices tend to fall to a group of management employees. It follows that the more one understands about the owner-managers of smaller firms, the better one's grasp on the prognosis for new leading actors in business philanthropy to emerge.

In *Millionaire Next Door: The Surprising Secrets of America's Wealthy*, best-selling authors Thomas J. Stanley and William D. Danko reveal one of those secrets: that America has no fewer than 3.5 million millionaires. They own more than 50 percent of the total of $22 trillion of personal wealth that had accumulated in the United States by 1996. Although only 20 percent of Americans are self-employed, 80 percent of millionaires can be so described. Most are either professionals (lawyers, physicians, and accountants) or small business owners.[4] Many have been catapulted to affluence by employment in high-technology firms that are sources of extraordinary wealth for tens of thousands of Americans. Some of these firms, like Intel, Microsoft, Sun Microsystems, America Online, Yahoo, and Netscape are less than forty years old; others are even younger. Their employees and their professional and small-business counterparts that keep them company are generally first-generation millionaires, having inherited little if any funds from parents or other relatives.

It is from the decisions of the burgeoning professional and small-business millionaire class and those on the way to joining their ranks that charitable contributions increasingly flow. It is in them that great expectations for future growth are placed, for their amassed wealth is simply staggering and unprecedented. Such affluence renders philanthropic generosity more affordable than ever before in American history. That this already large cohort of millionaire professionals, entrepreneurs, and small business owners is likely to expand from five to seven times faster than the general population is a fundraiser's fantasy come true.

What's more, authors Stanley and Danko found that a major ingredient of success for the millionaire next door is fastidious attention to savings and investing. He or she saves at rates of 15 to 20 percent of annual income, or about four to five times more than the average American. He or she invests from 20 to 40 percent of household wealth in common stock. These are the habits of the affluent and those who aspire to that status. They work—and never with more telling results than from roughly 1991 to 1998.

A Dow Jones Industrial Average that took a full sixteen years to double from 500 (March 12, 1956) to 1,000 (November 1972) and another fifteen years to add another 1,000 points, reaching 2,000 (January 8, 1987), experienced 1,000-point advances henceforth with amazing speed. The next 1,000-point jumps occurred in relatively brief intervals of four years each (April 17, 1991, and February 23, 1995). Then, the increase from 4,000 to 5,000 took only nine months (November 21, 1995). Only eleven months later, the 6,000 threshold was crossed (October 14, 1996). By February 13, 1997, the Dow had climbed to 7,000, reaching 8,300 later that same year.[5] And on Friday, April 10, 1998, the Dow topped 9,000 for the first time.

Such a prolonged and vital bull market, breathtaking in the rapidity of its advances, reflects extraordinarily favorable conditions: low unemployment and inflation; high corporate earnings, productivity, and competitiveness; and a strong dollar. The stock market's extraordinary rise and the conditions contributing to it help explain the vast accumulation of wealth by investment-minded professionals and owners of small business. The wherewithal to give generously abounds. The secrets of America's millionaire class bode well for alert and energetic fundraisers. Indeed, the prospect for record-breaking growth in small-business giving is strong, provided Third Sector institutions are organized, mobilized, and galvanized to ask—early, often, and well.

The third source of evidence pointing to the potency of small business as a community-minded, active, and proud philanthropist comes from the Business Committee for the Arts. *BCA Report: 1995 National Survey of Business Support to the Arts* contains some remarkable findings about how robust business support of the arts has been, with small firms leading the way:

> Businesses with annual revenues of $1 million and more gave $875 million, a record high, to the arts, in 1994. Nearly half the businesses surveyed supported the arts, and allocated an average 19% of their

philanthropic budget to the arts. *Nearly three-quarters of the total dollars contributed to the arts in 1994 came from companies with $1 million to less than $50 million in annual revenues* [emphasis added].

Businesses with annual revenues of $1 million and more gave $518 million to the arts in 1991. In 1991, 38% of businesses surveyed supported the arts and allocated an average 11% of their philanthropic budget to the arts.

The median dollar amount contributed to the arts in 1994 was $2,000, compared to $1,000 in 1991.[6]

Such figures are larger than those reported by the Contributions Council of the Conference Board and by *Giving USA*. Because these sources asked only large companies about their charitable support of the arts and generalize from that sample, they miss the high-growth philanthropic story. America's fast-growing small-business sector is its leading indicator.

There is a lot more to know about the small businesses of America in terms of both their existing philanthropy and their potential. What has been recently discovered, however, is enough to encourage nonprofits to solicit this part of the business community more energetically. Its members are sure to write new acts in the unfolding drama of business as benefactor.

Much of small business giving is obligation-based. Many small business owners locate their operations in or near their home towns. As members in good standing of the community, they are responsive to the needs and aspirations of their customers, who are also often friends, suppliers, and colleagues. The appeals of the local Boy and Girl Scout troop, baseball and soccer teams, community center and arts ensemble, for example, are difficult to turn away. When loyal customers solicit support for heartfelt causes and concerns, their requests can hardly be ignored or greeted with indifference. Campaigns for the United Way, the town social service organization, and the neighborhood Meals-on-Wheels operation gain momentum from peer solicitation, modeling, and pressure. Over time, contributions to charity come to be seen as something expected of small-business owners.

Real excitement is generated, however, when small and mid-size firms move from thinking of charitable contributions as societal dues to viewing them as business opportunities. Creativity and generosity blossom as philanthropy is extended as a form of enlightened self-interest as well as an expression of altruistic impulse. The ability to shape the support of nonprofit institutions and causes so as to motivate employees, enhance brand image, involve customers, and garner good will needn't be confined to large corporations. Three outstanding examples prove the point.

Take the case of Noah's Bagels.[7] A fast-expanding chain of retail breakfast and luncheon shops located principally in Los Angeles, the San Francisco Bay area, Washington, and Oregon, Noah's Bagels has built authentic notions of charity and community service into the core operations of each of its sixty outlets. Acknowledging its Jewish roots, the company explains that *tzedakah* (the Hebrew word for charity) means the moral duty to establish justice by helping those less fortunate. In a brochure available at every store, entitled "Caring Is Always Kosher," Noah's Bagels explains how its people practice *tzedakah* in the communities in which the company does business.

> For example, when a new store is opened in a community, Noah gives the crew who works in the store paid time off for community service projects in the neighborhood. (Painting homes for seniors, teaching art to homeless children, and tree planting are just some of the projects we've done.) Each store manager can also earn matching cash bonuses for the neighboring charity of choice.
>
> Helping others can taste good too. We built an urban farm where homeless families could grow crops. And unsold bagels are donated to homeless members of the community.

Each quarter, Noah's Bagels issues a customer newsletter, *Noah's News: All the Bagels Fit to Eat.* It is filled with examples of creative community service inspired by being part of the Noah Bagel family of employees and customers. A few headlines from the fall 1996 edition provide a sense of the fun, the enthusiasm, and the widespread participation engendered by the slogan "In Old New York It Was Kosher to Care. Same Thing Goes Today":

> Customers, Crew and Noah's Send 122 Kids to Camp
> Noah's Crew Hikes—and Bikes—to Fight AIDS
> "Bagels for Books" Open Up New Worlds for Oakland Kids.

The Noah's Bagel Foundation awards grants quarterly to "groups that strengthen the fabric of the community through services, education and the arts; expand opportunity for disadvantaged youth; and seek creative and entrepreneurial approaches to the problems our communities face."[8] Customers who know of worthy grantees are asked to offer their recommendations. Indeed, in all its literature, Noah's Bagels emphasizes how much it welcomes customer comments, suggestions, and ideas about community affairs and philanthropic activity.

Noah's fills the hole in their bagels with an energetic altruism that bonds the small-business enterprise to its customers and employees. The company's philanthropic activity benefits from being rooted in specific communities defined by geography.

It is also possible for small or mid-size firms to use advertising and direct mail appeals to associate the corporate image with public service. Working Assets, for example, is a long-distance company that claims to offer "the same reliability, the same savings, the same features" customers would receive from competitors like AT&T, Sprint, or MCI.[9] What makes it exceptional, however, is that it's socially responsible, devoting a portion of its charges to nonprofit groups working for "peace, equality, human rights and the environment."

In its sales literature, Working Assets claims to have given $7 million of donations over its decade-long business history, from 1986 to 1996. Company advertising and marketing campaigns highlight the work of such notable organizations as Handgun Control, Inc., Greenpeace, Human Rights Watch, and Doctors of the World. Mixed in with explicit pitches for business are testimonials from selected beneficiaries of Working Assets philanthropy, among them Marian Wright Edelman, the president of the Children's Defense Fund, and Randy Hayes, the executive director of the Rainforest Action Network.

As long-distance telephone calls have become a commodity-like service and the offerings of competitors have become virtually indistinguishable, a sensible approach is to endow the company's products with something beyond their intrinsic worth. For Working Assets Long Distance, that difference resides in the support of progressive causes.

The difference is apparent not only in the company funds destined to reach charitable causes but also in other aspects of its operation. Working Assets highlights the fact that its bills and letters to customers are printed on "unbleached, 100-percent, post-consumer recycled paper with soy-based ink."[10] On each month's bill, Working Assets describes two public policy issues in the news and offers customers the chance to call decision makers every day of the week (two calls each day, five minutes in length), free of charge. And in addition to donating 10 percent of all customer telephone charges to nonprofit groups, it offers on its bill the opportunity to "round up your check" above the monthly price to $35 or more. The difference between the balance due and the check written is sent to designated charities.

AT&T, Sprint, and MCI also contribute to charity and regard themselves as socially responsible. They might well take umbrage at Working Assets's claim to exclusivity. But none of them highlight charitable activity as central to its business appeal. Working Assets has occupied that position and carved out that niche. Apparently, it aims to demonstrate quite literally that giving pays.

The versatility of philanthropy as an asset of small business is manifest as well in Hanna, a mail-order company founded in 1983.[11] Hanna devotes itself to supplying "high quality children's clothing at the best possible price and to providing superior, informal customer service." To emphasize that Hanna's clothes are made to last and can be worn by more than one child, and to help needy families and their kids, the company developed a new idea. This was the Hannadowns program, a concept that merges the philanthropic instinct and the marketing imperative: If customers return their "Hannas" after their children no longer wear them, a 20 percent credit on the original cost is applied to any future purchase and all returned clothes are sent to needy women and children.

The Hannadowns program is mentioned in each issue of Hanna's direct mail catalogue. Customers return about 10,000 items each month and all receive Hannadowns credit. Since 1986, more than 500,000 items have been collected, and well over $2 million of customer credit has been redeemed. Hanna's is located in Portland, Oregon, whose foster care institutions, homeless shelters, and family centers receive the clothing. Clients are grateful for the help.

The same spirit of doing well by doing good informs Hanna's decision to donate annually in cash 5 percent of its pre-tax profit to charities and to match donations of its employees. Both are very rare practices for a small business. By year end 1995, Hanna's sales had reached $45 million.

Unlike patrons of Noah's Bagels, none of the customers of Working Assets and few of the buyers of Hanna's clothing have ever seen these companies' place of business or encountered one of their employees. But in all three cases, the business offering to customers embraces a spirit of giving that renders the offering firms readily identifiable and memorable.

These small companies have used philanthropy and community service to bond with their customers—inventively, creatively, and potently. The available evidence suggests strongly that their examples will multiply many times over in the years ahead.

Corporate Philanthropy: An American Export Grows Up

Among the few fast-growing components of corporate philanthropy is international giving. Starting at a very low funding base compared with such traditional categories of support as education, health, social services, and the arts in the United States, in total American companies increased overseas giving at rates of roughly 15 percent for each of the past seven years. The Conference Board reported that in 1988, the offshore donations of large firms had reached just $197 million. By 1995 that figure had roughly doubled to $400 million.[12] Considering that in these years overall corporate cash gifts to charity were essentially flat, this boomlet is impressive. Particularly so because it excludes financial support of overseas nonprofits from corporate expense budgets like advertising, marketing, sales, and public relations, and in-kind donations of equipment and personnel. Available data for those areas are fragmentary and unreliable, the more so because many companies direct international donations to U.S.-based nonprofits where they are credited to American domestic giving.

Something significant is underway. As they might ask in show business, does overseas giving have legs? Will it strengthen and endure? What business dynamics propel international philanthropy? What government policies and accomplishments undergird the commercial growth that will support it? And what has changed abroad to render philanthropy better understood and welcome almost everywhere?

One of the most dramatic transformations of American business in recent decades is its so-called globalization. Since the 1960s, the overseas international transactions of American companies have roughly tripled as a percentage of Gross Domestic Product (GDP), rising from 6 percent in 1964 to 17 percent in 1996. Another sign of the intensification of American commerce overseas is the expansion of U.S. investment. American-owned foreign assets grew threefold, from less than $1 trillion in 1982 to about $3 trillion by year-end 1993.[13] Such explosive growth is evidence that more and more American companies are traveling along an international commercial continuum with such destinations as a mature domestic business, a U.S.-centric business with some overseas operations and investment, a multinational business, and a truly global business.

Both a cause and consequence of this phenomenon have been major reductions in the cost of transportation and communication and the virtual elimination of tariffs and other barriers to international merchandise trade. Accelerating these trends of market openness and export expansion has been a major theme of the Clinton administration's foreign policy. It reflects a priority high on the agenda of American business. Indeed, recent achievements of the U.S. policy are important indications of even more American overseas commercial activity in the years ahead.

In the Clinton administration's first term, what has been described as an international trade "triple play" was sharply executed.[14] The United States negotiated and the Senate approved a global treaty embodying a major new round of tariff reductions on goods, the creation of a World Trade Organization equipped with dispute resolution authority, and a commitment to begin in earnest unprecedented negotiations about reducing barriers to trade in services. This worldwide agreement was complemented by the formation of two major regional trade alliances of which the United States is a leading member—the North American Trade Agreement (NAFTA), a formal treaty that received Senate approval, and the Asia Pacific Economic Cooperation (APEC) accord. Both NAFTA and APEC members are committed to widening and deepening trade among its members.

The Clinton administration views these pacts as indispensable to promoting the growth of U.S. exports. The pacts embody a shared belief that competition, market openness, and deregulation are essential to global prosperity. Immediately after President Clinton's reelection, U.S. trade negotiators pushed forward on two important fronts. First, they consummated two international copyright treaties designed to protect intellectual property in digital form and as transmitted by cable, satellite, VCR, and over the Internet. The treaties protect publishers, record firms, and entertainment companies that market their product overseas; they also hold out the promise that the content originated by those industries will be fairly compensated. Both await ratification.

Several weeks later, on February 10, 1997, Charlene Barshefsky, the U.S. Trade Representative (USTR), announced a breakthrough global pact on liberalizing telecommunication services. Most countries deliver telephone services to their people and businesses through government-owned monopolies. They are now committed to genuine competition. Foreign carriers are assured of gaining market entry and of the opportunity to invest substantially in existing dominant carriers. Incipient competition combined with deregulation is expected to yield huge reductions in the price of international long-distance calls and in transmitting data across national borders. As a result, demand for these services will soar.

The compromise resolution of tough issues like market access, foreign investment, and the overall rules of competition in the telecommunications industry marks a major turning point in widening world trade. It would not be surprising if such momentum leads to comparable global agreements in insurance, financial, and travel-related services. Also on the agenda for the future is the accession of countries to NAFTA, beginning with Chile; implementing the free trade goals of APEC; and serious exploration of a new economic alliance with the Europeans, or TAFTA (Trans-Atlantic Free Trade Agreement).

The federal government's resolve to help expand U.S. international trade extends beyond the USTR. The State Department has given the subject high-priority attention. Foreign service officers, historically unfamiliar with business and economics, are doing their homework on the interests of American firms in the countries to which they are posted. Former secretary of state Warren Christopher's pledge to have State Department officials view U.S. business as a principal client of their work has been redeemed so quickly that pundits now refer to the diplomatic corps as "peddlers in pinstripes." His successor, Madeleine Albright, places a premium on commercial diplomacy as well. At the Commerce Department, export promotion has always been a key mission. Under Commerce Secretaries Ron Brown and William Daly, it was pursued energetically and tenaciously. The special focus has been on the big emerging markets, like China, Malaysia, Indonesia, India, Russia, Brazil, Mexico, Poland, Turkey, and Argentina. Even the president and the vice president have not been hesitant to involve themselves personally in advancing America's business abroad whenever their intervention was necessary to ensure fair treatment.

All this activity closely corresponds to the cardinal importance placed by U.S. businesses on enlarging their overseas markets and improving their global competitive position. It is no accident that many of America's most successful firms derive substantial portions of their revenues from outside the United States. Of the twenty companies at the top of *Fortune* magazine's most-admired list for 1997, fifteen either already receive more than 40 percent of their total revenue from outside America or are well on their way to achieving that objective: Coca-Cola, Merck, Microsoft, Johnson & Johnson, Intel, Pfizer, Procter & Gamble, 3M, Hewlett-Packard, Corning, Levi-Strauss Company, Walt Disney, McDonald's, General Electric, and Boeing.[15]

Because corporate philanthropy is closely aligned to business interests, one would expect to see a wider role for corporate contributions in advancing international business. Not only is that very dynamic fully at work, it will also become a mainstay of American corporate philanthropy over the next decade.

Typically, the involvement of philanthropy in foreign affairs begins with a corporate connection to American nonprofits that employ experts on international politics and economics and on the specific countries in which a company wishes to conduct business. The growth in number and influence of American nonprofit think tanks devoted to a better understanding of foreign nations owes much to corporate participation and financial support. With such terms as export quotas, foreign exchange rates, unilateral economic sanctions, GATT, WTO, NAFTA, and APEC entering the working vocabularies of more and more business executives, they are often found at gatherings where such matters are intelligently discussed.

Organizations and institutions like the Berkeley Economic Roundtable, the Council on Foreign Relations, the American Enterprise Institute, the Center for Strategic and International Studies, the Brookings Institution, the Institute for International Economics, the Japan Society, and the Asia Society house and attract experts on the facilitators and inhibitors of global trade. In addition to these and many other freestanding public-policy organizations, corporations find it useful to associate with university-based institutes devoted to the study of industries, countries, and issues of international interest. These nonprofits provide not only a sanctuary for learning from resident subject matter authorities but also a place to network with both American movers and shakers and their foreign counterparts. In addition, the task forces they convene, the studies they commission, and the policy recommendations they advance do much to shape the climate of opinion in Washington and in overseas capitals.

A second form of expression of early interest in nonprofits by companies exploring overseas market entry is support for foreign-based public policy organizations and the overseas affiliates of U.S. nonprofits. Aspen Berlin, Aspen Tokyo, and Aspen Italia, the World Economic Forum with its now-famous annual global conference in Davos, the Trilateral Commission, the Royal Institute of International Affairs, and the Bildersberg Group are among those that attract senior executive involvement. As in America, corporate philanthropy helps open the doors to such institutions and provides them a share of the wherewithal to conduct business or to undertake specific programs and projects of mutual interest.

The third area of early philanthropic involvement for American companies in international matters is responding favorably to calls for humanitarian assistance wherever in the world the companies are intent on building a business. Offers of cash, food, medical supplies, drugs, and equipment to help the victims of natural disasters or assist the casualties of manmade calamities (civil wars, ethnic rivalries, and social disorder) are not uncommon for American companies. The city of Kobe, in Japan, along with Bosnia and Rwanda were major sites of worldwide humanitarian assistance in 1995 and 1996.

Firms with operations or aspirations in particular countries might choose to assist U.S.-based nonprofits that provide emergency relief services. Often referred to as NGOs (nongovernmental organizations), nonprofits like CARE, the International Red Cross, the International Rescue Committee, the U.S. Committee for UNICEF, and Catholic Relief Services are the beneficiaries. Other companies choose to direct support to NGOs organized inside the afflicted country. Still others steer their funds to multilateral institutions like UNICEF or the United Nations Development Program.

It is a sign of increased voluntary philanthropic interest that American NGOs are becoming far less reliant on federal government funding than was the case only a short time ago. In late 1995, the General Accounting Office reported that whereas international humanitarian NGOs had received 42 percent of their budgets from the U.S. government in 1982, a decade later only 13 percent of their funding came from federal sources.[16] These NGOs have successfully appealed to foreign governments and to private philanthropy, including corporations, in an effort to broaden and diversify their support.

These manifestations of corporate contributions activity frequently broaden as firms expand their business overseas. As their employment grows, as office space is leased and factories built, and as foreign firms are retained to supply goods and services, corporate operations cast burdens on public facilities. Consequently, companies are asked to contribute to building expansion or curriculum enrichment at schools in which the children of their employees are enrolled. They are approached to assist health care organizations located close to where employees live and work. They are solicited to help celebrate local holidays and support leading cultural events. Rare is the American company unwilling to discharge such minimal community obligations.

As in the case of small business, the most enduring impact of philanthropic engagement comes as firms recognize the opportunities and not just the duties of being a good corporate citizen. Companies with a substantial overseas presence need to source not just their goods and services but their human talent as well. Alert firms ask how philanthropy can connect them to foreign universities and, therefore, to the best and brightest of their graduates and the research products of their laboratories and institutes.

Companies wishing to become or remain important and recognized players in overseas markets need to cultivate relations with key figures in business, government, and the media. How can philanthropic support of home-grown nonprofit institutions facilitate coming to know these individuals and help command their attention?

Companies seeking acceptance as indigenous economic forces rather than as branches of a U.S.-centric operation find advantages in being viewed as citizens in good standing of the countries in which they do business. Being responsive to societal needs and joining others in helping to satisfy them through culturally appropriate ways and means offers a competitive edge.

A handful of American firms have appreciated both these obligations and benefits for decades. The reputation of Chase Bank in Latin America for the promotion of its gifted visual artists is widespread. IBM, celebrating its eightieth anniversary of continuous operations in countries like Japan and Germany, enjoys a well-earned high regard for its many societal contributions as well as its business leadership. Citibank's underwriting of the European, Asian, and Latin American tours of the New York Philharmonic demonstrate the potency of using the arts to entertain customers and influential groups overseas. The major, $5 million commitment of American Express to the "Save the Monuments Campaign," a program for the restoration and repair of a hundred long-neglected national landmarks located on seven continents, is an impressive piece of philanthropy.

What's new, then, and what's different?

The vigorous pursuit of business interest abroad continues to render international philanthropy desirable for U.S. companies. But around the world, the extraordinarily rapid growth of the Third Sector makes such giving possible and increasingly sought after. The leading scholar of the size and scope of nonprofits overseas, Lester Salamon, has characterized their recent rise as nothing short of revolutionary:

> From the developed countries of North America, Europe and Asia to the developing societies of Africa, Latin America and the former Soviet bloc, people are forming associations, foundations and similar institutions to deliver human services, promote grass-roots economic development, prevent environmental degradation, protect civil rights and pursue a thousand other objectives formerly unattended to or left to the state.
>
> The scope and scale of this phenomenon are immense. Indeed, we are in the midst of a global 'associational revolution' that may prove to be as significant to the latter twentieth century as the rise of the nation-state was to the latter nineteenth. The upshot is a global third sector: a massive array of self-governing private organizations, not dedicated to distributing profits to shareholders or directors, pursuing public purposes outside the formal apparatus of the state.[17]

Although new nonprofits are proliferating throughout the developing and developed world, it is important to recognize that they supplement an embedded base of existing institutions. Many Americans are surprised to learn of their number. Take Western Europe, for example. Whereas in the United States Third Sector employment as a percentage of the national total is 6.8 percent, comparable figures for France (4.2 percent), the United Kingdom (4 percent), Germany (3.7 percent), and Italy (1.8 percent) are hardly insignificant. Another indicator of the economic role of nonprofits is to weigh its expenditures as a proportion of GDP. Here, too, the United States leads at 6.3 percent. But to the surprise of many, the United Kingdom at 4.8 percent, Germany at 3.6 percent, France at 3.3 percent, and Italy at 2 percent register Third Sector organizations as a substantial part of their respective economies. All of these figures exclude organized religions and the charities associated with them. Their inclusion would lift Third Sector impact noticeably.[18]

My optimism about the future growth and maturation of international philanthropy is rooted in a recognition of the enormous scale and influence of existing nonprofit organizations, combined with the new cohort of charitable institutions on the scene. Their collective clout is being felt as a recognition spreads that the problem-solving capacities of government acting alone are severely circumscribed, for several reasons. Public resources are finite. Taxpayer resistance to new taxes is high. Voluntary associations are forming or strengthening as vehicles for self-improvement, self-expression, and self-help; they have tapped new societal sources of energy and initiative complementary to the indispensable exercise of state power.

Corporations will pay attention to such a major social transformation. The most astute among them will figure out how to ally themselves with what are sometimes called "nonstate actors." It hardly goes unappreciated that today's NGOs deliver more development assistance to Third World countries than does the entire U.N. system. When the time comes to renew China's Most Favored Nation (MFN) trade status, corporations cannot help but observe that Human Rights Watch and Amnesty International, for example, receive a respectful hearing. When NAFTA was being negotiated, the Bush administration was compelled to respond to a broad coalition of NGOs concerned about pollution, health and safety, immigration, and child labor. Ultimately, the agreement incorporated labor and environmental issues.

In numbers alone, the ascension of nonprofits abroad makes their presence dramatically different in degree. Their collective influence on the delivery of services and on public-policy decisions makes their impact different in kind. Jessica Matthews, the president of the Carnegie Endowment for International Peace, makes the case:

> At a time of accelerating change, NGOs are quicker than governments to respond to new demands and opportunities. Internationally, in both the poorest and richest countries, NGOs, when adequately funded, can outperform government in the delivery of many public services. Their growth, along with that of the other elements of civil society, can strengthen the fabric of the many still-fragile democracies. And they are better than governments at dealing with problems that grow slowly and affect society through their cumulative effect on individuals—the "soft"

threats of environmental degradation, denial of human rights, population growth, poverty and task of development that may already be causing more deaths in conflict than are traditional acts of aggression.[19]

This combination of quantitative impact and qualitative clout, of service delivery potency and government influence is the kind of development that changes minds and moves resources. Bullishness about the common stock of overseas business philanthropy is fully merited. Expect, therefore, for continued growth in the corporate share of the $2 billion of American philanthropy directed to international affairs as of 1995. More companies will join the early pioneers of overseas giving. To do otherwise isn't just uncharitable; it would deprive these companies of an important business asset.

Technology Ascendant, Philanthropy Transformed

A vast swath of uncharted territory awaits nonprofit adventurers and explorers, philanthropists not least among them. What do technological advances portend for soliciting gifts, for grantmaking, and most important, for the aspirations and operations of nonprofits? Surely, this consequential and tantalizing question is high on the agenda of every forward-looking Third Sector organization.

What will be the collective impact of such technological innovations as e-mail, voice mail, fax, compact (digital) disk, cellular phone, beeper, VCR, cable (and interactive) television and computer software generation on philanthropy in general and on corporate philanthropy in particular?

How will ease of access to the Internet, to surfing the Web, to accessing information from multiple data bases, to using digital video disk, and to encountering ideas and people in cyberspace affect the Third Sector's constituent institutions? How will using multimedia devices facilitate learning and accelerate the processing of work? How will easy access to interactive modes of communication to express views and respond to questions help condition the new environment of philanthropy?

From a commercial perspective, it is not yet at all clear whether the World Wide Web will become an advertising medium, a subscription medium, a transaction medium, or constitute some blend of these business arrangements. If the electronic relationship of buyers and sellers is fuzzy, equally obscure is how grantors and grantees and nonprofits and their clients will be affected by the awesome capabilities of emerging technology. Hardly a sizable educational, health, social service, or arts institution and scarcely a substantial foundation is not in the throes of considering this very question.

Already, significant change has taken place, evident in the ubiquity of voice mail in business; the extraordinary levels of market penetration of telephone answering machines, cable television, the computer, the fax machine, the VCR, the pager and the wireless phone at home and at work; the growing number of people who telecommute at least several days each week, if not full time; and the exponential increase in Internet access subscribers and of calls to toll-free databases. The rapid proliferation of corporate, private foundation, and nonprofit Web pages is noteworthy. Something is going on when Third Sector professionals compare notes on how many "hits" their Web page enjoyed last week.

But these are merely illustrations of early adaptation to the possibilities afforded by technology. Compared with what is shortly to come, they are elementary and rudimentary. The unprecedented speed and comprehensiveness of technological change carries profound consequences for nonprofits. Some are imaginable. Most are simply unknown.

Pilot experiments in interactive media with U.S. families that were conducted by companies like Time-Warner, Disney, and Microsoft are revealing. They suggest that Americans are eager to use these powerful new means of communication to learn about what's going on in their towns and neighborhoods and to stay in touch with the movers and shakers of their immediate environment. If it is true that access to the Internet and to other multimedia channels of communication will be used at least as much to discover the news from the local school, church, community center, Boy Scout troop, or theater as to learn about a national event or an international development, then the salutary contribution of nonprofits to social cohesion could be even more far-reaching in the future.

In what ways this digital revolution will influence how we govern nonprofits, deliver services through their good offices, reach to those with a need or an interest, and spur involvement, even stimulate generosity, represents an almost virgin field ready for cultivation. Bold pioneers, venturesome cartographers, and thoughtful gardeners will be in high demand.

Will the Internet help even the playing field among competing grant applicants by allowing all comers equal and timely access to donor information, through means far more accessible and up to date and far less costly than is now the case with predominantly printed materials?

Will the Internet significantly increase the interaction among grantors, among grantees, and between donors and donees? Will the Internet encourage conversational learning between philanthropic staff and nonprofit executives? For example, a donor might release draft guidelines to a target audience of nonprofits seeking comments and criticisms before releasing them in final form. Or, donors might create "chat rooms" for subsets of their donees to explore a problem or exploit an opportunity. Since turnaround is fair play, a group of nonprofits might address an issue of shared philanthropic concern by using the Internet to project messages to an audience of donors?

Other questions arise: How conducive will the Internet be to improving the efficiency and effectiveness of processing foundation business? How much will it reduce travel? To what degree will it allow common questions and concerns to be handled by electronic broadcast bulletins rather than by one-on-one correspondence, phone calls, or meetings? In what other myriad ways can the labor- and paper-intensive processes of philanthropy be re-engineered, using technology to cut expenses, add value, and speed decision time?

Each passing month records startling advances in the capabilities of software and communications technology. But for the vast preponderance of foundations and nonprofit organizations, the revolution in technology has not yet begun to transform the way business is conducted, let alone altered how it is conceived. That time fast approaches, however.

It would be well for the corporations whose inventiveness and innovations gave rise to these capabilities to turn some of their philanthropic attention to possible Third Sector use. A few do, but they need a lot more company. Helping to realize the potential gain to nonprofits from using technology well is a mission worthy of many enlightened corporations. The benefits include increased organizational effectiveness. Another advantage is the ability for companies to reach their employees, clients, customers and volunteers faster, more reliably, and at lower cost, or to bring their social agendas to the attention of targeted audiences. By such supportive undertakings business has within its power the capacity to prove beyond any doubt that giving works.

Employee-Driven Philanthropy

Conventional wisdom has it that the diffusion of modern technology to the American workplace and home has empowered employees, enabling authority to be spread widely throughout the corporation. Access to information has never been easier and quicker. Managers much closer to the customer or to a production process can make informed and timely decisions on the spot. The delays and distortions associated with orders emerging from the upper reaches of a distant hierarchy to the workers below are now regarded as anathema. Modern corporations are oriented more horizontally, less vertically. Action is taken more in deference to who knows what, rather than who knows whom, or where someone happens to be situated on an organization chart.

The same hardware and software capabilities that are helping to convert the workplace more to a participatory environment hold promise as well of transforming the relationship of employees to corporate philanthropy. Testing the sentiments of a segment of employees about the value of potential philanthropic initiatives is easy, fast, and inexpensive. E-mail and teleconferencing simplify the process of eliciting employee views on possible community relations projects. Convening employee focus groups to discuss the implications of a projected change in matching gift rules is as simple as setting up a "chat room" on the subject or combining fax transmissions with telephone conference calls. To reverse field, reaching employees with news about opportunities for voluntary service or with requests for assistance to help meet sudden community needs is no more than an audio broadcast or Internet message bulletin away.

The abundance of communication options available to corporate philanthropists will alter not just how and how often employees are informed and engaged. It will transform existing policy in many firms. The following example should help enliven this prediction.

At most companies in 1997, the United Way continues to monopolize the charitable payroll deduction program. This remarkable invention encourages employees to reach a decision only once each year about their level of charitable contribution. After they do, portions of every paycheck are automatically deducted and electronically transmitted to the United Way. In no small measure, the powerful advantages of reaching captive audiences of employees with a charitable appeal and offering them a convenient way to give explains how United Way became a $3.5 billion annual fundraising juggernaut.

The next decade will see the end of United Way's privileged insider use of payroll deduction and dominance of highly visible employee workplace solicitation. Irresistible pressures will arise to give other selective groups of charities, like united arts drives, environmental coalitions, and disease-specific appeals, opportunities to reach employees and to invite use of the charitable payroll deduction in their name. Just as matching gift eligibility rules have been significantly liberalized to allow not just colleges and universities but many kinds of charitable organizations to participate, so too will openness and choice come to characterize the diversity of nonprofits having access both to employees and to payroll deduction plans.

The employee who, on any given day, can change with a single phone call how his or her 401(k) savings plan is invested or several times a year change health insurance features by tapping on a computer keyboard will find charitable paternalism inexplicable and intolerable. Choice beckons.

Technology enables employees of any income class to be better informed about available options when they decide how to donate funds and to volunteer their time. It permits those in charge of the philanthropic function to determine employee preferences and increase employee awareness and knowledge as never before. Concurrently, the American economy has produced hundreds of thousands of executives and small-business owners who are themselves able to be important individual philanthropists. So record-breaking have been corporate earnings, so buoyant and long-lasting has been the rise in the American stock market, and so conducive to private wealth creation are deferred compensation schemes and stock option set-asides that trillions of dollars will transfer between generations over the next decade.

The corporation as benefactor may become less important to nonprofits than the corporation as identifiable network through which wealthy and, it is hoped, charitably generous businesspeople are reached. The nonprofit that sees a business as a medium through which to access a significant and growing number of affluent individuals as well as a purely institutional source of support will gain a sustainable fundraising advantage. The corporate philanthropist, eager to maximize the favorable public impact of the firm will regard senior executives not just as institutional allies and partners but as potential large-scale benefactors able to give generously on the strength of their own considerable resources.

To put it plainly, the charitable contributions record of Microsoft, Berkshire-Hathaway, Time-Warner, and Nike, for example, may well matter less to Third Sector organizations than the generosity of their respective chairmen and senior officers—Bill Gates, Warren Buffett, Ted Turner, and Phil Knight. They number among the roughly seventy-five members of a relatively new but fast-growing "club" in America, one composed exclusively of billionaires. That growing cadre and the some 250,000 American decamillionaires collectively wield far more philanthropic clout than the companies that spawned their wealth. Insiders who are in a position to influence the size and direction of the giving of such Americans will perform an extraordinarily valuable service.

The wholly unprecedented accumulation of private affluence over the past decade and a half promises to open a new era in the annals of American philanthropy. The current generation's equivalent of Andrew Carnegie, John D. Rockefeller, and Julius Rosenwald are barely identified. Who will join George Soros and Walter Annenberg as the new giants of philanthropy? The numbers of Americans with the capacity to give away $10 million or more each year is simply staggering.

Corporate philanthropy has never constituted *more* than 7 percent of total cash charitable contributions in any given year. Individual donations have never been *less* than 84 percent. One way to articulate a major challenge both to corporate philanthropists and to fundseeking nonprofits is to ask this question: How can the resources of the modestly growing 7 percent be leveraged to expand significantly the sums contributed by individuals? Casting the issue this way offers another powerful reason to place employees in general, and wealthy executives in particular, at the center of the corporate philanthropic enterprise. For they will determine more than any other force whether giving grows at rates consistent with America's economic good fortune or drifts into an era of complacent self-indulgence.

In the future, corporate philanthropists will be judged not only by the charitable performance of their business but also by how well employee contributions in time and treasure were encouraged and rewarded. In the future, nonprofits will assess their corporate fundraising not just by what a target business opted to donate but also by how many of its employees give substantially. The burgeoning affluence and economic comfort of millions of Americans remind us that insofar as philanthropy is concerned, individuals are the dog, companies the tail.

Creating a corporate culture of caring will redound to the benefit of generosity all around. Employees will take pride in knowing that the business that absorbs so much of their time and attention stands for something beyond the undiluted pursuit of self-interest. Companies will reflect in their giving the public-spirited inclinations of their employees.

Whether from their perspective as donors, volunteers, or customers, employees are emerging as leading forces in recasting the role of corporate philanthropy for the new millennium.

THE FOUR NASCENT TRENDS JUST DEPICTED are animated by corporate philanthropy as a dynamic and growing enterprise. It is an endeavor hardly confined to large business or circumscribed by America's borders. It is a craft soon to be transformed by the deployment of affordable innovations in communication and information-processing technology. And it is an undertaking driven by the dedicated efforts of employees. They bring their values about giving and volunteering to the workplace. Throughout the year, they demonstrate that business success is not at all incompatible with the exercise of social responsibility—quite the contrary.

The unbounded potential of corporate philanthropy and related activity is woven into the American creed that a free people can organize to solve problems collectively. An indispensable expression of that solidarity is democratic self-government. Another critical and pre-existing form of social compact is manifested in voluntary activities organized for public benefit. Employees may arrive at work each morning believing that there is no reason the companies that retain them cannot help to advance American democracy and enrich its pluralistic Third Sector. At the end of the day, a healthy polity and a thriving social order set the context for personal fulfillment and professional success. Contributing to these outcomes is both benevolent and self-interested. It is the product of an optimistic, can-do attitude. It is also the result of minding one's business.

AT&T: *OnStage*®

Request for Proposals
1999

Since 1985, AT&T: *OnStage*®—along with the AT&T New Plays for the Nineties Project—has reflected AT&T's long-standing commitment to innovation and diversity in the theater arts, with particular attention to the work of women and artists of diverse cultures. Sixty-seven new works have been supported at sixty-nine theater organizations in the United States, United Kingdom and Canada through AT&T: *OnStage*®. (Chronology enclosed.) AT&T is proud of its collaboration with these works and theaters and looks forward to the continuation of its AT&T: *OnStage*® initiative.

Invitational Process

A select group of theater companies in the United States, Canada, Singapore and the United Kingdom have been invited to submit proposals for work scheduled for mainstage presentation during calendar year 1999. Theaters selected for invitation are located in areas where AT&T has a major employee or business presence, and are noted for their outstanding artistic achievement, commitment to the production of new work, and ongoing work with women and artists of diverse cultures.
An advisory committee of distinguished members of the theater community will assist AT&T with the selection process for this initiative.

Eligible Productions

AT&T: *OnStage*® is an initiative aimed at supporting fully produced mainstage productions, not at the developmental stages of new work. Proposals will be eligible in three categories:

- **premieres of new plays or music/theater works in mainstage productions.** These new works must not have previously received critical reviews or notices as fully staged productions, though they may have had readings and workshops during a developmental phase;

- **productions of less frequently performed, preexisting theatrical material,** for which full-scale remounting offers the potential to expand the canon of literature available for the theater;

- **newly commissioned English language translations** of plays not frequently performed in English in the eligible countries.

Co-productions of new work are invited and encouraged. Two or more theaters that have been invited to submit work for AT&T: *OnStage*® may team as co-producers, but only organizations that have been invited may participate.

In general eligible works should be scheduled for production during **calendar year 1999**, but in any case, with a first performance date no earlier than November, 1998.

Support for Production and Promotion

The AT&T Foundation will fund a portion of production expenses connected with the mainstage production of a new play or music theater work. Grants will be based upon overall production budgets and will generally range from $25,000 to $75,000 (U.S.).

This premiere production will be considered part of the international AT&T: *OnStage*® initiative. In some but not all cases, in addition to grant support, AT&T may elect to provide advertising and/or special events for the production. Theaters in the United Kingdom should note that the AT&T Foundation awards grants rather than sponsorship support, and therefore, the value-added tax is not applicable.

Support for Playwrights and Composers

In addition to the production award and promotional support to the theaters, the author, translator and/or composer of an AT&T: *OnStage*® production is eligible to receive an individual award of $5,000 (U.S.) each. These grants must be over and above commissioning or other fees that have been negotiated between the theater and the artist(s). No more than $10,000 (U.S.) will be granted to the authors of any work; if there are more than two persons involved, the $10,000 (U.S.) will be divided equally among the writers and composers. The grant to the author(s) will be made to the theater for subsequent payment to the writers.

The theater should include a request for this regrant in its proposal and proposal budget. Theaters are requested to encourage the playwright, translator and/or composer to utilize these grants to be in residence during the production's rehearsal period and previews.

Crediting

Plays and musicals selected for production will be presented as part of AT&T: *OnStage*®, AT&T's international theater program. AT&T will collaborate with the theater to obtain maximum recognition for the production and AT&T.

AT&T must be the primary corporate sponsor for the first-time mainstage production, though there may be non-corporate donors. The play or musical must be recongnized by the theater company as being produced as part of the AT&T: *OnStage*® program, which must be acknowledged as the primary corporate sponsor. Appropriate recognition of AT&T: *OnStage*® and AT&T must be provided in all subsequent productions of the work where the premiering theater is credited.

Eligibility Requirements for Invited Theaters

Theater companies must meet the following criteria to be eligible to submit works for consideration:

- If based in the United States, the theater company must be a non-profit, tax-exempt organization under Section 501(c)(3) of the Internal Revenue Code.

- If located in a country other than the United States, the theater company must demonstrate that it is engaged exclusively in charitable, educational, literary and/or public service activities. No part of a theater company's income may benefit any private individual, and no substantial part of its activities may consist of efforts to influence governmental legislation or candidates for public office.

- The theater must have been in operation for at least five years as a professional company, compensating both managerial and artistic personnel.

- The theater must be located in community where AT&T has a major presence.

Deadline

The deadline for receipt of proposals is Friday, June 12, 1998. **This is not a postmark deadline.** Proposals must be **received** by the AT&T Foundation on or before this date.

How to Submit a Work for Consideration

Theaters submitting a proposal for <u>AT&T: *OnStage*</u>® should submit the following information:

1. <u>Three copies</u> of the script or book. The script or book should be **unbound** on 8 1/2" by 11" white paper, typed **on one side only** and ready for duplication. Please number the pages.

2. <u>Three copies</u> of complete project proposal which should include:

   - production description with full history of readings, workshops, and other development of the play or musical;

   - estimated production budget of the play or musical in U.S. dollars;

   - biography of the author, playwright, and/or composer;

   - other pertinent production information such as director, designer, musical director, choreographer, etc.;

   - personal statement by the company's artistic director reflecting his/her thinking in selecting and producing the play or musical, and as well as the theater's plans for audience educational programs.

3. <u>Three copies</u> of a demonstration tape of songs or other selections from the score or any incidental music for the score of a musical.

4. *One copy* of the company's most recent audited financial statement.

5. For theaters located in the United States, *one copy* of the Internal Revenue Service determination letter for Section 501(c)(3) tax-exempt status.

6. For theaters located in other countries, *one completed copy* of the accompanying AT&T Foundation Instructions for Non-U.S. Charitable Organizations form.

Questions concerning this request for proposals may be directed to:

Valerie D'Antonio	OR	Valerie Bové
212-387-6562		212-387-4872
vdantonio@att.com		vbove@att.com

FAX:
212-387-4236

These materials should be submitted under one cover to:

<u>AT&T: *OnStage*®</u>
AT&T Foundation
32 Avenue of the Americas, 24th Floor
New York, NY 10013
ATTN: Valerie Bové

AT&T: *OnStage*®
Chronology

1996 – 1997

The Cripple of Inishmaan by Martin McDonagh (Royal National Theatre—London)

The Cider House Rules Part II by Peter Parnell (Seattle Repertory Theatre)

Violet by Brian Crawley and Jean Tesori (Playwrights Horizons—New York City)

Wedding Dance by Dominic Taylor (Crossroads Theatre—New Brunswick, NJ)

The Wake by Tom Murphy (Royal Court Theatre—London)

Whispering to Horses by Jo Carson (7 Stages—Atlanta)

Tongue of Bird by Ellen McLaughlin (Intiman Theatre Company—Seattle)

1995 – 1996

Ballad of Yachiyo by Philip Kan Gotanda (Berkeley Repertory Theater and South Coast Repertory—Costa Mesa, CA)

The Hunchback of Notre Dame: 1482 by Robert Rosen, Paul Walsh, Steve Epp (Theatre de la Jeune Lune—Minneapolis)

Unmerciful Good Fortune by Edwin Sanchez (Northlight Theatre—Chicago)

Slaughter City by Naomi Wallace (Royal Shakespeare Company—London)

1953 by Craig Raine (Almeida Theatre—London)

The Ends of the Earth by David Lan (Royal National Theatre—London)

A Park in Our House by Nilo Cruz (Magic Theatre—San Francisco)

The Innocence of Ghosts by Rosanna Staffa (Pan Asian Repertory Theatre—New York City)

1994

Seven Guitars by August Wilson (Goodman Theatre—Chicago)

Love! Valour! Compassion! by Terrence McNally (Manhattan Theatre Club—New York City)

The Wooden Hill by Don Hannah (Canadian Stage Company—Toronto)

Hiro by Denise Uyehara (East West Players—Los Angeles)

Bandido! by Luis Valdez (El Teatro Campesino and the Mark Taper Forum—Los Angeles)

The Woman Warrior adapted by Deborah Rogin (Berkely Repertory
	Theatre)
Dream on Monkey Mountain by Derek Walcott (Guthrie Theater—
	Minneapolis)
A Small World by Mustapha Matura (Arena Stage—Washington, DC)
The Devils by Liz Egloff (American Conservatory Theatre—San
	Francisco and NY Shakespeare Festival)

1993

El Greco by Bernardo Solano & William Hudson Harper (INTAR
	Hispanic American Arts Ctr.—New York City)
Chatsky by Alexander Sergeyerich Griboyedov (Almeida Theatre—
	London)
Bluebeard's Castle by Bela Bartok and *Erwartung* by Arnold Schoenberg
	(Canadian Opera Co.—Toronto)
The Butcher's Daughter by Wendy Kesselman (The Cleveland Play House)

1992

The Baltimore Waltz by Paula Vogel (Circle Repertory Company—New
	York City)
My Favorite Year by Joseph Dougherty and Stephen Flaherty (Lincoln
	Center Theatre—New York City)
Dream of a Common Language by Heather McDonald (Berkeley
	Repertory Theatre and The Women's Project—New York City)
Today by Valetta Anderson (Jomandi Productions—Atlanta)
Flyin' West by Pearl Cleage (Alliance Theatre—Atlanta)
The Gigli Concert by Tom Murphy (Almeida Theatre—London)

1991

A Wonderful Life adapted by Sheldon Harnick and Joe Raposo (Arena
	Stage—Washington, DC)
The Winter's Tale: An Interstate Adventure, a musical adaptation
	(Cornerstone Theater Company—Santa Monica, CA)
The White Rose by Lillian Garrett (Old Globe Theatre—San Diego)
The Heliotrope Bouquet by Scott Joplin and Louis Chauvin by Eric
	Overmyer (Center Stage—Baltimore and La Jolla Playhouse—San
	Diego)

Back to the Blanket by Gary Leon Hill (Denver Center Theater
    Company)
All for Love by John Dryden (Almeida Theatre—London)
When We Dead Awaken adapted by Robert Brustein (American Repertory
    Theatre—Cambridge, MA and Alley Theatre—Houston)

1990

Search and Destroy by Howard Korder (South Coast Repertory Theatre—
    Costa Mesa, CA)
Johnny Pye and the Foolkiller by Mark St. Germain and Randy Courts
    (George Street Playhouse—New Brunswick, NJ)
Square One by Steve Tesich (Second Stage Theatre—New York City)
Once on This Island by Lynn Ahrens and Stephen Flaherty (Playwrights
    Horizons—New York City)
Each Day Dies with Sleep by Jose Rivera (Circle Repertory Company—
    New York City and Berkeley Repertory Theatre)
Jekyll & Hyde by Leslie Bricusse and Frank Wildhorn (Alley Theatre—
    Houston)
Love Life by Kurt Weill and Alan Jay Lerner (American Music Theater
    Festival—Philadelphia)

1989

On the Town by Leonard Bernstein, Betty Comden and Adolph Green
    (Arena Stage—Washington, DC)
Mixed Blessings by Luis Santeiro (Coconut Grove Playhouse—Miami)
Dream Jumbo: Working the Absolutes by Robert Longo (UCLA Center for
    the Performing Arts—Los Angeles)
The Talented Tenth by Richard Wesley (Manhattan Theatre Club—New
    York City)

1988

Utamaro: The Musical a collaboration with the Japan America Theater in
    Los Angeles
Elmer Gantry by John Bishop and Mel Marvin (Ford's Theatre—
    Washington, DC and La Jolla Playhouse—San Diego)
AT&T: *OnStage*® at the Joyce Theatre—New York City presented *Green
    Card* by JoAnne Akalaitis (Mark Taper Forum—Los Angeles), *Six
    Characters in Search of an Author* adapted by Robert Brustein and

Big Time: Scenes from a Service Economy by Keith Reddin (American Repertory Theatre—Cambridge, MA)

The Grapes of Wrath by Frank Galati (Steppenwolf Theatre Company—Chicago)

"The 1987 New Plays Festival" at the Los Angeles Theater Center produced *The Film Society* by Jon Robin Baitz, *The Stick Wife* by Darrah Cloud, and *La Victima* by El Teatro de la Esperanza, and staged readings that included *Etta Jenks* by Marlane Meyer

Tango Apasionado by Graciela Daniele (INTAR Hispanic American Arts Center—New York City)

1986

Ajax adapted by Peter Sellars (American National Theater—Washington, DC)

Shout Up a Morning, based on music by Nat and "Cannonball" Adderley (La Jolla Playhouse—San Diego)

Roza by Harold Prince (Center Stage—Baltimore)

1985

Coyote Ugly by Lynn Seifert (Steppenwolf Theatre Company—Chicago)

In the Belly of the Beast based on the writing of Jack Henry Abbott (Wisdom Bridge Theatre—Chicago)

AT&T: *OnStage*®

1999 Application Cover Sheet

Theater Name: _____

Address: _____

_____

Contact Person: _____

Telephone: _____ Fax: _____

*Please collate the following items into **three sets**.*
(Do Not Bind, Staple, or Punch with Holes and Leave a 1" left margin)

☐ Three copies of the Application Cover Sheet.

☐ Three copies of the introduction/cover letter.

☐ Three copies of the personal statement by the theater's artistic director (maximum pages, 2).

☐ Three copies of the development history of the play or musical (maximum pages, 1).

☐ Three copies of the brief synopsis of the play or musical (maximum pages, 1).

☐ Three copies of the bios of the playwright and/or composer.

☐ Three copies of the production budget of the play or musical in U.S. dollars.

☐ Three copies of the script.

☐ Three copies of a demonstration tape of songs or other selections from the score or any incidental music for the score of a musical.

*Please collate the following items into **one set**.*

☐ One copy of the theater's overall outreach education program and/or evidence that the theater's programs are accessible to all segments of the community (maximum pages, 1).

☐ For theaters located in the United States, <u>one copy</u> of the Internal Revenue Service determination letter for Section 501(c)(3) tax exempt status.

☐ For theaters located outside the United States, <u>one copy</u> of the completed form: **AT&T Foundation Instructions for Non-U.S. Charitable Organizations.**

☐ <u>One copy</u> of the theater's Board list with affiliations.

☐ <u>One copy</u> of the theater's most recent audited financial statement.

☐ <u>One copy</u> of the theater's annual report.

Preface

1. These data are drawn principally from two sources: Virginia Hodgkinson et al, *Nonprofit Almanac, 1996–1997: Dimensions of the Independent Sector* (San Francisco: Jossey-Bass Publishers, 1996) and AAFRC Trust for Philanthropy, *Giving USA: 1996* (New York: AAFRC Trust for Philanthropy, 1996).

2. Lester Salamon, *America's Nonprofit Sector: A Primer* (New York: Foundation Center, 1992).

Introduction

1. These data are derived from three different sources: Virginia Hodgkinson et al, *Nonprofit Almanac, 1996–1997: Dimensions of the Independent Sector* (San Francisco: Jossey-Bass Publishers, 1996); AAFRC Trust for Philanthropy, *Giving USA: 1996* (New York: AAFRC Trust for Philanthropy, 1996); and, *Giving and Volunteering in the United States, Volume II: Trends in Giving and Volunteering by Type of Charity* (Washington, D.C.: Independent Sector, 1994).

2. These five key roles played by nonprofit institutions are usefully depicted in Lester Salomon's *Holding the Center: America's Nonprofit Sector at a Crossroads* (New York: The Nathan Cummings Foundation, 1997), 7–9.

3. AAFRC Trust for Philanthropy, *Giving USA: 1997* (New York: AAFRC Trust for Philanthropy, 1997).

Chapter 1

1. AAFRC Trust for Philanthropy, *Giving USA: 1997* (New York: AAFRC Trust for Philanthropy, 1997).

2. The business literature is replete with critiques of board performance ranging from failure to assess CEO performance to lax oversight of senior executive compensation. See, for example, the article by Arch Patton and John C. Baker, "From the Boardroom: Why Won't Directors Rock the Boat?" *Harvard Business Review* (November–December 1987): 10–18.

3. AT&T distributed to every employee its statement of mission and values, entitled "Our Business Ethics: Living Our Common Bond." It was issued in the

second year of Robert E. Allen's tenure as Chairman and CEO. Widely disseminated and discussed, few if any employees were unaware of its key themes.

4. Excerpt from AT&T's statement of mission and values, "Our Business Ethics: Living Our Common Bond," document undated, issued around 1995.

5. Peter F. Drucker, *The Practice of Management* (New York: Harper and Row, 1954), 34–88 and *Management: Tasks, Responsibilities, Practices* (New York: Harper and Row, 1954), 58–94.

6. Under the leadership of Bruce Jeffries-Fox, AT&T's director of public relations research, a wide variety of studies were completed and surveys commissioned about the impact of philanthropy on customer perceptions of the company. According to poll respondents, employees play a key role as carriers of the firm's reputation.

7. Ralph Nader, *Unsafe at Any Speed: The Designed-In Dangers of the American Automobile* (New York: Grossman, 1972).

Chapter 2

1. These two schools of thought labeled here as purist and utilitarian are portrayed at greater length in an article I wrote entitled "Caught Between Two Poles: Corporate Grantmakers Must Strike a Balance Between Idealism and Institutional Self-Interest," *Foundation News* (May–June 1985): 58–59, 63.

2. *A.P. Smith Manufacturing Company* v. *Barlow*, 13 N.J. 145 (1953).

Chapter 3

1. This excerpt is drawn from a widely circulated internal statement of AT&T's corporate mission and values entitled "Our Business Ethics: Living Our Common Bond."

2. Other nonprofits that welcomed AT&T's New York and New Jersey based senior executives to their boards of directors in the early years after divestiture included: Brooklyn Polytechnic Institute, the American Council for Education, the American Institute for Contemporary German Studies, the Merce Cunningham Dance Company, the New York City Opera, the Robert Wood Johnson Foundation, the Tri-State United Way, the United States Chamber of Commerce, and Tufts University.

3. Fred Hechinger, "Turnaround for the Public Schools?" *Harvard Business Review* (January–February 1985): 136–144.

4. The results of such corporate advocacy yielded news headlines like these: "Business Executives Urge More Spending on Nutrition for the Poor" — Associated Press; "Corporate Chiefs Promote Infant Care. Concerned About Future Work Force, CEOs Urge Increase in Program for Poor Children" — *Washington Post;* "Top Executives Urge Congress to Expand Nutrition Aid for Poor" — *Newark Star Ledger;* and, "Executives Sell Social Program" — *New York Newsday.*

5. Quoted in news story by Paul Taylor and David Broder, "New Drive to Aid Children Often Cuts Adult Programs: Spending Priorities Shift in Budget Squeeze," *Washington Post,* 27 March 1991.

Chapter 4

1. Growth in chamber music and opera is no less significant. In the decade 1979 to 1989, Chamber Music America claims its membership grew from 20 to 578 ensembles. According to Opera America, the audience for opera in the United States had swelled to 7.2 million in the 1994–95 season. American audiences and benefactors at that time supported no fewer than 136 professional opera companies.

2. These nationwide figures become perhaps even more vivid and consequential when cast in local terms. For example, according to a study conducted by the Port Authority of New York, in the New York metropolitan area alone nonprofit arts groups employed 27,000 people, spent $1.3 billion and yielded a total economic impact of $2.7 billion in 1992. Over the decade 1982–92, more than $1.3 billion was spent on the capital projects of nonprofit arts organizations in the region. See "The Arts as an Industry: Their Economic Importance to the New York–New Jersey Metropolitan Region," *Part I of Tourism and the Arts in the New York–New Jersey Region* (New York: The Port Authority of New York and New Jersey, 1993).

3. In the bestselling book by John Naisbitt and Patricia Aburdene entitled *Megatrends 2000: Ten New Directions for the 1990's* (New York: Avon Books, 1990), 76–78, much is made of the arts outpacing sports as America's dominant leisure activity.

4. Ibid., chapter 2, "Renaissance in the Arts," 50–86.

5. An excellent example of this body of work by Lou Harris and Associates from which the data is drawn regarding both arts attendance and public funding is *Americans and the Arts: Highlights from a Nationwide Survey of the Attitudes of the American People Toward the Arts* (New York: American Council for the Arts and the National Assembly of Local Arts Agencies, June 1996).

6. Ibid., 5.

7. Newspaper coverage of successful arts fundraising campaigns are extensive. The data that follows was drawn principally from the *New York Times,* the *Washington Post* and the *Los Angeles Times.*

8. See the *New York Times* front page story by Judith Miller, "Big Cultural Institutions Heating Up Efforts in Large-Scale Fundraising," 3 February 1997.

9. Rich Frank, "The Next 42nd Street," the *New York Times* op. ed., February 1998.

10. For comparative data on public expenditures to support the arts in European countries and the United States please see Naisbitt, *op. cit.,* 70–71; Robert

Hughes, "Why America Shouldn't Kill Cultural Funding: Pulling the Fuse on Culture," *Time*, 9 August 1995; and, Alan Riding "Europe Still Gives Big Doses of Money to Help the Arts," the *New York Times*, 1 May 1997.

11. Alan Riding, op. cit.

12. Naisbitt, op. cit., 63.

13. A superb source of data and analysis on giving to the arts and humanities can be found in Nina Kressner Cobb's *Looking Ahead: Private Sector Giving to the Arts and the Humanities* (Washington, D.C.: President's Committee on the Arts and Humanities, 1996).

14. Ibid., and the 1992, 1995, and 1996 editions of *Giving USA* (New York: AAFRC Trust for Philanthropy, 1992, 1995 and 1996).

15. *Business Committee for the Arts 1996 Survey of Member Companies* (New York: Business Committee for the Arts, 1996).

16. James Fallows, *Breaking the News: How the Media Undermines American Democracy* (New York: Pantheon Books, 1996).

17. Similarly, AT&T OnStage has granted funds to such well-established nonprofit theatres as Chicago's Steppenwolf Theatre Company and Windsom's Bridge, the LaJolla Playhouse, Washington D.C.'s Arena Stage, Lincoln Center Theatre, the Berkeley Repertory Theatre and Houston's Alley. Just as gratifying has been assistance to the lesser known George Street Playhouse in New Brunswick, New Jersey; the Alliance Theatre of Atlanta, Georgia; the Cornerstone Theatre in Santa Monica, California; New York's INTAR Hispanic American Arts Theatre; Theatre del la Jeune Lune of Minneapolis, Minnesota; San Francisco's Magic Theatre; and El Teatro Campesino of Los Angeles.

18. The other twenty "New Art/New Vision" winners in 1992–93 were: Long Beach Museum of Art, Long Beach, California; Museum of Contemporary Art, Chicago, Illinois; High Museum of Art, Atlanta, Georgia; the Houston Museum of Fine Arts, Houston, Texas; the Corcoran Gallery of Art, Washington, D.C.; the Studio Museum in Harlem, New York, New York; the Museum of Fine Arts, Boston, Massachusetts; the California Afro-American Museum, Los Angeles, California; Air Tower Mito Contemporary Art Center, Tokyo, Japan; Centrum Sztuki Wspclozesne Zamek Ujaztowski, Warsaw, Poland; the Detroit Institute of Art, Detroit, Michigan; the Ansel Adams Center of Photography, San Francisco, California; the Museum of African American Life and Culture, Dallas, Texas; the Museum of Contemporary Art, Los Angeles, California; the Museum of Modern Art, New York, New York; the Mexican Museum, San Francisco, California; the Newark Museum, Newark, New Jersey; the Pacific Asia Museum, Los Angeles, California; the Vancouver Art Gallery, Vancouver, British Columbia, Canada; and, the Walker Art Center, Minneapolis, Minnesota.

Chapter 5

1. The most complete articulation of this argument was advanced by Milton Friedman in *Capitalism and Freedom* (Chicago: University of Chicago Press, 1962).

2. The most thorough, detailed, and consistent source of such criticism of corporate philanthropy from the right wing of the political spectrum has been generated by the Capital Research Center. Its reports on American business and its charitable endeavors have been consistently negative.

3. Faye Wattleton, *Life on the Line* (New York: Ballantine Books, 1996), 419–423.

4. Albert J. Dunlap, *Mean Business: How I Saved Bad Companies and Make Good Companies Great* (New York: Random House, 1996), 200.

5. Ibid., 199.

6. Ira Millstein and Paul W. MacAvoy, "Corporate Philanthropy vs. Corporate Purpose," in *Corporate Philanthropy: Philosophy, Management, Trends, Future, Background* (Washington D.C.: Council on Foundations, 1982), 26.

7. Ibid., 26.

8. Albert J. Dunlap, op. cit., 200.

9. This excerpt is quoted from the decision in the landmark case *A. P. Smith Manufacturing Company v Barlow,* 13NJ145 (1953).

10. Although this chapter only quotes from three different *Patterns of Corporate Philanthropy,* the consistency and longevity of this right-wing critique of American philanthropy renders it especially noteworthy.

11. The summary quotation is taken from Stuart Nolan and Gregory P. Conko, *Patterns of Corporate Philanthropy: Executive Hypocrisy* (Washington, D.C.: Capital Research Center, 1993), 1.

12. Capital Research Center, *Patterns of Corporate Philanthropy* (Washington, D.C.: Capital Research Center, 1990).

13. Peter Frumkin, "A Distorted Portrait of Corporate Philanthropy," *Foundation News and Commentary,* March–April 1996, (Washington, D.C.: Council on Foundations, 1996).

14. Stuart Nolan, op. cit., 16.

15. Charles Murray, *On Losing Ground, American Social Policy, 1950–1980* (New York: Basic Books, 1984).

16. The stationery of the House of Representatives is to be used for official business purposes only.

17. It is perhaps significant that AT&T is the only company cited in the notes of Faye Wattleton's memoir, *Life on the Line,* op. cit.

18. Reynold Levy letter to Faye Wattleton, 12 March 1990.

19. This brief quotation is selected from a full-page advertisement that appeared in the *New York Times,* among other newspapers, during the week of April 23, 1990.

20. Planned Parenthood, letter to members and supporters, March 1990.

21. This advertisement appeared in the *New York Times,* among other newspapers, during the months June through September 1997.

22. Reynold Levy, reply letter to Alan Pifer in or about May 1990.

Chapter 6

1. The best way to discern corporate giving trends are to read carefully the reports of the Conference Board and of *Giving USA* (New York: AAFRC Trust for Philanthropy). They track the ebb and flow of cash philanthropy and how such movement relates to corporate earnings, hiring trends, and the national inflation rate, among other factors.

2. The author is indebted to the Conference Board and to Peter Malkin and his associates for these statistics. Mr. Malkin, together with Paul Newman and Ben Cohen of Ben and Jerry's, is organizing an effort to increase the level of corporate contributions to an average of 22% of pre-tax net profit for contributing firms. Mr. Malkin's father-in-law, Lawrence A. Wien, an accomplished lawyer, investor, and philanthropist, now deceased, headed the Committee to Increase Corporate Philanthropic Giving from 1979–84. It was credited with raising the consciousness of CEOs and boards of directors of *Fortune* 1000 firms to the value of and need for corporate philanthropy. As of this writing, the new initiative—not yet named—has developed an excellent case statement from which the cited data are drawn.

3. These data may be found in an unpublished case statement of the Malkin initiative described in note 2, above. The document is entitled "The Foundation for Corporate Social Investment: A Case Statement."

4. "Proof" is a song that can be heard on Paul Simon's *The Rhythm of the Saints,* Warner Brothers Records, Inc., 1990.

5. AAFRC Trust for Philanthropy, *Giving USA 1996* and *Giving USA 1997* (New York: AAFRC Trust for Philanthropy, 1996 and 1997).

6. U.S. Labor Department statistics as quoted in the *New York Times* in January and February 1996.

7. Melissa Berman, "Corporate Contributions," 29 April 1998, the Conference Board, Inc.

8. Quoted from Business for Social Responsibility brochure and membership application, May 1998. BSR's national headquarters is located at 1683 Folsom Street, San Francisco, California 94103-3722 (415-865-2500). Its president and CEO is Robert Dunn.

9. Milton Friedman, *Capitalism and Freedom* (Chicago: University of Chicago Press, 1962).

10. Robert Kuttner, "Of Our Time: Taking Care of Business," *The American Prospect,* July–August 1996, 8.

11. This polling data was cited in a 1993 internal analysis of corporate social responsibility entitled "Corporate Social Responsibility" written by Bruce Jeffries-Fox, Research Director, Public Relations, AT&T. It reviewed a wide range of sources on the subject.

12. James P. Shannon, *Corporate Giving: The Views of CEOs of Major American Companies* (Washington, D.C.: Council on Foundations, 1982).

13. James A. Joseph, *The Climate for Corporate Giving: Current and Future CEOs Talk About Giving in Today's Environment* (Washington D.C.: Council on Foundations, 1988).

14. AAFRC Trust for Philanthropy, *Giving USA 1996* (New York: AAFRC Trust for Philanthropy, 1996), 95–96.

15. Quotation taken from a speech of Robert C. Goizueta, "The Real Business of Atlanta," addressed to the Commerce Club, 17 March 1994, 9.

16. I am indebted for these figures to Gary Doran, an able division manager at AT&T, who has been associated with the corporation's philanthropy for almost two decades. He gathered the data at my request from published sources and through telephone interviews.

Chapter 7

1. In an unpublished but widely circulated study, Brian O'Connell, then President of the Independent Sector, now a professor at Tufts University, argued that private foundations were much more adequately staffed than were corporate contribution units.

2. The description of the work of LISC and data on its accomplishments are drawn from the organization's annual reports and other literature. LISC was a grantee of the AT&T Foundation while I served as President and trustee.

3. Frequent reference to this demographic "bulge" of school-age children and its consequences for primary and secondary schools were made by Albert Shanker, the president of the United Federation of Teachers and his successor, Sandra Feldman, in their "advertorials" that appeared weekly in the Sunday *New York Times*, among other newspapers around the country.

4. The description of the work of Teach America is derived from its literature. Teach America was a grantee of the AT&T Foundation while I served as President and trustee.

5. The Brooklyn Academy of Music's description is drawn from three sources: its literature, my experience as a member of BAM's audience, and BAM's status as an AT&T Foundation grantee while I served as President and trustee.

6. The profile of dimensions of the work of the Harvard University School of Public Health is drawn from its literature and its standing as a beneficiary of AT&T Foundation funds during my tenure there.

7. James A. Smith, *The Idea Brokers: Think Tanks and the Rise of the News Policy Elite* (New York: The Free Press of Macmillan, 1994), 58.

Chapter 8

1. The tendency of philanthropists to meet together and become in-grown and self-satisfied is a pet peeve of Gerald Freund. His recent book *Narcissism and*

Philanthropy: Ideas and Talent Denied (New York: Viking, 1996) offers a useful critique of the habits of professionals in the field.

2. Frances Ostrower, *Why the Wealthy Give: The Culture of Elite Philanthropy* (Princeton: Princeton University Press, 1995), 8.

3. Brian O'Connell usefully reviews roles of government and the Third Sector in "Reexamining the Roles and Relationships of Voluntary Organizations and Government" (occasional paper, Lincoln Filene Center for Citizenship and Public Affairs, Tufts University, 7 April 1995).

4. Frances Ostrower, op. cit., 136.

5. Frances Ostrower, op. cit., 18.

6. Julian Wolpert, *What Charity Can and Cannot Do* (New York: Twentieth Century Fund, 1995).

7. The figures in this chart were taken from AAFRC Trust for Philanthropy, Giving USA: 1984 Annual Report (New York: AAFRC Trust for Philanthropy, 1984), 33 and AAFRC Trust for Philanthropy, Giving USA: 1995 (New York: AAFRC Trust for Philanthropy, 1995), 79.

Chapter 9

1. The marked tendency of the board of directors of nonprofit institutions to expand in number during the 1970s and 1980s is noted by Francie Ostrower in her book, *Why the Wealthy Give: The Culture of Elite Philanthropy* (Princeton: Princeton University Press, 1995), 10. Ms. Ostrower's study focused on nonprofits located in New York City.

2. Dwight F. Burlingame and Patricia A. Frishkoff, "How Does Firm Size Affect Corporate Philanthropy?" in *Corporate Philanthropy at the Crossroads,* Dwight F. Burlingame and Dennis R. Young, eds. (Bloomington and Indianapolis: Indiana University Press, 1996), 86–101.

3. Ibid., 93.

4. Thomas J. Stanley and William D. Danko, *The Millionaire Next Door: The Surprising Secrets of America's Wealthy* (Atlanta: Longstreet Press, 1996).

5. Dow Jones Industrial Average quotations drawn from daily *Wall Street Journal* issues.

6. Business Committee for the Arts, *The 1995 National Survey of Business Support for the Arts* (New York: Business Committee for the Arts, 1996), 2.

7. Descriptions drawn from Noah's Bagels extensive literature on its community service activity available free in every retail store. Pamphlets are displayed prominently in racks to draw consumer interest and attention.

8. Noah's Bagel Foundation printed guidelines, 1996.

9. Description drawn from the advertising and direct mail marketing of Working Assets.

10. Quotation taken from sample monthly bill of Working Assets.

11. The Hannadowns program is portrayed well in David Bollier's *Aiming Higher: 25 Stories of How Companies Prosper by Combining Sound Management and Social Vision* (New York: American Management Association and the Business Enterprise Trust, 1996), 23–26.

12. Linda B. Gornitsky, "Benchmarking Corporate International Contributions: A Research Report" (New York: The Conference Board, Report Number 1103-96-RR, 1996).

13. C. Fred. Bergsten, *America in the World Economy: A Strategy for the 1990s* (Washington, D.C.: The Institute for International Economics, 1988).

14. Statement of C. Fred Bergsten and Jeffrey J. Schott, Director and Senior Fellow, Institute for International Economics, before the Subcommittee on Trade of the House Committee on Ways and Means, US House of Representatives, 11 September 1997.

15. *Fortune*, 27 October 1997, contained its annual feature story on America's "most admired" companies.

16. Shepard Forman, "Paying for Essentials: Resources for Humanitarian Assistance," (background paper presented at a conference held by the Center on International Cooperation, New York University, Pocantico, NY, 11–12 September 1997).

17. Lester M. Salamon, "The Global Associational Revolution: The Rise of the Third Sector on the World Scene," (occasional paper, no. 15. Baltimore: Johns Hopkins University Institute for Policy Studies, April 1993).

18. Lester M. Salamon and Helmut K. Anheier, *The Emerging Nonprofit Sector: An Overview* (Manchester and New York: Manchester University Press, 1996).

19. Jessica T. Matthews, "Powershift," *Foreign Affairs* 76, no. 1 (1997): 63.

What's Really Worth Reading:

A Highly Recommended Booklist for
Philanthropists and Fundraisers

Arnott, Jan Corey et al. *Evaluation for Foundations: Concepts, Cases, Guidelines and Resources.* San Francisco: Jossey-Bass for the Council on Foundations, 1993.

Bellah, Robert N. et al. *Habits of the Heart: Individualism and Commitment in American Life.* Berkeley: University of California Press, 1985.

Bollier, David. *Aiming Higher: Twenty-five Stories of How Companies Prosper by Combining Sound Management and Social Vision.* New York: American Management Association, 1996.

Bremner, Robert H. *American Philanthropy.* 2nd ed. Chicago: University of Chicago Press, 1988.

——. *Giving: Charity and Philanthropy in History.* New Brunswick, N.J.: Transaction, 1994.

Burlingame, Dwight F., and Lamont J. Hulse, eds. *Taking Fund Raising Seriously.* San Francisco: Jossey-Bass, 1991.

Burlingame, Dwight F., and Dennis R. Young, eds. *Corporate Philanthropy at the Crossroads.* Bloomington: Indiana University Press, 1996.

Carnegie, Dale. *How to Win Friends and Influence People.* New York: Simon and Schuster, 1936.

Clotfelter, Charles T., ed. *Who Benefits from the Nonprofit Sector?* Washington, D.C.: Partners for Livable Spaces and the Rockefeller Brothers Funds, 1983.

Crimmins, James C., and Mary Keil. *Enterprise in the Nonprofit Sector.* Washington, D.C.: Partners for Livable Spaces and the Rockefeller Brothers Fund, 1983.

Freund, Gerald. *Narcissism and Philanthropy: Ideas and Talent Denied.* New York: Viking, 1996.

Gardner, John W. *Excellence.* New York: Harper and Brothers, 1961.

——. *Self-Renewal: The Individual and the Innovative Society.* New York: W. W. Norton, 1981.

Hodgkinson, Virginia A., and Richard Wibyman, eds. *The Future of the NonProfit Sector.* San Francisco: Jossey-Bass, 1989.

Muller, Jerry Z. *Adam Smith: In His Time and Ours—Designing the Decent Society.* Princeton: Princeton University Press, 1993.

Nielsen, Waldemar A. *The Big Foundations.* New York: Columbia University Press, 1972.

——. *The Endangered Sector.* New York: Columbia University, 1972.

——. *The Golden Donors: A New Anatomy of the Great Foundations.* New York: E. P. Dutton, 1989.

——. *Inside American Philanthropy: The Dramas of Donorship.* Norman, Okla.: University of Oklahoma Press, 1996.

Novak, Michael. *Business as a Calling: Work and the Examined Life.* New York: The Free Press, 1996.

O'Connell, Brian, ed. *America's Voluntary Spirit: A Book of Readings.* New York: Foundation Center, 1983.

Odendahl, Teresa ed. *America's Wealthy and the Future of Foundations.* New York: Foundation Center, 1987.

O'Neill, Michael. *The Third America.* San Francisco: Jossey-Bass, 1989.

Ostrower, Francis. *Why the Wealthy Give: The Culture of Elite Philanthropy.* Princeton: Princeton University Press, 1990.

Payton, Robert L. *Philanthropy: Voluntary Action for the Public Good.* New York: Macmillan, 1988.

Salamon, Lester M. *America's Nonprofit Sector: A Primer.* New York: Foundation Center, 1982.

Schervish, Paul G., ed. *Taking Giving Seriously.* Indianapolis: Indiana University Center on Philanthropy, 1993.

Shannon, James P., ed. *The Corporate Contributions Handbook.* San Francisco: Jossey-Bass, 1991.

Weisbrod, Burton A. *The NonProfit Economy.* Cambridge: Harvard University Press, 1988.

Wolpert, Julian. *Patterns of Generosity in America: Who's Holding the Safety Net.* New York: Twentieth Century Fund, 1993.

Wuthnow, Robert. *Acts of Compassion: Caring for Others and Helping Ourselves.* Princeton: Princeton University Press, 1991.

——. *Learning to Care: Elementary Kindness in an Age of Indifference.* New York: Oxford University Press, 1995.

———. *Poor Richard's Principle: Rediscovering the American Dream Through the Moral Dimension of Work, Business and Money.* Princeton: Princeton University Press, 1996.

Substantive concepts from the notes are referenced in the index by the page(s) on which they occur followed by *n* or *nn* and the note number(s).

Reynold Levy is the president and CEO of the International Rescue Committee, a leading nonprofit institution devoted to the relief and resettlement of refugees in twenty-five nations around the world and in the United States. Levy spent 1984–96 with AT&T, beginning his tenure as the founder and president of the AT&T Foundation and ending as the senior officer in charge of AT&T's international public affairs. From 1977–84, he was the executive director of the 92nd Street Y, a major cultural, educational, and social service organization located on Manhattan's Upper East Side.

A graduate of Hobart College, Levy holds a Ph.D. in government and foreign affairs from the University of Virginia and a law degree from Columbia University. An active member of the Council on Foreign Relations, he is also the chairman of the board of the Nathan Cummings Foundation and a trustee of the Manhattan Theatre Club and Phipps Houses.

Levy is the author of *Nearing the Crossroads: Contending Approaches to American Foreign Policy.* He is married to Elizabeth A. Cooke. They have two children, Justin and Emily.